OUR HARVARD

OUR HARVARD

Reflections on College Life
by Twenty-two Distinguished Graduates

Edited by Jeffrey L. Lant

TAPLINGER PUBLISHING COMPANY
NEW YORK

OR 11/82

First printing
Published in 1982 by
TAPLINGER PUBLISHING CO., INC.
New York, New York

Copyright © 1982 by Jeffrey L. Lant
Printed in the United States of America
Designed by Ganis and Harris, Inc.

Library of Congress Cataloging in Publication Data
Main entry under title:

Our Harvard: reflections on college life.

   1. Harvard University—Addresses, essays,
lectures. I. Lant, Jeffrey L.
LD2134.095   378.744'4   81-18471
ISBN 0-8008-6139-6   AACR2

The editorial on page 19 is reprinted by permission of *The Harvard Crimson* and the Harvard University Archives.

CONTENTS

INTRODUCTION

Here, somewhat in advance of the 350th anniversary of the founding of Harvard College in 1636, is a collection of essays that should throw some light on what has happened to the College in this century. Twenty-two distinguished graduates, ranging from the class of 1917 to that of 1981, have contributed reflections on their undergraduate years. The result is a significant piece of social history, not just about undergraduates at America's premier college but about America itself.

It might be argued, indeed some critic (probably from Harvard!) will argue, that men of the College are in no sense representative: that is why they go to Harvard in the first place. Yet the final result belies any such caviling. Each voice, each remembrance in this collection is authentic, completely recalling its proper period. This authenticity confirms my belief that each of us embodies in a small way the spirit of his age. What distinguishes the contributors, however, from others is that they are not only representative but also wonderfully precise and articulate. That is why their words are worth attending to.

The book itself opens upon a world that is gone forever, the era of Georgian America, when, as Buckminster Fuller points out, "Human beings were 'rooted' creatures," and the air was pungent with the smells of unwashed bodies and horse manure. There was, such pungency notwithstanding, a sweet grace about those days, a measured pace, and a gentle inevitability about much that happened. For Fuller, this inevitability meant Harvard; he was, after all, the scion of seven generations of Harvard men, and there was, therefore, no question about where he would matriculate.

What he found when he entered in the fall of 1913 was not so very different from what undergraduates had been finding for half a century. The College had, to be sure, grown during those years; it now extended beyond the quiet confines of the Yard, even as far as the Gold Coast of Mount Auburn Street, where richer undergraduates found housing in fireproof, multistoried, private dormitories. Here was an oasis among ramshackle boardinghouses where their less fortunate classmates made do. Charles William Eliot (recently retired as president in 1909) was a man with grand visions for Harvard University; he had, however, let lesser matters in the College, including undergraduate housing, take their course. As a result, in Fuller's day Harvard College was still small, comfortably inward looking, yet rather uncomfortably split between the two worlds of the exclusive club men and other collegians.

World War I, which came shortly afterward and felled a tenth of Fuller's 1917 classmates, did not disturb this pleasant universe. It seems to have quickened its pace, just perceptibly, but the impression overall was of some honored place, distinguished by a careless plenitude, existing to crown youth, which was beautiful and fleeting. *Gaudeamus igitur* . . . Dreamy and translucent, as John Finley remembers, "This was neither the old Harvard of the Yard nor the later Harvard of the Houses but something in between, a place of discovered sympathies, of lights and shades, and of occasional sun-flecked shafts as from some high window."

Into such a world, too soon gone, it behooved undergraduates to move, not with callow insouciance but with an alert reverence, as David McCord did when he first approached

the brick gate across from Plympton Street, with its horta-
tory, admonitive message: Enter to grow in wisdom. "Inside
that gate the Harvard Yard, serene in the company of surviving ancient elms, artfully dotted with younger ones now
grown along with me, I stood . . . speechless." Freshman
McCord was struck, I think, for a thrilling, daunting instant
with that which has awed so many Harvard men in similar
circumstances; that is, by an abiding insight that we are
now and forever a part of a notable tradition, in which the
many significant hopes we have for ourselves will be not
only awaited but also expected from this great establishment that will now and afterward give us in return its ample,
continuing sustenance.

There was, however, a pernicious aspect to this sun-
touched world. As John Finley has written, "The pre-House
College was not hospitable to everyone." Those who were
what Thomas Boylston Adams calls Mandarin fared best in
this best of worlds—that is, those with resonant names,
social entrée, and money bearing no trace of its origins.
Such men walked secure in the knowledge that they would
get into a club, "the object of coming to Harvard," in Adams's
phrase.

For those who should have been in a club, and they knew
who they were, doing so in that George Apley world held a
gripping significance hard to recapture today. Buckminster
Fuller, whose great-grandfather had been a founding member of the Hasty Pudding, whose father had been a popular
club member in the class of 1883, was club timber. His
father's premature death and the reduction in his family's
circumstances, however, effectively precluded membership, leaving him "a social outcast, in the midst of the
club-bound one-seventh of my class."

Thomas Adams, "who was very shy," did get into a club,
"for no other reason except that his brother had been a
member and some of his friends from the School were going
into it." It was, he recalls, "as pleasant a place as he would
ever know," with companionable friends, sharing compan-

ionable prejudices, delicious meals, and, despite the inhibiting Prohibition, "as much liquor as anyone cared to drink."

This smug little world was jolted by two considerable forces: Abbott Lawrence Lowell and the Great Depression.

Lowell, unlike his presidential predecessor, looked to the College as the generous heart of the University, and the undergraduates, his undergraduates, sensing this enthusiasm, responded to him warmly. Little wonder. David McCord recalls Mr. Lowell's good, democratic manners. "He would," he remembers, "greet his visitor, however young and shy, however old and seasoned, with instinctive warmth and sympathy, and address him always man to man, not ever as president to freshman or president to men named Croesus or Harkness." Robert Fitzgerald, younger than McCord, has a touching story, extraordinary to any of us today who have cooled our heels in the impersonal antisepsis of Stillman Infirmary, of Mr. Lowell calling there on his ailing undergraduates. This was a man who might well excite an almost primal loyalty.

Such a man took no delight in the invidious barriers within the College, barriers fostered by the clubs. His vision of what Harvard College should be ran to something more unified, more truly collegiate in spirit and in reality. And so when Mr. Harkness, a humane plutocrat with an idea so recently (if temporarily) rebuffed at Yale, made an offer to construct Houses at Harvard, Mr. Lowell promptly accepted. Club men, reluctantly forced to live in these Houses, found—without much difficulty, one hopes—that the men they had previously tried so hard to avoid were not, on the whole, so bad after all.

At the same time, the Great Depression laid low a good many of those clubbable Mandarins who had been, in the bountiful post–Civil War era, lords of creation. Part of their extensive, expected inheritance was Harvard, but a Harvard that came to them by unchallenged right and where they succeeded without particular effort. This Harvard did not fare well in the 1930s. Internally, it was challenged by Mr.

Lowell's curricular reforms, which made the College, through concentrations, or majors, and tutorials, rather more academically demanding. Externally, the Great Depression ushered in a troubling world where the glittering prizes were more often reserved for those who would work and fight hard for them, though this extraordinary situation prevailed less at Harvard than elsewhere.

There was little joy and much bitter irony among the Mandarins thus beset that another Mandarin, a man of the College and indeed a member of the Fly Club, should preside over such a Götterdämmerung. Arthur Schlesinger, Jr., remembers that when this Mandarin, Franklin Roosevelt by name, visited Cambridge before the 1936 election, he was greeted, as a traitor to his class and college, with a resounding chorus of boos.

This Harvard, which welcomed the assiduous James Bryant Conant as president in 1933, was not a very taxing place to be, particularly for those young men who had had no other notion but that at college they would have to do a little work. Because, after all, the work was not so very arduous and the life was so very good.

E. J. Kahn, Jr., recalls that "it was possible to get through Harvard almost without doing any work at all" and remembers a classmate who received an A in an Old Testament course not by attending lectures and such like, but, provokingly, by doing no more than perusing Kahn's own "skimpy" notes the night before the exam—provokingly, because Kahn himself, who had done somewhat more preparation, received only a B. Arthur Schlesinger remembers that "the [academic] transition to Harvard proved far less agonizing than the transition had been in 1931 from the Cambridge Latin School to Exeter." And Thornton Bradshaw recalls his righteous rages, while writing for the *Advocate*, against the tutoring schools in Harvard Square. These schools could, he writes, help undergraduates distracted by other, more pressing concerns obtain "the gentleman's three C's and a D." That they were able to deliver on their promises, with students whose minds were determinedly elsewhere, was "due in some measure to the low level of teaching at Harvard at the time." Such undemanding courses left undergraduates free to pursue their own interests in concert with companionable friends. These interests, these friends were, for so many, more important than dreary classroom stuff.

Robert Fitzgerald, afire with his literary obsession, cultivated poems in an "inky chaos." "In the small hours when the rumor of other life had subsided and only the wind over the glow of the avenue gave an occasional buffet to my panes, I sat under my goosenecked lamp, incapable of anything but this work of the ear and the sixth sense—queerly most fully alive when most nearly dead."

Ah, this was living.

E. J. Kahn, chastened by the example of his New Testament classmate, was thereafter motivated not to study, either. *He* wished to comp for the *Crimson* and would have, too, had its Jewish quota not been already filled. Instead, he wrote for the rival Harvard *Journal*, "a feisty daily that kept those of us happily associated with it on the go, day and night, often all night, for thirteen heady weeks."

That the classroom could compete at all against such agreeable pursuits was due largely to certain professors who were, in the best tradition of Harvard, larger than life.

Robert Fitzgerald remembers Irving Babbitt, "a big bent old man with no nonsense about him . . . quoting effortlessly from Malherbe and Boileau, rubbing and seeming to scratch or even lightly to pick his distinguished nose, while he glared over his low spectacles at the handful of incipient romanticists before him." Babbitt was, like so many others, suitably monumental and awe-inspiring. So were, for Kahn, John Livingston Lowes and George Lyman Kittredge; for Schlesinger, Perry Miller, F. O. Matthiessen, and Bernard De Voto; and, for Bradshaw, Arthur Holcombe, Carl Friedrich, and Roger Bigelow Merriman, sometime Master of Eliot House, fondly called "Frisky" by the young men whose hats he would knock off with an ivory-tipped pointer. "His

History I—from the fall of the Roman Empire to the present day—," Bradshaw remembers, "was a *tour d'horizon*, a sweeping view of history. It was said that if a student sneezed he might miss the entire twelfth-century renaissance. No one who took History I will forget that life in the Middle Ages was 'slow, slow, inconceivably slow!' "

Here then was the College world as it stood: "subject," as Bradshaw writes, "only to the modest restrictions imposed by selection of a field of concentration," Harvard's undergraduates were left to do as they liked. Study, of course, was possible, even encouraged, and should one have a mind for it there were academic titans at hand to provide both information and inspiration. But it was not, in that thoroughly agreeable place, absolutely necessary. Thank goodness, too, for there were so many other, compelling matters to attend to: clubs, athletics, dramatics, and, always, girls. What interest there was in politics, Schlesinger recalls, was directed far from the Yard, to national and international issues, never to things closer to home. "Even those Young Communists who met conspiratorially to overthrow the capitalist system apparently never dreamed of doing anything to revolutionize their immediate environment." So, while they spun their ideas of revolution, these visionaries continued to let the biddies clean their rooms, continued to wear jacket and tie to the dining halls and to observe "without protest parietal rules of inconceivable stringency and absurdity." "The world was changing," Bradshaw writes, "and Harvard with it, but not yet."

T. F. Bradshaw graduated in 1940. Ineffaceable change was very, very near. Before it arrived, however, harsh and unwelcome, there was still a little time to enjoy that which made this Harvard such a gentle, enviable place.

In the fall of 1940 the class of "Double Four" arrived in Cambridge. It was to have, for reasons its members could not have then foreseen, a special significance, which had nothing to do with soon posting the highest percentage of men on the dean's list in the history of the College. Its retrospective importance came instead from the fact that it was, according to Anton Myrer, "the last class to enjoy a full year of the 'old' Harvard, the leisurely, nonchalant Harvard of unlimited cuts, relatively relaxed fields of concentration, uncrowded dormitories . . . and the casual, disinterested pursuit of knowledge."

Everything that took place that year had happened before, even the glorious victory over Yale. Yet each event assumed an unexpected aureole as the men of "Double Four" realized that life would never be the same—not just for them but for everyone. This sad, confounding realization came all at once on "that Sunday," in December of 1941. Anton Myrer looked at his roommate and saw "an eerie mélange of shock, anger, dread, grim acceptance," the same emotions that played on his face, the same feelings that shot through his classmates.

Gone, gone forever was the leisure, the blithe casualness, the feeling that the future, a good future, was "simply to arrive," in John Finley's phrase. A renewed American purposefulness, tough and unrelenting, was born on that Sunday and instantly found a home at Harvard. Myrer remembers that "the phrase you heard everywhere on campus was 'What are you going to do?'" Undergraduates had always asked this of one another, of course, but now there was an insistence in the question that had never been there before.

The pace, hitherto an ambling one, was now discernibly quicker. "Everything was accelerated," Myrer remembers, "classes, courses, meals, drinks, dates, love affairs." John Simon recalls how in the fall of 1942, when he arrived, "there was still table service in the dining halls; by the next semester, or shortly thereafter, one had to stand on a chow line as if one were in the army." To this drumbeat of urgent change, young men went off to war, or, too young to fight, stayed to witness, disconsolately, innovations that became, in short order, unsparing.

John Simon went out for rugby. It was discontinued. He switched to fencing. It, too, was abolished. So was crew. Only hubba-hubba physical training remained, "from which," Simon recalls, "one could not wash out." So much for the gentleman athlete, an early wartime victim of Harvard's slide into "comparative barbarism."

Was there, then, no benign innovation in these years? That depends, of course, on how one looks at things; but girls seemed, and perhaps really were, more accessible.

In Myrer's day, there was a fixed code regulating the relationship between men and good girls; it prescribed that he should "venture as far as he could until the girl invariably stopped him; then, protesting, he dutifully stayed within those bounds, whereupon the evening turned into a tortured, interminable ritual of kissing and groping about that left both parties dizzy, panting, half-stunned." This code, one of the few things that did return to its prime state after the war, was now buffeted, too, a little. Radcliffe, Simon remembers, now had a group called the Dirty Thirty. Patriotic, its members seem to have reserved their charms for servicemen rather than undergraduates, but some few of these, honored too, were witness to slow progress "in those pre-sexual-revolutionary days."

Otherwise it was all bad.

When Myrer returned to Harvard in 1946 things were very, very different. "Compulsory attendance, roll calls—roll calls!—in class. No auditing." It was, indeed, a new, unexpected place to those who had been there before. " 'Fish or cut bait,' a dean—a new, strange dean with a large square mouth, whose beady eyes glinted with unconcealed glee— told three of us. 'We've got no time for that prewar folderol.' "

"This was not the Harvard we had known and loved."

But it couldn't be, for the College, the entire University, was populated now by men—some of them freshmen as old as thirty-six!—who had recently been participants in death and mayhem. Their concerns were different, serious, unlike the ones that they, as mere boys, had had so recently. In seriousness they approached the task of education, which severe circumstances had given them an ability to appreciate in a way they could not have done before the war.

Robert Coles, when he arrived at Harvard in 1947, was

only seventeen, too young to have served. He did not, therefore, immediately understand or appreciate the moral earnestness of his veteran classmates, one in particular: a man
in his middle twenties who had fought at Guadalcanal. This
man, now just a sophomore, reminded Coles that "we were
both fortunate to be alive, to be living in America, to be well
fed and well clothed, to be able to speak freely to each other
without fear of some dictatorial intrusion, or worse, and, of
course, to be at Harvard." Coles's response to this outburst?
"First I was bored. Then I became annoyed. Why do I need
to hear all that? . . . Why was he so talkative, so *emotional?*"

Here so close as to make one squirm was American purposefulness—powerful, demanding, frankly proselytizing.
It was vital, so very earnest, and not yet construed as somehow dangerous. This purposefulness was a very compelling
thing, indeed, and weekly Coles confronted it in the lectures
of Perry Miller and Werner Jaeger, professors who left an
indelible mark.

Miller, his voice sometimes cracking with emotion, called
upon America, as the Puritans of old, to be as a city on a hill,
a shining example to all the world. Jaeger, who sang "with
an unashamed baring of soul," spun tales of the ancient
Greeks, of the strong and brave, of moral principles or intellectual and moral passion. And so challenged the undergraduates to live better lives. "Both Perry Miller and Werner
Jaeger kept telling us, in their classes, that multiple-choice
factuality and even the well-rounded and carefully eloquent
exam essay were but a prelude to something else—to a
moral life we must find for ourselves as we go slouching
toward Jerusalem." As with the Puritans, however, this Jerusalem could not just be obtained; it must be won—by hard
work.

As the decade ripened, as the war-tested veterans de-
parted, as a new postwar normalcy settled on Harvard,
undergraduates may, from time to time, have forgotten why
they were working so hard. But they didn't stop working.
The undergraduates of the fifties were, like John Spooner's

roommates, a very intent lot on the whole. "They had been highly motivated and competitive since kindergarten, told by parents and teachers and coaches that they had to be the best, that there were kids all over America breathing down their necks, waiting to take their place if they faltered." Erich Segal was part of that generation, and he remembers "working like a fiend," asking his roommates please not to talk before 10:00 P.M. (because he was studying) or after 10:15 (because he was sleeping).

Told regularly that the fate of the civilized world hung on such grave matters as their ability to memorize irregular Greek verbs or run a five-minute mile, it is little wonder that there was tension in these undergraduates—or that it often was released in undesirable ways. Hence a partial explanation of the social "horror shows" of the era. So much went into creating these events: selfishness, exuberance, pleasure, irresponsibility, and release from the new, unceasing pressures that came with American hegemony and the suddenly increased expectations for the men of Harvard.

That many adults understood this complicated situation probably did them little good when they were actually confronted with the havoc-wreaking undergraduates. Did the hostess whose hands had been tied above her head by "one member of the Porcellian, whose family owned most of a major midwestern city" think to blame Sputnik? Did the police sergeant, cocking his gun over a recumbent undergraduate who had illegally entered a Concord house and fallen asleep, leaving this note: "I am a drunken Harvard student, not a thief"? Did the gentleman acting as host to Peter Prescott's D.U. brothers, as he watched these young leaders of Harvard bounce glasses down the elegant stairway at the Club of Odd Volumes? Probably not. No doubt they all bewailed, as the decorous mature will, the end of decency and the advent of a new adolescent uproariousness, just as their counterparts did in *Bye Bye Birdie*: "Why can't they be like we were, perfect in every way? Oh, what's the matter with kids today?"

Antisocial though so many undergraduate activities were in those days, they were, nonetheless, laced with something very good and utterly characteristic of the period: massive self-confidence. It was the best part of the period, even if it manifested itself in curious ways.

John Spooner recalls his roommate, the Beast, who from an armchair in the middle of Storrow Drive "directed traffic with one hand while the other brought a bottle of Early Times frequently to his lips." He was convinced, with a self-confidence drawn from the deep wells of youth, Harvard, and American might, that "no ill could befall him." Jonathan Larsen felt the same when he opened the gas tank on his motor scooter, struck a match, and peered in. "Why I was not blow sky high I'll never know."

For nigh on twenty years, there was an unshakable feeling among undergraduates that they were the chosen people of a chosen nation. "We had a certainty that this was only the beginning of triumphs," Spooner recalls, "that . . . we would leave our roistering behind us and move on to accomplishments that were serious, far-reaching, and special." This feeling animated even dining hall table talk, so Michael Barone remembers. "It seems almost absurd as I think back on it, but I remember arguing with fellow undergraduates at the *Crimson* and in dining halls about the future course of the Common Market and President de Gaulle's politics. . . . There was . . . a sense that was not wholly without foundation that we were—or were about to be—in control of the course of the major institutions of society, that the major decisions of the future were ours to make. We had," Barone continues, "confidence in our ability to rule as well as confidence in the people who then seemed to be ruling our nation and so much of the world." It was, without doubt, a very wonderful, thrilling time to be at Harvard—if one fit in.

But not everyone did.

John Spooner remembers that "There were virtually no Jews in the Hasty Pudding . . . or in any of the better final clubs. . . . If you were black at Harvard in the late 1950s, unless you were the president of Nigeria's son, you kept a low profile, did your work, and moved on quietly to the business of real life."

To be homosexual, however, was worst of all. Postwar Macho America brought with it many unsavory things, but one of the worst was an attitude of vindictive discrimination against homosexuals. Harvard's opinion on this matter mirrored that of the country at large.

There had been a certain prewar tolerance for homosexuality at Harvard; many genteel people, after all, were quiet participants. So long as it was not flaunted, homosexuality was not found particularly objectionable; indeed, it gave many a piquancy they would not otherwise have possessed. Thus, it seems to have been fairly common knowledge that F. O. Matthiessen was gay (although Arthur Schlesinger, Jr., as an undergraduate didn't know it), and John Simon recalls Henry Wadsworth Longfellow Dana. He was, Simon remembers lightly, a "way-past-menopausal but still hopeful homosexual" who seems to have made no bones about his interest in winsome undergraduates, many of whom he entertained at his mansion on Brattle Street. True, he was dismissed from Harvard, but only in part for his sexual tastes, Simon writes; more likely, it was his pacifism and communism that were held against him, just as they had been at Columbia, which also gave him his congé.

Amused tolerance, however, was swept away in the postwar period; remember the beady-eyed, square-faced dean, who had no time for that prewar folderol, including, it seems, knowing when to leave well enough alone. Under the new regime, with its strict expectations about male behavior, homosexuality became something malign and insidious.

Jonathan Larsen recalls an incident at the Fly Club. There a European, "one of the richer and more infamous students at the College, had decided to play Pygmalion to a young, naive varsity swimmer from the Midwest." It was just the thing to enrage the wholesome: "At best the relationship seemed ambiguous, a page out of Henry James, in which the more sophisticated European toys with and dominates an innocent American. At worst, it looked like a homosexual affair trying to come out of a closet that the culture was not yet ready to open."

Years later James Fallows, then on the *Crimson,* wrote an "absolutely vicious" review of Stephen Kelman's book *Push Comes to Shove* in which he suggested that Kelman's "hostility to SDS might be due to an unrequited homosexual love for Mike Kazin, an SDS leader in the class of 1970." It ought to be noted that Fallows later apologized for this review and that he and Kelman have since become friendly.

Andrew Holleran writes especially poignantly of his sense of shameful separateness. "Marooned in a complicated adolescence," he found himself sunk in that "gloom common to homosexual youths before they have come to terms with themselves: the conviction that I was the only one in the world." Even seeing the Lowell House playwright "walking into the foggy courtyard with his arm around another young man" and knowing, instinctively, they were lovers, didn't help, for he was unconnected yet and still caught between devastating incompatibilities: to give in to desire meant, perhaps, relatedness and, with luck, peace. It also meant permanent estrangement from the assured success Harvard promised, for a wayward commitment to homosexuality presupposed, he thought, "giving up the promise one had in life, a promise that Harvard itself symbolized; it meant to surrender the future."

That there was a future, a luminous future, was, of course, never doubted in the early 1960s. These were transcendent years of promise and boundless confidence, with only the likes of Michael Harrington, that gadfly, reminding undergraduates that in the midst of so much plenty there was still much shocking want.

The existence of such want did not prove disconcerting to undergraduates; neither, at first, did the burgeoning Vietnam War, which began to be, in the middle of the decade, a matter of concern. Why such Olympian detachment? "Our perspective during all these debates," Michael Barone recalls, "was that of the policymaker. We did not think of ourselves as people who could be affected directly by Vietnam, certainly not as people who would be killed there."

Once the undergraduates *did* begin thinking of themselves as possible combatants, possibly corpses—once, that is, the draft became an inevitability—things changed very rapidly. Suddenly the war, which had so intrigued them as policymakers, seemed a much more menacing event and one that had to be stopped, at once. As the war widened and the draft drew off its engorged quotient, the demonstrator, the militant, the radical undergraduate all sprung to life.

In years past, these militants, like junior members of the establishment before them, would have gladly taken sherry with senior members, so many of them graduates of the College. But the war changed things dramatically. Disagreeing Harvard men now came to view each other warily. Most (usually older) viewed the rest (usually undergraduates) as capable of any outrage against prevailing mores and as subverting the "bourgeois civil liberties" they had gone to war themselves to preserve. In turn, the undergraduates thought their antagonists immoral perpetrators of an iniquitous war and an oppressive social order from which they benefited too greatly. As the war escalated, so did the divisiveness, until there emerged implacably hostile camps, each distinguished by what has always distinguished Harvard men: ringing self-confidence and an assuredness, deeply felt, that their point of view was the correct one.

The stage was thus set for the bitter years of the late 1960s and beyond.

Three clusters of events stand out in these years: the seizure of University Hall in April 1969, the "trashing" of Harvard Square a year later, and all that followed the invasion of Cambodia and the Kent State killings just a little later still. James Fallows, Stephen Kelman, William Martin, and I, in our very different ways, were caught up in these events.

Fallows covered them for the *Crimson,* often coming face to face with "the great stone-faced Nathan Pusey, [who] tried to conceal his utter astonishment at the passions tearing up his university." Kelman, far from being a conservative himself, worked hard with a compact group of followers against the galloping radicalism of SDS and thus became, so he writes, "the single undergraduate most hated" by that zealous organization. Martin, a freshman in 1969, felt like so many other undergraduates that the radicals were destroying the Harvard he had come for, but like most students he was "politicized" when the administration ordered the police to retake University Hall. "We had all hoped that, somehow, the issue could be resolved without an army of police. Then, the crowd began to roar its anger. One of my friends, a rather quiet, conservative student, began to scream, 'I can't believe this is Harvard! They've brought in the pigs!' "

The next morning I awoke, on the opposite coast, to find bold newspaper headlines about what had happened. Just accepted as a graduate student in the history department, I now found myself worrying, too, about what was happening to America's proudest university. Surely, after I had waited so long to be a part of it, it would not be sundered? I thus looked forward to Harvard somewhat grimly and with my heart set against the radicals who were disrupting the life I so wanted to share.

In fact, these radicals and their determined business affected me, or the University, very little, though I do remember several incidents from those days quite clearly. One concerns nothing more than a rumor, though it was chilling to those of us whose lives centered on the Widener Library. We heard that campus radicals were going to attack the library's card catalogs and so destroy all research capability. Who knows where such a canard originated? It was, however, earnestly believed by graduate students who felt such monstrous ingenuity perfectly in keeping with what we knew of the militants and their selfish behavior.

I remember, too, a balmy night in April 1970 when the debate raged about what Harvard students should do to protest the invasion of Cambodia and the Kent State killings. I spent the evening walking a morally concerned friend around the Yard as he agonized over whether to finish his work and get a master's degree or join the growing boycott of classes and so protest what was happening. Because I held out staunchly for finishing and thought the boycott foolish, he branded me an insensitive realist. He never did get his degree.

Finally, I was present at the "trashing" of Harvard Square, which also took place that spring. This occurred when a motley array of revolutionaries and delinquents, sensing their opportunity, marched from a rally on the Boston Common and protested America's war in Vietnam by creating chaos in Cambridge. Heedless of what might happen to casual observers, I watched the melee from behind a locked gate at Lehman Hall and got, as a result, my only whiff of teargas.

As William Martin reports, this mindless violence and destructiveness ended the moral ascendancy of the radicals, for they were no longer "bringing serious demands to the University"; they offered only anarchy. That June the University prepared for the disruption of commencement by SDS sympathizers hostile to Stephen Kelman, who was delivering the English Oration. The disruption that actually occurred, however, was arranged instead by disgruntled Cambridge tenants protesting the University's expansionary policies, not by antiwar radicals. They wound up their tumultuous years at Harvard with nothing worse than a sound booing of Kelman.

When the class of 1970 left, things suddenly got much quieter, and it was possible to enjoy the Harvard I had come for. Thanks to the Signet Society and Dudley House I got my full measure.

At the Signet, where I was an associate member, I came to know Archie, the steward, as generations of undergraduates had done; I also met other luminaries: Norman Mailer, his arm in a sling from some recent, raucous encounter; Peter Ustinov, who glanced over the failure of his newest production using rich, compelling language; Robert Lowell, who advised us that to be a poet one must have sloth. I was present the evening Michael Tilson Thomas outraged the club by talking of his grandmother's bejeweled abortion needles and sang "Swanee" (and made us sing, too) while wearing a T-shirt. It was the same evening Henry Cabot Lodge refused to join the standing ovation for Arthur Schlesinger, Jr., who gave a ringing speech on the need to dismantle the imperial presidency of Richard Nixon.

At Dudley House, which I served as a resident tutor, I encountered Lodge again. This time I arranged a luncheon for him. He arrived early and to general confusion; the lunchroom was filled with acrid smoke from a malfunctioning fireplace, and the crowd from a morning coffee party for Margaret Hamilton was hilariously departing. Jean Mayer, the Master, attempted to introduce the departing actress to the arriving Brahmin, but forgot her name. "Mr. Ambassador, may I present . . ." And then inspiration: ". . . the Wicked Witch of the West!" Lodge gave the ebullient lady a cold hand and an opaque glance; she sensibly declined a hurried invitation to luncheon.

I remember so much about Dudley House, which enabled me to have a close association with many undergraduates and to organize many agreeable activities. There was the public reading and subsequent private luncheon I arranged for Anne Sexton; like Jonathan Larsen with W. H. Auden, I ended up pouring vodka into a water glass. Unlike Larsen, I also spent late hours on the telephone with a very tormented soul I knew not how to comfort. There was the evening I arranged for Humberto Cardinal Medeiros, that often underappreciated cleric, who almost upset all my plans and did produce an unexpected demonstration by dismissing the popular Roman Catholic chaplain a few days before coming to campus. I remember less weighty events, too:

Jack Weeks, a never-unobtrusive undergraduate from Southey, swinging into a party on a sheet rope, quite nude, to the accompaniment of *Appalachian Spring*. It infuriated him that nobody noticed. And John Marquand, the very rotund senior tutor, waltzing into my office in Apley Court, in a green bathrobe, complaining about the plumbing, while I was entertaining a numerous company assembled in honor of a visiting English historian. It infuriated *him* that everyone did notice.

I came to have, while living the monastic, restricted life of most graduate students, a palpable feeling for the under-graduate universe, and I was witness to the move to career-ism that occurred in the middle of the decade. Some under-graduates, of course, were still deeply committed to radical ventures, but there were yearly fewer of them. Most others, cynical now, retreated into their work and used their years at the College to leverage better, more secure futures. Mark O'Donnell, who arrived in the fall of 1972, remembers: "Going barefoot was still a political statement, and the final clubs were still bashful about their elitism, but the fear of abandonment that would lead to *Self* magazine was already eating up the baby boom's will to Worry About Others." O'Donnell bucked this trend and joined the *Lampoon*, which he admired for its "tradition of absolute scholastic negligence. . . . It opened a world of adult irresponsibility to me that my sterling childhood would have swooned at rather than imagine." John Adler, the youngest contributor, moved into the Signet Society and there worked hard "to escape the prevailing attitude of joyless grade-grubbing, which pro-duced a lot of tedious people who will undoubtedly make millions of dollars and someday return for reunions to recall the good old days they never had."

O'Donnell and Adler share a common credo: "Never let academics disrupt more important matters." In this regard, they are the authentic representatives of a significant Har-vard tradition: the tradition of the College as a place where gifted young men are free to explore, free to fail without fear of repercussion, where casual brilliance is valued, where style is important, where there remain time and resources abundant enough to waste without remorse, where the focus is on a valued past and an exciting present, where undergraduates are not prematurely burdened shoring up security against an uncertain future.

This tradition is an important part of what makes Harvard great. It is therefore good to know that sensible men like O'Donnell and Adler uphold it against narrow, determined classmates whose years at Harvard constitute one giant cram session directed toward the alphabet exams on which they suppose their futures rest: LSATs, MCATs, GMATs. Someday, this malign careerist trend will thankfully wane. Someday, guiltless undergraduates will again be free to indulge their untrammeled animal spirits and their exuberant, if unformed, intelligence. Essentially pedestrian minds will find such a thought affronting and, being in the saddle now, will urge more zealousness, more tight control, and more right-minded planning for the future. But in the whirligig of time, the day of these grim men will in due course set, and another golden age of Harvard College will inevitably follow. I plan to be here to savor it.

Jeffrey Lant, Ph.D. '75
Cambridge, Massachusetts

Buckminster Fuller '17

Buckminster Fuller was born in 1895 in Milton, Massachusetts, and, after graduating from Milton Academy, entered the class of 1917. He went on to earn worldwide recognition as an inventor, mathematician, author, architect, and cartographer and was appointed to the Charles Eliot Norton Professorship (Poetry Chair) at Harvard in 1961–62. Forty-five honorary doctorates have been conferred on him as well as many awards that include the Gold Medals of the Royal Institute of British Architects, the American Institute of Architects, the National Institute of Arts and Letters, and the American Academy of Arts and Sciences, the Plomado de Oro of the Society of Mexican Architects, and Honorary Phi Beta Kappa, Harvard University (Alpha chapter). He has written sixteen books, which include Operating Manual for Spaceship Earth *(1963),* Synergetics: Explorations in the Geometry of Thinking *(1975),* Synergetics 2: Further Explorations in the Geometry of Thinking *(1979), and* Critical Path *(1980).*

I may be Harvard's oldest living undergraduate. If so, I do not consider that a distinction. I consider it to be an inestimable privilege. I am still learning at an ever-multiplying rate. Thank Harvard and God. With the exception of a few compulsory freshman year subjects, my curricula have been entirely elective and most often unlisted in the catalog.

I grew to Harvard entry age with my own idealized assumption that, in contrast to elementary and college preparatory schools—where the subjects of study and their respective passing grades are all prescribed—in college the scholar undertakes self-education. I assumed that in college the individual—advantaged by magnificent libraries—consults with or listens to the lectures of distinguished scholars. By and large, the collegians schedule their own explorations and preoccupations. Many of the technological, psychological, social, and aesthetic experiences essential to developing a constantly ever greater comprehension of the omni-inter-relatedness of all phenomena exist only outside the college grounds.

That an institution like Harvard had to have an orderly plan of operation and behavioral tolerance limits seemed to me to be as necessary as it is for parents to have operating

schemes for their families—schemes whose limits, however, are as flexible as may be the limits of their love-inspired
understanding. I assumed the difference between Harvard
and all other institutions of higher learning to be a greater
tolerance for stretching of the rules—a Harvard-family wisdom and love, which could stretch the rules to accommodate unprecedented, nondestructive initiatives and innova-
tive explorations of its sons.

That my working assumption did not correspond with
1913 reality was probably a product of my having been born
into a Harvard family. Steeped in fascinating stories about
Cambridge life, I assumed from the beginning that I was a
Harvard son. I was the eighth Harvard generation in a direct
line of father, grandfather, great- and multi-great-grandfa-
thers for seven generations before me—eight of them on my
father's side and two more on my mother's. They were
members of the Harvard classes of 1883, 1840, 1801, 1760,
1744, 1740, 1739, 1721, 1698, and 1683. In addition, I had a
score of uncles and great uncles as well as five living cousins
who had attended Harvard.

All ten of my direct Harvard parental-line forebears were
born and lived their lives within a twenty-five miles, one-
day's walking distance of Cambridge.

The family reminiscing and the many pictures, diplomas,
and other Harvard trophies on the walls of our Milton home
and on the walls of my Fuller grandparents' home at 13
Hilliard Street and Fuller Place in Cambridge combined to
produce a vivid picture of Harvard and Cambridge. My
picture was also influenced by the published experiences of
my great aunt Margaret Fuller with Emerson, Thoreau,
Channing, and other early nineteenth century transcendentalists. I developed an idealized concept of Harvard,
which I assumed was everyone else's. In due course my
concept of Harvard proved to be quite different from those of
others.

All my Harvard forebears had been lawyers or ministers,
until my father became the first merchant among them. He

imported leather and tea from India and leather from the Argentine, all via the last of the clipper ships. He sold his fine leathers to the large shoe-manufacturing industry of greater Boston and, having introduced Darjeeling tea to his many Bostonian friends, he found a private household demand for the lead-foil-lined, steel-edge-banded, cubic teakwood chests of that Himalayan-grown tea.

In the fall of 1913, after eight years in Milton Academy's lower and upper schools, I entered Harvard with A's in physics, mathematics, and biology; B's in English, history and German; C in French; and D in Latin. I have not yet officially worked off that "condition" in Latin—a C grade minimum was compulsory in 1913—but I have worked it off to my own satisfaction. My Latin has been truly useful to me throughout the years.

Nineteen-thirteen was the next-to-last year of the Victorian era, an era that ended in Europe in 1914 with the outbreak of World War I. In 1913 the American population had no inkling, or thought, of an imminently impending outbreak of a world war—the first ever. World War I was not realistically felt in the U.S.A. until America entered it in 1917. Since the Civil War had closed half a century earlier, Yankeeland had experienced an era of peace broken only by the—compared with the Civil War—musical comedy–scale Spanish War touched off by the sinking of the U.S.S. *Maine* and the subsequent o'erwhelming of the Spanish enemy in naval engagement at Santiago and the charge of Teddy Roosevelt's Rough Riders at San Juan Hill.

Closing out the post–Civil War era, my generation danced the turkey trot to the accelerated tempo of "Alexander's Ragtime Band" and many others of that catchy style of music emanating from New Orleans. In 1912 Deep-South jazz was invading the deep North to displace or be added to New England's inheritance of such dignified European dances as the English Portland fancy, Vienna waltzes, Polish mazurkas, and German polkas; the two-step and waltz survived.

The first American automobile was produced the year I was born (1895). With the turn of the century, the first car came into Milton, seven miles outside Boston. Eight thousand cars had then been produced somewhere in America. Local cartwheel-rutted, dirt roads surrounding the cities in which automobiles were manufactured, plus frequent blowouts, did not invite immediate touring.

When we entered Harvard in 1913, the number of automobiles in the United States had just reached one million. The U. S. population was 100 million; only one in 100 Americans had a car. U.S.A. humans were walking an average of eleven hundred miles a year and were riding by some means of transportation only six hundred additional miles a year. Humans were "rooted" creatures. It was stylish for wealthy individuals to travel away from home, but poor people who traveled were good-for-nothings, hobos, gypsies, or suspect fortune-seekers. "Good citizens" owned their own homes and stayed there. In 1913 the around-the-globe, geographically remotest-from-one-another Earthians, employing the then swiftest extant means of travel, were six months apart. The then-popular—and now for the moment popularly unremembered—Kipling wrote, "East is East and West is West, and never the twain shall meet." In 1913 everybody believed that. In 1910 Harvard's just-retired President Eliot and his wife, granddaughter, and a young Harvard graduate escort established a world record by being the first-ever private-citizen family to accomplish a world-around trip via the regular services of transoceanic passenger ships and continental railway links. The newspapers published their successive safe arrivals. As I write this today, seventy years later, my work has taken me in forty-seven zigzagging encirclements of our earth. Over ten million other humans have an equal experience. Almost every college graduate now goes around the globe as a common experience.

In 1913 what humans spoke of as reality was all that could be seen, heard, smelled, and touched.

As I was born, Marconi discovered the invisible "wire-less," but it was not put to practical use for some time. I was twelve when the first SOS was radio broadcast by an ocean steamer in distress. When I was three years of age, the electron was discovered—it was the beginning of human-ity's operation within a new invisible reality. When I was eight, the Wright brothers first flew. Until that moment I had been told by my elders that it was inherently impossible for humans to fly.

I had a sister three years older than myself who in 1910 became one of Boston's two dozen debutantes. This was three years before I entered Harvard. She had wealthy Har-vard undergraduate beaux who came in their automobiles to call on her in Milton. One had a 1912 Mercer, another a 1910 Crane-Simplex, another a stripped-down 1908 Buick racer, another a 1912 (Belgian) Metallurgique, and one other, a 1910 Packard runabout. I felt myself very lucky. I spent hours studying those cars outside our house in the Columbine Woods of Milton.

The early automobiles titillated my exploration-eager genes. I noticed that humans were born with legs and not roots. I dreamed automobile driving as I walked. I pretended to myself that my bicycle was a car.

To the best of my knowledge, when I entered Harvard in 1913 only two in our class of seven hundred had automo-biles in Cambridge. Some of the rich out-of-towners may have had cars at home. One of the two who had cars in Cambridge was Ray Stanley, whose father had invented and was then producing the Stanley Steamers.

Our home telephone number was Milton 10. The doctor's number was Milton 37. Our Milton house was built before the days of electricity. We used kerosene lamps and wax candles.

As I entered Harvard in 1913, most fundamentally indica-tive of the technical changes occurring in the human envi-ronment was the just-then opened subway from Cambridge to Boston. It took only seven minutes to reach Park Street,

Boston (then the end of that line). This was phenomenal as compared to my great grandfather's horse-and-buggy-driven, overnight round trips from Cambridge to Boston via Watertown Bridge, or my grandfather's and father's all-day trips from Cambridge to Boston by horse and buggy or on foot over the Cambridgeport–West Boston bridge.

The Harvard stadium was built in 1903, when I was eight. It was America's and possibly the world's first large reinforced-concrete structure. I remember going to a football game in the stadium with my father when it first opened. The smell of its new concrete environment was strong. The smell of the new concrete in the Cambridge-to-Boston subway seemed to be the typical environmental smell at the portals of a new age into which we all were entering.

I was tempted by and frequently sought entrance into the new age. I invented the HCKP Club, named for the Boston-bound subway's terminals and way stations—Harvard, Central, Kendall, and Park. Brought up in one of its affluent country suburbs, I knew naught of the realities of city life. Boston fascinated me.

I could tell from the shingles hanging in my father's den that he had been a very popular club member in the class of 1883; my great-grandfather had been one of the founding members of the Hasty Pudding Club. My father had an 1879 crimson glazed china pitcher with a bronze Harvard seal let into its front belly. I learned that its hue, Harvard's official crimson, was only settled upon in my father's time. I have as yet a flag of the newly official crimson silk made by one of my father's Cambridge girl friends in 1879 with "Harvard" in black ribbon letters sewed on it.

Because there was then little indoor plumbing, body bathing by the poor was a troublesome routine. It was not frequently accomplished. The odors were powerful in the trolley cars and along the city streets. In almost every city block, there was a saloon. The smells of the people and the beer and the horse manure were powerful. In Boston Harbor there was an island where they burned the carcasses of the dead horses. Sadly, we often saw horses fallen dead on the streets. As you entered it, Boston became smellier and smellier—and you could sense the difference between the mercantile districts. The shoe-and-harness-making areas had strong aromas. So too had the linen, tea, coffee, and other districts. Luckily, some were pleasant. Some of the pleasantest came from the ship chandlers on the waterfront. Ropes, tar, and other seagoing equipment had particularly pleasing aromas. Cambridge had a much cleaner smell. It was, however, an old-building fragrance. Each of the old college buildings had its unique brand of ancient fragrance.

I was particularly dismayed by the color of buildings in general. Greater Boston and Cambridge had many wooden tenement houses, and they almost always were painted dismal yellows, browns, or grays. Frequently the very rich residences also were painted the same yellows, browns, and grays. Those yellows looked like vomit to me. I disliked the looks of the buildings themselves. They looked wrong. Almost all boats, ships, and water craft looked right and wonderful to me. Land buildings had evolved from progressively demilitarized fortresses. Yellow-painted, wooded battlements and shirt-front buildings, crammed tightly into real estate lots, looked "just like that." I did think the old buildings in Harvard Yard to be beautiful. I liked the pure-goldleaf-coated dome of the State House that shone above all Boston.

My family were not wealthy enough to have their own horses and carriages. When we needed them we hired them from the livery stable. The favorite livery driver of Harvard students was John Cusick. Many who went into Boston by subway in the evening rode out to Cambridge in or on top of John Cusick's cab.

Starting at about the time I was born, the Irish began migrating to Boston. The Irish girls found employment as maids. Their wages must have been very low. In addition to our wonderful old Irish cook Johanna, there was a waitress and a second maid—a downstairs helper. There was also an upstairs chambermaid. While young, the children had nurses. For a while we had two. It was a large household.

I found my home and family life a warm, loving experience. I thought everybody else's houses I went into were quite inferior to my own, although they were often much bigger and belonged to very rich people. There didn't seem to be as much love loose around in their houses as in mine.

Poverty was so prevalent in 1913 that the number of girls who could afford, and knew how, to dress—as neatly and as charmingly as can any girl today—was so small that everybody in Boston knew who "that girl" was.

My parents continually reminded me of my good fortune in not being one of the vast number of poor. They warned me not to be wasteful or we too would become poor. The fact that all the servants in our house seemed happy and loving obscured from me as a child that there was indeed a class system. My father worked hard at his office and worked hard in the garden when he came home. My mother seemed very busy managing our household. She was the head worker.

At ten, I realized that there was a working class. I saw an enormous number of poor, a very few really rich, and an in-between set of socially cultivated but nonrich, to which class my family belonged. When Anne Hewlett, a tenth-generation New Yorker, and I, a Bostonian, were married in 1917, the newspapers called it a "moth-ball aristocracy wedding."

There had been very large fortunes made during the nineteenth century by Bostonians and Salemites who owned clipper ships. The clipper-ship owners' family names were all around us. There were a number of clipper-ship family sons and grandsons among my freshman classmates. In 1913 the new world of finance capital had come in, and clipper ships had gone out. The banker, lawyer, stockbroker sons of clipper-ship families were in great prominence in Boston's social affairs.

That year Boston's was still predominantly a harbor of sailing ships. Few of the old square-rigged clipper-ships were to be seen. There were many primarily fore-and-aft rigged schooners of two, three, four, five, and six masts. I saw the ill-fated seven-masted *Thomas W. Lawson* as she first lay at anchor in Boston Harbor.

My father suffered a series of strokes when I was ten and never recovered. He died on my fifteenth birthday in 1910. My mother dismissed all the servants except our cook, Johanna. She dismissed the furnace man and the gardener. From then on, I did all the workingmen's chores—running the furnace, beating the rugs, cutting the grass, raking the driveway. My mother and I did the gardening. She kept me on at Milton Academy.

My sister's automobile-driving beaux were members of Harvard clubs. She later married a member of the A.D. She took pains to tell me that I would not get into any Harvard clubs because our family was not wealthy and I had no father or relatives to work at getting me into a threshold or final club. I had neither a distinguishing athletic capability nor an engaging enough personality to induce those who controlled the club system to take me despite my impecunity. I was alarmed when my sister said that my failure to be taken into a club would greatly reduce the Boston community's regard for our family.

When I did get to Harvard, I found my rich former Milton Academy classmates—now my Harvard freshman classmates—letting me know how sorry they felt for me because they had just learned that I was not going to be taken into the clubs as were they. This had an inordinately dismaying effect. I couldn't stand the idea of my friends being sorry for me. For this reason, I boasted the superior privileges to be enjoyed in my own HCKP Club and attracted some excellent members. My trouble was that I had attended not only a vastly rich men's school but was of a "poor but proud" family keeping up only superficially with the life-style of the rich. My 1917 classmate Brooks Atkinson said to me years later that, because he came into our 1917 Harvard class from a public high school in a nonaffluent suburb of Boston, he knew nothing about the club system, regarding which he had no interest whatsoever when later he learned of it.

With my older sister about to be married and I "off to college," my mother sold our Milton home. She procured excellent freshman rooms for me in Randolph Hall facing Mount Auburn Street opposite the *Lampoon* Building. This location was then known as the Harvard Gold Coast. The Gold Coast had a row of four then-modern, fireproof, multi-storied, private dormitories—Russell, Randolph, Claverly, and Ridgely Halls—within which the rich freshmen rented quite sumptuous quarters. There were no freshman dormitories or houses in Cambridge at that time. The foundations for the first freshman dormitories—now Kirkland and Winthrop Houses—were being laid in 1913. There I was, a social outcast, in the midst of the club-bound one-seventh of my class. It has taken the major class reunions of sixty years plus hundreds of fortunate happenings for me to meet and know many of the wonderful human beings constituting the other six-sevenths of Harvard 1917—less, of course, the 10 percent who perished in World War I.

In the autumn of 1913 came my first real awareness of the existence of a social class system. I had not realized, nor had anyone pointed out to me, that the controlling forces and the epistemological atmosphere of the Harvard of my forebears—the Harvard of lawyers and ministers and scholars—had been altered, as had the social, moral, and aesthetic atmosphere of America. The second half of the nineteenth century's steel, steam engine, and railroad-building era's financial underwriting wizards had become America's new power structure. Its leading banker, J. P. Morgan, and his partners underwrote the inauguration and building of Harvard's new, ever-more-specialized graduate schools. The names of those Morgan partners were given to the graduate school buildings.

Until I entered Harvard, I had never had an allowance. I had no experience in planning my economic year. Now, I had my whole year's allowance of one thousand dollars deposited for me in a Cambridge bank by my mother. With both a checkbook and a fountain pen in my pockets, I prepaid both my full year's rent and my Harvard tuition. The latter was then $150. I tried eating on a weekly basis at the several places then available to Harvard undergraduates: the Union, Memorial Hall (then the biggest, most popular, and lowest in price), Jimmy's food bar in the basement of the then very active *Harvard Lampoon,* or the Waldorf Lunch on the Square. You could buy coupon books for an adequate week's eating at an average price of five dollars.

I decided that I already had a sufficient grasp of the most effective ways of pursuing mathematics, physics, and biology to be able to pursue those subjects entirely on my own. I would read the advanced books on those subjects. In addition to taking compulsory Freshman English A, I selected for my formal subjects of study Government I, an excellent course with lectures by Monroe and Lowell; English 28, a literature class; the theory of music; chemistry; Fine Arts Appreciation I; and German literature.

I went out for cross-country running. My coach, Al Shrub—then the world's ten-mile champion—came running alongside one day and said, "Why are you running with your hands?"

I replied, "I am not."

He said, "Why then are you clenching your fists? You are wasting energy." I relaxed my hands. He kept looking me over and relaxing other parts of my body while putting all my energy into effective running. I found myself almost floating along with little effort. He said, as he left me, "Take it easy and go faster." I have never forgotten this. It has helped me through many difficult moments when I was worrying and trying too hard.

My English 28 section assistant taught me never to pretend to myself that I could guess the meaning of an unfamiliar word by its contextual implications. "Always find it in the dictionary. Always write it out with its dictionary meaning. Most important, write a sentence using the word. Once you

have used the word as a tool of your own, you will never lose
it from your spontaneous vocabulary." I have followed his
advice for sixty-seven years.

If I had stayed in Cambridge every evening, I might have
succeeded in going through Harvard in a conventional manner, but my puerile pride and my as-yet-hurting jilting by
my first-ever fallen-in-love-with girl, plus my titillated wan-
derlust, sent me scurrying into my HCKP Club's Harvard-
end entrance. From its Park Street exit, it was about a
five-minute walk southward on Tremont Street by the Hotel
Touraine, Boston's turn-of-the-century senior tenderloin
hostelry. Passing into the heart of the theater district, one
turned naturally into The Nip, the Harvard students' favorite Boston bar. Until founding the HCKP, I had never
"stepped up" to any bar. With but one of Nip proprietor
McGrath's personally shaken "nips," I was magically con-
verted into a real, live millionaire. My imagination conceived of ways of making my Cambridge Club initiates
realize the superiority of my HCKP Club. My just-married
sister, off to Honolulu for a six-month honeymoon, had left
her Russian wolfhound, Mitzi, in my care at a Cambridge
kennel. I hired a Western Union messenger to fetch Mitzi to
me. In the theater across the street from The Nip was
playing *Passing Show of 1912.* One of its minor stars was a
girl named Marilyn Miller, later to become one of Ziegfeld's
greatest-ever stars. I took Mitzi to the stage door. After the
show, every female member of its cast exiting the stage door
stopped to admire my Russian wolfhound. Marilyn Miller
and her mother were particularly intrigued with Mitzi. I
asked them to supper at the Touraine. They accepted.
Stunned by success, I was approximately speechless
throughout the evening, but the Millers seemed to enjoy
themselves and bade me contact them again. I walked back
to Cambridge with Mitzi, feeling that I had accomplished
that which many of my contemporaries would envy. They
did. I felt better.

With Harvard's then-famous football team's champion-
ship year ended and Christmas past, along came midyears. I
might have gone on successfully in this way had not my
bank account diminished too rapidly. I saw that I had not
enough to take me through to the September beginning of
my next year. I decided to expand my studies beyond Cambridge for a while. I withdrew my remaining money from the
bank, cut my midyear exams—knowing that the dean's
office would have to "fire" me—entrained with the whole
company of *Passing Show of 1912* as they shifted into their
New York opening, gave a dinner for the entire chorus at a
Broadway restaurant, took a room at the old Waldorf-Astoria
Hotel, then situated at Fifth Avenue and 34th Street where
the Empire State Building now stands. Suddenly I was out
of money and had not enough to pay my hotel bill. I tele-
phoned a rich relative of my father's age in Boston. He sent a
private detective with money to bail me out and return me to
Boston. My mother being away in Bermuda with my youngest sister, I was sent off by other Harvard 1883 classmates of
my father to be apprenticed to Lancashire, England, machine fitters who were about to assemble all the cotton-mill
machinery for a new factory whose empty building had just
been completed in Sherbrooke, Quebec. Those Lancashire
men were good teachers. I learned to assemble by myself
each of the different types of machines used in the process.

All the machines were imported from England or France.
During overseas transport, many machines were broken. I
was given the job of discovering on my own how to get
replacement parts made in foundries and machine shops in
Sherbrooke. This gave me an extraordinary development in
metallurgy and the full range of machine-tool operating. I
stayed to help get the mill in operation. I finished that job in
July. In August, World War I began. All my family and the
Harvard officials were enthusiastic over the glowing reports
of my Canadian development. I was invited back to Harvard.
This time as a "drop freshman"—dropped into the class of

1918. This in-Cambridge phase of my Harvard education again lasted until midyears, which I again cut and forced myself to be fired again—an extravagant way of signing out.

I went to work for the Chicago meat-packing house, Armour and Company, serving successively in all twenty-eight of their greater New York City wholesale market branch houses. These opened daily at 3:00 A.M. to provide fresh meats for the retail butchers' daily needs. The branch house work ended any time after 5:00 P.M. My salary was fifteen dollars a week. I had very real experience working in all the different departments of that business—learning how New York was fed. Again, I did so well that Harvard was willing to take me back, but the U.S.A.'s entry into the war was by then imminent. I joined the navy. Out of our 700-member class of 1917, only 45 were left in Cambridge to graduate. There was no GI Bill after World War I. Because I had done well in the navy, Armour and Company took me back as their assistant export manager.

During World War I, I was sent to a special three-month course at the U.S. Naval Academy. There were three requirements for such an appointment: 1) must be a college student, 2) must have had war-zone duty, 3) must be nominated by a captain or admiral.

Assuming that students had already acquired a conventional college education, the Annapolis course consisted of subjects taught only at the Naval Academy: navigation, ballistics, strategy, handling of ships, everything necessary to become an officer-of-the-line familiar with the duties of all officers of all ranks and levels of responsibility and able, if all other officers are killed, to take over the fleet.

Every split second was employed, and the strictest physical disciplines were maintained. It was the most difficult training of my life. Many flunked out. I was gratified to finish among the leaders and ahead of all other Harvard men present. This seemed to validate my self-educating strategy.

While the regular colleges were training individuals to be specialists, the Naval Academy in those days was training its graduates to be comprehensivists. I decided to continue as a comprehensivist. My successive in-out-and-in-again Harvard experiences gave me a key idea of how to accomplish comprehensivity. The strategy was based on the following fundamentals:

The successive discoveries of Copernicus, Kepler, and Galileo made possible Newton's discovery of the only mathematically expressible interattraction existing between any two celestial bodies, which varies inversely as the second power of the arithmetical distances intervening. Sum-totally, these four scientists had discovered several constant interrelationships existing between parts of a system not discoverable by the separate consideration of any one part of the system. Such a phenomenon is called synergy.

Nothing in the behavior of an atom, considered only by itself, predicts atoms compounding to form a molecule. Nothing in a molecule per se predicts biological protoplasm. Nothing in protoplasm per se predicts camels and palm trees, as well as both their lives being dependent upon the respiratory gas discharges of one serving as the other's sustaining respiratory gas and vice versa.

It is evident that the whole universe operates only synergetically in its only nonsimultaneously occurring, overlapping complexity of omnieverywhere and everywhen nonsimultaneous intertransformings. Considered only all together do these nonsimultaneous intertransformings manifest the eternal regenerativity of universe. The 100 percent efficiency of the cosmic system is manifest only by the totality of the energy involved, which never increases or decreases.

The whole educational system operates in reverse of synergetic persuasion. We fractionate comprehensive knowledge into what we call "elementary" education, which deals only in separate parts.

This fractionation came about aeons of eras ago when the greatest muscle and cunning constituted the power structure. The power structure's grand strategy has always been:

"Divide to conquer. To keep conquered, keep divided." Fearing the bright ones but in need of their help, the power structure instinctively divided their numbers by making them all specialists. Thus was developed an educational system that isolated the brilliant in ever more finely angled compartments. The power structure reserved total intelligence for its own exclusive advantage.

The power structure said to the scientists: "Don't mess around with that undignified applied science. Stick to pure science. You may get a Nobel Prize. You lay eggs; we will decide what to do with them."

I did not wish to be a specialist. Determined to be a comprehensivist, I realized that there are only a few generalized scientific principles governing the universe. If I could become a master of all the known generalized principles, then, with a little ingenuity, I could break through the ethnic, professional, and industrial language barriers and comprehend all special-case realizations of the generalizations.

I set out to do just that. It worked. I found that I could talk cogently in depth with any scientist regarding his specialization.

After a decade of vital experiences and developments, I was invited in 1929 to return to Cambridge by the founding members of Harvard's Society of Contemporary Arts—Lincoln Kirstein, Edward Warburg, and John Walker. I was asked to give five lectures a day for three weeks in the society's rooms on the top floor of the Harvard Coop building. I was exhibiting and explaining my new Dymaxion House.

The following editorial from the *Crimson,* Wednesday, May 22, 1929, tells the story:

THE HARVARD CRIMSON

Entered at the Boston Post Office, Boston. Mass., as Second Class Mail Matter, December 1, 1887.

Crimson Printing Company, Plympton Street, Cambridge 38, Mass.

WEDNESDAY, MAY 22, 1929.

DYMAXION

Mr. Buckminster Fuller's Dymaxion house is being shown this week at the rooms of the Harvard Society for Contemporary Art. When the first rumors of its marvels began to circulate in Cambridge, there was more cynicism and discountenance than even at Brancusi's Golden Bird, or at the Modern French pictures. Consider a house which is primarily a machine to live in, which can be manufactured in mass, assembled at service stations and delivered in 24 hours, costing as a minimum $500 a ton. Its translucent walls of casein, its inflatable doors and floors, its collapsible mast, its bathroom cast in a piece—all these were fantastic items to catch the imagination. However as many architects from the school and offices of the vicinity have honored the 4D plan with more than an incredible smile.

Its basic principle of decentralization, its independence of power resources, electric light, its amazingly simplified practicality in the perfection of detail has convinced many of the most obdurate, and has frightened many of the most farseeing. For in its widest implication the Dymaxion house is rather a frightening phenomenon. It threatens the architectural aesthetic found on an accumulative tradition, of Roman, Romanesque and Renaissance design. It dispenses with contracting engineers, with servants, with such domestic appendages as laundries, custom built furniture, electric light bulbs, carpets. It threatens the present economic system of centralized control of natural resources. It may mean the dissolution of the suburbs, the population of seemingly inaccessible parts of the earth. Personal independence of drudgery, allowance for a doubled leisure, a more civilized manner of existence, all depend on the Dymaxion House. Mr. Fuller has created the possibility of a new civilization, a new world of people, one only wonders with Shaw what man would do with his new found leisure.

Indeed Mr. Fuller has reinvented all the appurtenances of workaday life. The only thing left for him now, is the discovery of that elixir, by which man can double his span—so that he may satisfactorily enjoy the inevitable Millenium.

Since that editorial's writing, without any assist from me, life expectancy has almost doubled.

All my five daily lectures were to a packed room. I saw many famous Harvard professors and numbers of Boston's leaders in my audience. The late George Sarton, then Harvard's professor of the history of science said that he remembered me in my 1913–14 Cambridge-on-campus-phase, and he recalled that he had thought then that I had promise.

In 1930 Harvard University's Arts and Architecture Department asked me to give a lecture series in the Fogg Museum. In 1931 the Harvard Engineering Society asked me to speak to them at Boston's Harvard Club and made me a member of the society. In 1950 I was asked to give a general university lecture series in the Fogg Museum. In 1951 I was asked to give a series of mathematical lectures on my synergetic-vectorial geometry in the old Phillips Brooks House. In 1960 I was again asked to give a general university lecture series. In 1962 I was appointed Harvard's Charles Eliot Norton Professor of Poetry. In 1967 I was asked to speak to the Choate Club of the Law School. In 1967, my 1917 class's fiftieth anniversary year, our class officers nominated me for honorary membership in Harvard's founding chapter of Phi Beta Kappa. I received my key and diploma at the reunion.

In 1970 Harvard's Graduate School of Social Studies' New Curricula Planning invited me to lecture to them. In 1973 the business school's Century Club asked me to be their spring speaker. In the fall of 1973 I was asked to address the law school's Forum. In 1974 I was asked to be the evening's speaker at the joint dinner meeting of Harvard Business School's Graduate Association and the University of Pennsylvania's Wharton School of Finance Graduate Association held at New York City's Harvard Club. In 1978 Harvard University's Houghton Library of rare books acquired my limited edition, *Tetrascroll*. In 1978 I was asked to speak on synergetics in the Old President's House, and in 1979 Mrs. Fuller and I were invited to be the week-long guests of the Master of Lowell House.

In 1913 Harvard's dean of students assembled our entire 1917 class. He informed us that there is a subject called "sex," into which we would not inquire until after graduation. For 320 years Harvard maintained that sex vitiated study. Any student who married was immediately dismissed. When the post–World War II GI Bill came into effect, paying universities well for taking married GIs, Harvard decided to yield. In 1956 it announced with astonishment that the married students were demonstrating much better scholarship than the unmarrieds.

What I have learned from my eternal Harvard undergraduate education is that the courage to adhere to the truth as we learn it involves the courage to face ourselves with clear admissions of all the mistakes we have made. Mistakes are sins only when not self-admitted. The sin is the omission. Admission is education. An angle is a sinus, an opening, a break in a circle, a break in the integrity of the whole. Trigonometrically, the sine—sin—of an angle is the ratio of the length of the chord facing the central angle considered as ratioed to the length of the radius—taken as unity $= 1$. Epistemologically speaking, the considered angle is the angle of error of viewpoint of the individual whose circular integrity has been violated.

Human beings were given a left foot and a right foot to err or veer first to the left, then to the right, then left again and repeat. Between the overcontrolled steering mistakes, they inadvertently attain the (between the two) desired direction of advance. This is why physics has found no straight lines; it has found a physical universe operating only wavilinearly—veeringly.

"Veritas" (veer-i-tas), the motto of our 345-year-old Harvard, suggests the exquisitely controlled veering of one's course. The V contains alternate angular redirectionings. Truth is approached (but never absolutely reached) by exercise of ever less tolerance of veering errors. This is the basis of the 34-year-old science of cybernetics.

The word *cybernetics* is derived from the Greek word for "steering a boat." It was first employed by Norbert Weiner to

identify the human process of gaining and employing information. When the rudder of a ship is angled to one side or
the other of the ship's keel line, the ship's hull rotates
around its pivot or deepest keel point. Since ships have great
weight, frequently in thousands-of-ton magnitudes, the momentum of that tonnage's pivoting tends to keep rotating
the ship beyond the helmsman's intention. He therefore has
to "meet" the ship's swing-altering of its course. He does so
by "putting the rudder over" into the opposite angular direction. This always produces contradiction of momentum and
a resultant course alteration to the opposite angular side of
the desired course. It is impossible to eliminate altogether
the ship's course realterations. It is possible only to reduce
the degree of opposite angular error-swinging by ever more
sensitive, frequent, and gentle corrections.

Norbert Weiner next invented the word *feedback* to identify the progressive discoveries of angular errors and their
spontaneously coped-with overcorrections. Governed by the
gyroscope's precessionally powerful "hovering" on true
north and interconnected by delicate hydroactivated or elec-
trically actuated servomechanisms, mechanical steering is
accomplished only by the high-frequency redirecting feedback, which only minimizes angular variance errors, and
not by eliminating errors or pretending that they do not
exist. Gyro-steering produces a net wavilinear course, but
always with errors of much higher frequency and much
shorter wavelength than those made by the human handling of the rudder and the rudder's inevitably greater left
and right veerings. Veering is counter-erring; steering is
successively paired errings.

All designing of the universe is accomplished only
through angle and frequency modulation. The DNA-RNA
codes found within the geodesic protein shells of the viruses
govern the designing of all the individuals in all the species
of all the biological organisms on planet earth. The DNA-
RNA codes consist only of angle- and frequency-modulated
instructions. The course adjustments of ballistic missile

trajectories are angle- and frequency-modulated instructions ever more quickly calculated by computered feedback data from the previous course-adjustment experiences. Each competent steersman, everywhere, ever accrues experience in more effectively delicate error correction, veering along the path toward truth.

I don't know of anyone who has made as many mistakes as have I. That has been my good fortune.

Incredibly, complexedly and exquisitely designed humans have always been also designedly born naked, utterly inexperienced, ergo absolutely ignorant. They are also designed to be repeatedly hungry, thirsty, and curious. They are thus programmed to be driven to learn only by trial and error. We humans have had to make myriad mistakes. Society has now made its greatest mistake in all history by maintaining that "nobody should make mistakes" and in punishing those who do. If humanity does not bravely and intelligently admit and veeringly correct the galaxy of errors characterizing our present world status quo, it will fail to pass its examination for further continuance in the cosmic scheme, the integrity of whose eternal regeneration is governed by *veritas*.

"Veerily, verily, I say unto you" that the epistemological and etymological wisdom and aesthetics that formulated the word *veritas* were thinking of the exquisitely high frequency of interalternating feedbacks necessary to hold our mutually envisioned "true" course.

Universe—uni-verse—"toward one."

"From the age that is past to the age that is waiting before," Veritas, fair Harvard.

David McCord '21

David (Thompson Watson) McCord, poet and essayist, has written forty books (eleven of them verse for children) and edited five. Twice nominated for the National Book Award, he received the first award of the National Council of Teachers of English for One at a Time, *his 450 collected poems for the young. Sometime editor of the* Harvard Alumni Bulletin, *now* Harvard Magazine, *McCord has been a Guggenheim Fellow, received a grant from the National Institute of Arts and Letters, a very substantial grant from the Littauer Foundation in 1980, the Sarah Josepha Hale Medal and various others, and has been Phi Beta Kappa poet at five colleges. In 1950 he gave eight Lowell Lectures on Edward Lear. Born in New York City, raised in Oregon, he spent forty-six years of what he calls his "gainful life" at Harvard: A.B., 1921; A.M., 1922; L.H.D., 1956. In 1977 in Boston he read his "Sestina for the Queen" to Queen Elizabeth II. He is a Benjamin Franklin Fellow of the Royal Society of Arts, Fellow of the American Academy of Arts and Sciences, member of the American Council of Learned Societies Committee on the* Dictionary of American Biography. *Two libraries (one in Canada) are named for him. In twenty-five years he has talked about poetry to tens of thousands of fourth- and fifth-graders from Boston to Chicago.*

It is easy to carp at colleges, and the college, if we will wait for it, will have its own turn. Genius exists there.
—Ralph Waldo Emerson, Class of 1821, Harvard College

Something totemic as well as personal is in the title of this book. For *Our Harvard* implies, or so it seems to me, not simply essays of recollection, but essays of the most intimate kind of recollection of time and place implicit in three Latin words: *laudator temporis acti*, and in the illusional sense of *déjà vu*.

If you are my contemporary in years, then my view of what happened to me at Harvard, or my reporting of the Harvard scene of fifty or sixty years ago, may strike you as plausible enough; but to a younger reader much of what I say will appear as strange—even as improbable—as what (in 1919 or so) I found both strange and improbable in the old class reports of the post–Civil War period as I looked them over. Indeed, I stare aghast at Harvard Square today: uprooted and disfigured by the feverish sandbox engineering involved in stretching subway tracks out north to Porter Square, as though some moles of huge proportions were at work in monstrous tunnels under a public lawn where a thousand frantic people can no longer play croquet. And so, as I consider this well-planned disaster and thread my way through labyrinths of prefab weird detritus, I wonder if my Harvard, when I knew and loved her, ever existed as a work of art. But it did exist. And all the more vividly to me because of my background. Harvard to me was revelation.

I was born in New York City, lived for several years on Long Island; for three in Princeton, New Jersey; and, having caught malaria in lower New York (as many did) from Italian workers on that city's pioneer American subway, I never advanced beyond the equivalent of grade six in two different private schools. Recurring malaria and much-needed though horrible quinine kept me out of the classroom for months at a time. Then suddenly, when I was twelve, my father, my mother, and I took off for my uncle's wild-as-Eden but godforsaken Oregon apple ranch—incredible for flowers, veins of gold, quail, blue grouse, cougar, wild hogs, pileated woodpeckers, jackrabbits; truly frontier nature to respect, fear, love, and marvel at—in the upper Rogue River valley, southwest Jackson County.

No school at all from twelfth to fifteenth year, save for some twenty weekends of tutoring in Latin, math, and English by a remarkable crippled German lady, named Celia Doerner, in nearby Grants Pass. In those three years I never actually saw, let alone spoke to, more than five or six youngsters my age in twelve months' time unless we drove to Medford or Grants Pass on business. If I learned about loneliness, I learned to value solitude as well; that love of solitude, a constant search for solitude even in the midst of a crowd, has been with me all my life. And what *is* solitude? A commodity unknown to most of us today; ununderstandable by the teenager or hippie lugging his portable radio going full blast on the street or in a bus. Silence by many is no longer to be endured.

So, on that unyielding apple ranch I came to understand something of the wilderness: how to milk a cow, swing an ax, pan gold, raise chickens, keep my bearings in a trailless forest, and (above all) how to fish with a fly for trout and steelhead in the clear swift water of the Rogue. Then followed three happy years in Portland where I went to Lincoln High School which, through a series of miracles, prepared me for and directed me to Harvard.

I say this much of myself because my account of *my* Harvard is that of a curiously shy and unsophisticated youngster, "magnificently unprepared" (in Frances Cornford's wondrous words) not "for the long littleness of life," but for private trailblazing through the enormous lost-and-found department of an ancient College.

Still a firm believer in Sir William Osler's notion of living in a day-tight compartment, I have spoken just now out of what to me seems a most spectacular silence as I pause to look and think back across the gulf of sixty-three years. Having once lived in Princeton, and even earlier in my boyhood become familiar with Washington and Jefferson College in Pennsylvania—for the sooty town of Little Washington was where my grandmother made her home—I was quite ready, in choosing Harvard, to discover what goes on *inside* a college. "Enter to grow in wisdom" read the sign over the gate which greeted me in cheerful welcome mixed with mild admonition back in 1917 as I emerged from a nonmalarial new subway operating in a pregraffiti age. Inside that gate the Harvard Yard, serene in the company of surviving ancient elms, artfully dotted with younger ones now grown along with me, I stood—I remember standing—speechless. Perhaps I failed to register the stark Euclidean order of the older dormitories—Hollis, Stoughton, and Holworthy in particular, for what at once took my eyes and imagination was not what Emerson, Thoreau, and tens of generations before me had remembered, but the twin symbols of my own inventive age: two stunning wireless towers atop the Cruft Laboratory. What else? For had I not learned the Morse code at seven? At fifteen I was a licensed amateur first-grade wireless operator. My steel-cutting lathe, with its superior Skinner chuck, which I had bought with a hard come-by thirty-two dollars out in Oregon, would soon be standing in the apartment which my mother had rented on Story Street, just three blocks from the Yard. It was my lathe

and the wireless apparatus I had built, plus my father's and
my uncle's engineering background that swung the needle
of my compass toward those towers.

"You will be concentrating in the classics?" asked my
elderly adviser, a distinguished member of the Department
of Romance Languages, noting from my college board
exams that the 84 in translating English into Latin—not
rendering unto Caesar the things which were Cicero's—
had some slight significance even against my 97 in solid
geometry. "No," I stupidly replied, "I think I shall—probably
using 'will'—be in physics." Why was I not asked what I
knew about physics (zero) and what were the (nonexisting)
reasons for my singular choice? My elderly adviser did not
even say, "Well, good luck." Nor did I tell him about beginning Latin at age ten or that I was given the lead (300 lines)
in a high school Latin play with the thrilling opening of
"Nunc, pueri, percipite quaeso diligenter quae dicam."

"London is many cities," said H. M. Tomlinson, that solitary titan among neglected English men of letters. Yes,
indeed: Harvard College is—or was in my time—many colleges. To me, ostensibly a commuter, though not from any
great distance, Harvard did not simply *appear;* it had to *loom*
across the Charles as did, in *Arabia Deserta,* Boreyda and its
mesjid toward the Wady er-Rummah. For in a disappointing
sense I never saw it truly from the inside as did most of my
1921 classmates who *lived* in Harvard College: first in the
newly opened so-called Freshman Dormitories along the
Charles, and later in the old Yard itself. This, in the androgy-
nous school language of all American colleges today, means
simply living on or off campus. My father having died in the
fall of 1916, I shared with my mother that four-room apartment on Story Street. Today I pay for garaging my car in
Boston more than twice what she paid out in rent! It is true
that in freshman year I *ate* in Gore Hall, one of President
Lowell's freshman dorms, or in Memorial Hall, or later on in
the Union or the Signet; but the night life of the average
three or four undergraduates assigned to a suite of two or
three rooms was glimpsed only on rare occasions.

Because I lived on very little money, I had set myself a rigorous schedule of six courses a year in order to graduate in three years: a plan which I held to in spite of a few months at Plattsburg in the infantry and at Camp Zachary Taylor in Louisville as a second lieutenant in the Field Artillery. I was but one half a course short of fulfilling that Spartan schedule by the end of my junior year, when something gave way in my resolve. I stayed on and completed my senior year with five courses, chiefly in Romance languages; but now with freedom for pursuing extracurricular activities: president of the *Lampoon,* for one.

Certainly those malarial years and their reward (no school, remember) on my uncle's ranch had clearly defined for me the profound distinction between loneliness and solitude. All my directives so clearly Thoreauvian, I had turned nonetheless to my grandfather's Emerson before I even heard of *Walden.* But not knowing a living soul in the Harvard College which I entered, I discovered quickly that loneliness and solitude were soluble. ROTC and inevitable enlistment to come had much less effect on me—and on my classmates, mostly two years younger than I—than one might think. I was over my head in a brand new world. Lonely at times, as I am sure my remarkable, brave pioneer mother must have been so very often, for me (as not for her) there was youth alive at every turn: even the classroom was exciting.

Some aspects of college life, of course, were difficult to understand at first. There were, for example, some twenty-five Exeter graduates in my class of 1921. They had the big hand in class politics as in different ways did other groups from Milton, Groton, St. Mark's, Nobles, St. Paul's, and Middlesex, though the group from Andover was too small to count. As a group of one from Lincoln High School way out in Portland, I could only marvel how, on certain October or November weekends, considerable numbers of my classmates left Cambridge to visit and feel again, as one-time big shots, the hypocaustal warmth of their several schools. Why? I asked myself. I had crossed a continent to enter

Harvard, that marvelous and complex synecological terminus to which all roads of life were made to lead and from which all roads through life appeared to depart.

My freshman year was untypical. The electronic side of physics had lured me—by casting a spell, it must have been—into concentration in that increasingly abstruse division of science for which I was in no way prepared. Pathetically immature in most ways, even if I could read the Morse code and loved the sound of words in that other musical code of prose and prosody, I carefully avoided taking any courses in English literature, save the prescribed and stuffy English A, because I fancied my own way of writing, such as it was—as it surely was *not!*—would be shaped by rules and influences easy to imagine, impossible to define. I had enjoyed elementary mathematics, but the months spent on analytical geometry I still consider a waste of time. By freshman year we all should have been well into differential, if not integral, calculus. But let me say that as a writer I now value—actually treasure—those three years in the physics laboratory even though I could often not distinguish the walls of glass from the walls of bronze. This more than half a lustrum spent in an exacting science has strengthened a relentless effort on my part to look for exact answers where there are (as in poetry) none.

It seems to me now, on reflection, that in those first few months in Cambridge I was constantly comparing the College, the Yard, and Harvard Square with what I remembered of Princeton (1907–10) and Washington and Jefferson (off and on during long and short visits (1903–17). Princeton favored Gothic architecture. The original Prospect Place, in my day the president's home, was my three-times great grandfather's house; and in it, I am fairly certain, the Congress of the young United States assembled for its first few sessions after withdrawing from Philadelphia fifty miles away. For that reason, the Princeton campus and the gracious stretch of Nassau Street (half a street, as they say of the more famous one in Edinburgh, familiar to the

Scottish president John Witherspoon) remained a part of me: secret and lovely as T. S. Eliot's rose garden. Nevertheless, Princeton as I had seen it, with sophomore-freshman hazing, undergraduate regimentation, and dominion of the clubs, failed to challenge now the absolute tranquillity I discovered in the Harvard Yard. On the other hand, Washington and Jefferson, where my grandfathers and uncles had gone to college, still held for me as late as 1916 the fascination of an informality years ahead of its time. The noisy fraternity just across the street from grandmother's old house proclaimed its splendid isolation from the world in winter when yellow tobacco juice spit from second-story windows would ring the building every time fresh-fallen snow was on the ground.

My early Cambridge days came back to me in unrelated flashes. Let me itemize at random.

Item. Today, whenever I visit the still peaceful Yard and cross some diagonal path from one building toward another, the place comes suddenly alive with ghosts—not for me the ghosts which Emerson recalls so eloquently, but my own shifty private trains of them, a thrombus in bright memory: George Lyman Kittredge, magnificent in carriage as of old; but now reduced, in visitation, to the well-trimmed white beard, the well-smoked black stogie; John Livingston Lowes of the piercing gaze, scarce taller than John Keats's five feet even, with the small man's bounce to his step, his corporate self so vividly kinetic, so clearly the well-indexed bundle of unreleased tension; or the great unhonored Irving Babbitt, heavier when stooped with no cluttered desk in front of him, perpetually lost in blinding thought; or President Lowell, always elegant, always the perfect image of portable aristocracy; or forbidding Copey, black bowler tightly pressed sideways under his right arm, wearing self-consciously his cool cucumber mask which, better than a bumper sticker, told you: "I am Charles Townsend Copeland. Who are you?"; or dear Edward Ballantine the musician, even in music truly a wit, whose infectious laugh was, in low register, one long indrawn stifled gurgle.

Item. Copey! I have only to conjure his gray shade, repeat in a whisper his three-decker name, to remember his lapidarian delight in—"fondling" is the word I want—in fondling strange syllables sandwiched between the Christian and given handles of, say, Francis *Peloubet* Farquhar, Charles *Macomb* Flandrau, Nathaniel *Southgate* Shaler, Sarah *Orne* Jewett, Minnie *Maddern* Fiske, Annie *Trumbull* Slosson, my Harvard classmate Stoddard *Benham* Colby, and Robert *Silliman* Hillyer, Copey's successor in the Boylston professorship.

Item. Copey should have been an actor: he *was* an actor, *Meopte ingenio* he might have, but did not, say of himself. Above his many readings towered the annual one he gave at Christmas: free, and a sell-out in box office terms. His friend and admirer Alexander Woollcott once introduced him at Christmas time in the Harvard Union. Of course Copey no more needed an introduction than did Will Rogers then or Bob Hope now. After lamp, chair, reading glasses, water glass, shades, all of what the Horatian in Copey referred to as "Persian apparatus" had been adjusted, and a long silence endured, the inevitable cough was heard, duly registered, and responded to by "Coughing does not help a reading." Another pause, broken by Copey: "I want none of this to get into the papers." He then proceeded to read from the Book of Ruth.

Only President Lowell could equal or excel Copey with the Bible. As the Master once said to me of John Barrymore in *Hamlet:* it sounded as though he had written it himself.

Item. The outdoor commencements in the twenties were appropriately climactic as something more than the logical conclusion of three days of festivity in the old Yard: brightness by day with the sparkle of two huge temporary fountains playing quietly against a lively band in a genuine bandstand; brightness again by night, and sentimentally a total dream world under the beautifully ukiyo-e spun web of Japanese lanterns—pure fairyland for which I would gladly trade today's huge hi-fi spectaculars assembled in massive anonymity, and trade them ten times over. I think of William James: "The curse of bigness." Charm is a dead duck now.

Item. Not being able to read music beyond knowing that the spaces in the treble clef spell FACE, I nonetheless tried out for the Harvard Glee Club in my sophomore year and failed to be accepted. In my junior year I learned the part which I would probably be asked (required) to sing in the trials and thereby became a risky member. I sang in my junior and senior years under Archibald (Doc) Davison, being lowered by him quite logically from a baritone to a second bass. Singing under the Doc, coming not only to admire him but to love him as a friend, was spiritually and artistically the greatest Harvard experience—*concentrated experience,* you understand—of my undergraduate days. I continued with the Glee Club during my single graduate year as well. The Doc stood then at the height of his inspirational power: concert by concert he was drastically changing uninspired collegiate choruses into the often dizzying instruments which they are today right straight across the country. I foolishly did not go abroad with the club in the summer of 1921 because of an Ivy Oration commitment. I regret that awkward decision—one of those "little decisions" of which I shall speak—gone wholly wrong. But I *did* have the long earlier trip in the Easter vacation to Cincinnati, Pittsburgh, Chicago, St. Louis, and elsewhere, including a fog-bound train wreck.

Item. I remember one time standing in Sanders Theater during a BSO concert. I think that Papa Monteux was conducting the Brahms Third or Fourth. One of my fellow

Glee Club members stood an arm's length away from me writing music on a sheet of paper pressed against the wall. Supposing that he was taking down what Monteux happened to be playing, just as an exercise, I asked him if my guess was right. It was not. He was composing, he said, a fugue of his own. That as yet unacknowledged Saint in One Act was Virgil Thomson.

Item. What happened "worldwise," as they say today, in 1921? Well, Harding was President, George V was king of England; David Lloyd George, prime minister; Robert Bridges, poet laureate. *The Birth of a Nation* was banned in Boston. Richard Wilbur, poet, and Peter Ustinov, actor, were born; E. B. White emerged from Cornell. Caruso died. O'Neill's *Anna Christie* opened, and I saw it, starring Pauline Lord. Three world figures won Nobel Prizes: Anatole France, Albert Einstein, Woodrow Wilson. Among the new popular songs was "Look for the Silver Lining." Among books published: Wells's *Outline of History,* Sinclair Lewis's *Main Street,* Edith Wharton's *The Age of Innocence.* Abbott Lawrence Lowell was president of Harvard; Le Baron R. Briggs, dean. The Harvard Glee Club under A. T. Davison toured Europe—a landmark, I think, for any American college chorus.

Item. Class reunions. At commencement, 1921, I and some classmates looked with awe if not with pity upon the class of 1896, twenty-five years out, still artificially spry and ambulatory, parading in columns of two. How could any people live so long? In 1971, at our own *fiftieth* reunion, I overheard one hippie remark to another as we straggled up from Dunster toward the Yard: "Incredible!"

Item. Henry Beston, '09, of *The Outermost House,* spent an hour in my Wadsworth House office during *his* twenty-fifth, then rose with a noticeable sigh of resignation and said, "Well, I guess I'll have to go out and smell Rover."

Item. ROTC. The spring of freshman year found me digging trenches out Fresh Pond and Waverly way and serving as assistant bayonet instructor. The only thing I ever killed with that instrument was a belligerent tarantula which jumped out of a bag of bananas on my bed at 2:00 A.M. as I was reading *Les Miserables* in French. I finished the tarantula with horror and the book with tears.

Item. Jimmy's Lunch, a popular hole-in-the-wall wooden shack abutting the Hasty Pudding Club, was the splendid dispenser of a late breakfast and midnight snacks. Jimmy's featured, and indeed was famous for, some peculiar offerings unduplicated anywhere. Examples: black and tans (thick chocolate paste on hot buttered whole wheat toast); seagoing black and tans (the same with peanut butter added); elephant milk (a very large glass of pasteurized— not yet homogenized—milk). Most glamorous was "Queen the Duke," the curt command for a spread of cream cheese and bar-le-duc. *Queen the Duke!* What a glorious sound! A glory undiminished, like, man, uno. Right?

Item. My classmate, the future geologist John Bradley, and I occasionally walked around Fresh Pond, and twice (thirteen miles each way), to Concord. He introduced me to Walden—book and pond. John was a master bass plug fisherman who scorned the use of an antibacklash reel. His prose style in that small classic *Parade of the Living* likewise shows the same perfectionist at work. John is dead now, but it pleases me that the oldest fossil known to man (a starfish) is named for such an ardent Thoreauvian as he.

Item. President Lowell, to my imperfect knowledge, was the only president of the five I have known to own a dog. His was a spaniel with a lofty, uncharacteristic plume for a tail. He answered to the name of Phantom. Phantom followed Mr. Lowell everywhere except up ladders leaning against new buildings under construction. When President and

Mrs. Pusey arrived to take over No. 17 Quincy Street in 1954, their taxi driver, recognizing the address, spoke of Mr. Lowell in the singular, but of Phantom in the plural. "President Lowell would always meet me at the front door, and I can hear his very words, for they were always the same: 'Watch out now for them dogs.' "

Item. At various times we heard, and sometimes met or dined in the company of such as Siegfried Sassoon, William Jennings Bryan, Gertrude Stein and Alice B. Toklas, H. G. Wells, AE, William Butler Yeats, James Stephens, T. S. Eliot, Robert Frost, Alexander Woollcott, Langston Hughes, H. M. Tomlinson, Stephen Vincent Benét, Robert Sherwood, Robert Benchley, Walter Lippmann, Heywood Broun, Waldo Pierce, Julian Street, Christopher Morley, Walter de la Mare, Rabindranath Tagore, Bernard Berenson, Amy Lowell, Louis Untermeyer, and (who could forget?) an English youth named Mallory, a Rupert Brooke-like young Apollo, soon to lose his life on Mount Everest.

Item. Dear old Dean Briggs! Among lesser teachers he shone like a star in my section of freshman English A—expository writing, with fringe benefits in terms of reading, lectures on grammar, usage, and the like. The dean once gave us a fatherly moral lecture, the contents of which, I later came to realize, both strongly and weakly resembled similar fatherly efforts (foolish efforts) in such plays as *Ah, Wilderness!* and *Life with Father.* The first published poet whom most of us ever heard reading or saying his poems was Joseph Auslander in English A: perhaps Robert Hillyer as well. It was a curious education for me (still with my shyness) to know and like as a friend Jack Wheelwright, one year ahead of me in college and a fellow editor of the *Lampoon.* He sometimes sought me out and read me his leftist poetry—poems just now, as we enter the penumbral shadow of 1984, gathered together and put openly on display by questing and questioning young critics. I met these friendly readings by Jack at sharp right angles, but I actually helped him get his single now quite famous poem, "There Is No Opera like Lohengrin," into the pages of *The New Yorker*. He was always more generous with my amorphous labors than I with his.

Item. Six courses a year for three years are not to be recommended. I could never do justice to any of my six. Tutorials were just then coming into the humanities, though not into the sciences; and I, unguided, was already over my head in physics, groping blindly toward the coming world of transistors; repeating in laboratory Milliken's famous experiment of the charge on the electron. At the same time, however, I was entirely free under the elective system to delve into geology, astronomy, anthropology, philosophy, fine arts, French, and comparative literature. I more than delved into French, choosing to reconcentrate in my finally unscheduled senior year; and I chose to concentrate this time in Romance languages. The primary criticism of my lustrum at Harvard is to deplore the lack of a continuing professor-adviser. None but a fool (see Maugham's *The Summing Up* on the subject) would waste two years studying Spanish. I could reasonably make out a Spanish paragraph simply through Latin and French. Two years of it, and half of *Don Quixote*, and all I can say with truth today is *No puede mas! Ich kann nichts dafür; J'en suis fâché.*

Item. George Washington Pierce in physics not only knew, wrote, read, and lectured in and on the calculus—he *spoke* the calculus, and was in no way impatient with an ungifted student. Were I to produce an essay to be entitled "Me and the Calculus Today," I would point to Professor Alfred North Whitehead respecting one concept of the Quantum Theory in action: "It is as though you could walk at three miles per hour and at four miles per hour, but not at three and a half miles per hour." In the calculus I walked (sometimes jogged) at three and a half miles per hour.

Item. Compared with my genuine surprise in being one of three undergraduates elected editors of the *Lampoon* in freshman year—a record which, I think, stood long unbeaten—my athletic career at Harvard was a dismal failure. Out in Oregon I had played hare and hounds, very popular at the time. And being one of the hares never caught by a future Princeton cross-country runner and star two-miler, I went out for cross country in my junior year. We used to change our clothes at the police station in Belmont and then struggle and straggle out over the Belmont hills. I once came in ahead of all the freshmen and behind all the varsity; but later on in Cambridge and Watertown, returning for some geographic reason through the small cemetery east of Mount Auburn, I came upon the first tenor of our barbershop quartet being sick on a tombstone. This dismal sight ended my cross-country venture. I wasn't even eligible to be included in the squad photograph. My father had been a champion golfer and stroke of his crew at R.P.I., and his brother captain of both baseball and football at Lawrenceville in New Jersey. I cheerfully disgraced them both.

Item. In my junior year I caught the measles, and during two weeks in quarantine at home I turned out, with the help of my steel-cutting lathe, a very compact, very small, very neat crystal wireless receiving set, in which the hinged lid of match-box dimensions was a functional part. On recovery, I took this tiny instrument over to Cruft Laboratory and tried it out on the big antenna which had beckoned me on that first day in the Yard. I expected to pick up code in my earphones and nearly fell out of the chair to hear someone playing the banjo—one of the earliest broadcasts of voice and music ever recorded in Cambridge. It issued from the Tufts station on Medford Hillside.

Item. Criticism. Sometime before this nightmare world we live and work in falls apart, the pressing of a single button will give us a printout (readout) of the digested conclusions of all certified critics respecting any book, subject, project, syndrome, invention, discovery, or what you will. But if I learned anything at Harvard it was to *weigh* the critic critically, for he or she is only human. Nothing that matters can be all good or all bad, to be tested or tasted like an egg. A bad poem may contain the splendid line or thought which shatters you. A beautiful theory may be childish in deduction at only one point—the point at which the knowledgeable judge will judge it. In my Harvard years I think we learned from the giants, or from just one medium giant on the faculty, to value values for exactly what they are; and to understand that even as we examine or admire the venation of a single leaf, a critic somewhere may be chopping down the tree.

Item. Recommended reading: Raphael Demos, a Platonist, urgently led me to *Of Human Bondage,* opening an early door to other books by Maugham. And if Maugham readers have missed it, I in turn recommend, in continuing the Demos chain of good advice, a travel book by him called *The Gentleman in the Parlour,* title out of Hazlitt, a very different and compassionate Maugham from the one you know.

In 1922 John Livingston Lowes looked unfavorably on *Moby Dick* as he did on Joyce. But because *The Road to Xanadu* (1927) was already in embryonic state and on display in Lowes's lectures, I read *Moby Dick,* and likewise all of Joyce, involving many midnight hours lost in Dublin fog over *Finnegans Wake.* I know that Lowes later changed his mind about Melville. I doubt if he ever yielded to *Ulysses,* even to *Dubliners.* I, on the other hand, easily yielded to his recommendations of detective stories such as *The Rasp* and *The Noose* by Philip MacDonald. What critic, incidentally, has made a specific study of xenolithic Joyce *and* Edward Lear in Lear's published letters? A gold mine for someone. Lowes had died before I could ask him about this.

Item. Once at a Leverett House dinner in the early 1930s a few of us lucky ones sailed briefly to Byzantium. Yeats was visiting Harvard while T. S. Eliot was serving his semester as Charles Eliot Norton Professor. At Leverett House I so well remember Yeats, whom I had never seen before, standing at the head of the receiving line. Eliot, whom I did know slightly through George Blake and Frank Morley of London, was just ahead of me in line. Yeats inclined his tall handsome self, with half-closed eyes, offering everyone a straight-arm downward defensive handshake. I thought perhaps he would say, "Hello, Tom," to T.S.E. But no. Mr. Eliot received in silence the same downcast eyes and downward handshake as the rest of us. *Juxta fluvium poteum fodit.*

Item. At one of Eliot's semi-inaudible Norton lectures, a friend of mine watched an elderly lady plumped down in front of him, with an open pad resting on the wide right arm of her seat. Once she bent over quickly and made a note while the great man was talking. My friend leaned down to see what she had written. She had written: "The Renaissance. Watch out for it."

Item. The awakening. Readers of Thoreau—and you will find this quoted in Emerson's *Journals*—may remember "What you seek in vain for half your life, one day you come full upon—all the family at dinner." Harvard in my day was a breeding ground for serendipity. Perhaps she still is. Associate Professor Richard Lauren Hawkins in an early French course, pausing one day to recite from memory, and apropos of nothing, a poem by William Cory (1823–1892), startled me:

> They told me, Heraclitus, they told me you were dead.
> They brought me bitter news to hear and bitter tears to shed. . . .

On leaving the classroom I hurried across to Widener, looked up the text. Mr. Hawkins had recited the whole of it; and so could I recite it before I left the library. Isn't this what lectures are really for: the lighting of unexpected lamps?

Item. What bookstores in Harvard Square today will graciously induct an inwardly curious and outwardly wistful young illiterate like myself into the delights not alone of book buying, but of book collecting? Years ago there stood genial—wise and genial—Mr. Moriarty in the old Harvard Coop building, inviting you simply by his presence into the small book-lined hole off the mainstream of best-seller counters, ready to express with a mingling of surprise and sorrow his personal anxiety over your personal ignorance of "the mystical mathematics of the Kingdom of Heaven," which could be yours, and yours extended through all six enchanting small English volumes of Sir Thomas Browne. These six, four of Synge, and a deeply treasured Gibbon from my classmate and first publisher, David W. Bailey, are about the only sets, as such, in my six-thousand-volume library. I scatter now the ashes of recollection across this page in memory of Mr. M.

Item. Nature. It was *Red Fox, The Kindred of the Wild, The Feet of the Furtive, Haunters of the Silences, The Watchers of the Trails*—perhaps but the very titles in themselves above and beyond all those handsomely bound and illustrated books by Charles G. D. Roberts of New Brunswick, Canada, read as a boy of eight, nine, or so—that made me want to try some day to be a writer. Of course, Sir Charles—he was one of the first three Canadians to be knighted—was a poet first of all. And if you can't guess that fact just by reading aloud to yourself five words: *The Feet of the Furtive,* you have not walked enough alone in woods to "feel the fell of dark" as I have felt it.

But busy with physics, geology, fine arts; struggling miserably with philosophy; deep in a new world as difficult at times to value as it is to think of $\sqrt{-1}$, it was not until my graduate year under Lowes, Babbitt, and George P. Baker that, quite on the side, a larger, ever-widening landscape opened to me through the door of Hollis 15. Certain figures moved across that landscape, and they were Conrad, Emerson, Thoreau, Parkman, Borrow, W. H. Hudson, Kipling, James Stephens, Tomlinson, Sarah Orne Jewett, and de la Mare. They seemed to move in chorus, though in totally different directions. They had in common the natural world, a glorious conflict of styles; and the catalyst in Copey stood behind them.

Item. Birds in the Yard. I suspect that in the stretch of 344 years certain undergraduates must have kept bird lists. I never did, but I have seen, beyond the expected sparrows, pigeons, crows, gulls, starlings, robins, blue jays, some few others: catbirds, chickadees, one barred owl, one brown thrasher, ruby-crowned kinglets, occasional flickers, an olive-backed (male) thrush, various warblers. I knew of, but failed to locate, the solitary shrike whose storage office was in President Conant's hedge. Queerly enough, when I once talked at Sweet Briar, I was told of a shrike in the Sweet Briar president's hedge! Two shrikes! I refrain from the obvious pun.

Item. More than sixty Harvard commencements have rewarded me with very few memorable citations introducing the recipients of honorary degrees just before they are handed their crimson-bound diplomas. None who heard it will forget President Pusey's for E. B. White: "Sidewalk superintendent of our time."

Somewhat ahead of Edmund Clerihew Bentley's invented verse form, which bears his name, the Harvard honorary degree citations began to follow a simple monotonous formula: the candidate's name, and then what he or she is noted for. An example of the concise Clerihew form is:

> Cimabue
> Was a bit of a roué.
> He used to get blotto
> With a bloke named Giotto.

My own rendition of the Harvard formula, though absurd, still strikes me as not unpleasantly accurate: "Long a breeder of Guernsey cows, he found a new way to bring cream to the top."

Item. Harry Starr, learned, devoted friend and classmate for whom a professorship at Harvard is now named, alerted me very early freshman year to F.P.A.'s famous "Conning Tower" in the old New York *World,* a truly intellectual paper: in short, a floating island of self-castaway young writers. Being alerted, I was not long out of graduate school when I began contributing to "The Conning Tower," a supremely tempting target to many young beginners. To me, no other target ever loomed so large. No excitement, I am sure, exceeded that of those of us who hit it now and then—most particularly the top of the column, where my first contribution was printed.

Item. Well, what *did* we get out of Harvard? What does *anyone* get out of Harvard in any generation? Never the same thing twice. Snowflakes, we say, resemble each other: and so they do in everything but shape. What we all get (and got) out of Harvard is a useful awareness of our ignorance and an awakening of intellectual curiosity. My worldly classmate, James N. White, tells me of what B.L.T. (Bert Leston Taylor), the brilliant F.P.A. of the *Chicago Tribune,* once quoted in his column. Respecting the city's motto—the sharp "We will!"—my classmate has given me ten specific words of some Midas of the Stockyards quoted by B.L.T.: "What's an orchestra? By God, we'll have one!" Beyond what Whitehead called those "irreducible and stubborn facts," through which we forced our way, new vistas suddenly came into focus, birds flew up out of the turret, doors swung open on Eliot's rose garden, on Conrad's *The Mirror of the Sea,* on the technical revelations of Gerard Manley Hopkins. We sensed for keeps the exponential possibility of imminent expansion in world geology, astronomy, botany, economics, electronics, the surgeon's breakthrough of mitral stenosis and tissue transplants and such miracles yet to come, all as dazzling as the vast vocabulary of the Eskimo, undoubtedly by now in swift and civilized decline. We learned to respect the rudimentary art of correlation, how to distinguish the first rate from the second rate, how to look at a painting, drawing, watercolor, or etching, how to listen to music, how to accept not wholly with sadness the deadly erosion of time, how to fly just a little on extended wings we don't in any way possess. And as to that last: how to read with equal pleasure the poetry of Wallace Stevens, Eliot, Frost, Edward Lear; the prose of Parkman, Doughty, C. S. Lewis, Chesterton, J. O. P. Bland, W. W. Jacobs, Max Beerbohm, Freya Stark, and *A Wrinkle in Time*.

Item. Of what use is an education? It may save you money. My physics saved me money once when I was fishing for salmon on the Miramichi in New Brunswick. Wading in fast water just over my knees, I fell behind a large rock in the young river, held my precious Thomas rod aloft, but got quite wet. Returning to camp I discovered that my new glasses—my first pair at forty-six—had escaped from my coat's upper pocket. Sixty feet below where I had fallen, the river tumbled in a noisy drop through a jumble of boulders. Various jokes were made about my accident. It was assumed that my new glasses were heading for the sea. I mentally considered their flatness, the hooks of the bows, the weight of the water and the probable differential between surface speed and bottom speed, turbulence, a so-called Reynolds number (velocity times distance over viscosity) which could suggest a bottom speed of one-seventh surface speed, and took immediate action. I returned to the site of the tragedy, tied my sunglasses to my leader, cast them over the spot where I had fallen, gave them slack line, and after several experiments in that open laboratory found that the angle of descent was constant and that the glasses each time came to rest. My unbelieving classmate and I then waded out upstream from just below where the sunglasses had come to rest, peered down through the clear northern water, and there shone my spectacles. Two of my ancestors knew Ben Franklin. I never knew even William James. We pragmatists are a solitary lot.

Item. From 1917 on down into the thirties, Boston was Mecca, Valhalla, and Paradise for anyone who loved the theater. Ten cents would take you from Cambridge to Boston and back; twenty-five gave you a seat in the balcony of the old Copley (Repertory) Theater, directed by E. E. Clive. It was there that I saw and heard most of, much of, or some of Shaw, Sheridan, Wilde, Galsworthy, Milne, Pinero, Lonsdale, Ian Hay, Maugham, Chekhov, and miniclassics like *The Ghost Train* and *Charlie's Aunt,* or was it *Bunty Pulls the Strings?* What a choice of theaters, thronged on opening nights, in that post–World War I period: Shubert, Wilbur, Majestic, Hollis, Plymouth, Cort, Colonial, Tremont, Copley, the Old Howard. Name another such galaxy in any English-speaking city, save London and New York! A golden age in that respect, and we at Harvard were in it.

Item. How simple, how peaceful, how *safe* was Harvard Square in 1917 to 1921. Today at the roaring high tide and bedlam of shuttled traffic it seems more like the Black Hole of Calcutta, but sixty-three years ago, so totally quiet, it impressed one as did a small town's simple cluster of stores surrounding a small college. Trolley cars would take you to seedy Central Square, past O'Brien's Funeral Home, past M.I.T., across the bridge, and on into Boston; or, with a few changes in another direction, all the way to Concord, perhaps to Worcester. Perhaps, for all I remember, having no carfare, to Hartford or Springfield. Who could tell?

Item. It is not always the brilliant lecturer who persuades. Out of the background of dullest monotone issuing from a dormouse sometimes the word, phrase, aphorism, or wise tangential observation strikes home because of contrast. Professor Conrad C. H. Wright on seventeenth-century

French literature was a deep, devote (not devout) man in scholarship: professionally dull in voice and delivery, yet strangely and memorably vivid by implication. All these years I have been grateful to him for the way he repeated three important words—vastly important to a writer—of Malherbe: *"Polisser et repolisser."*

Item. From 1921 on, Copey became my constant adviser until he died. I think often of those enchanted evenings in Hollis 15 with the petulant Master, and with (by us) unexpected visitors like Elizabeth Shepley Sargent (E. B. White's sister-in-law), Heywood Broun, Woollcott, Lee Simonson, Tomlinson, Philip Barry, Waldo Pierce, Stephen Benét; of an afternoon (two hours) with John Barrymore who sipped whisky (or whiskey) out of a small Listerine bottle and told us how, on a night train from Melbourne to Sydney or Brisbane or somewhere, he had read two acts of *Hamlet* for the first time and had said to himself, "Some day I must play this fellow." He was then playing in nightly sell-outs here in Boston in the old Opera House at the same high level of many other great Hamlets, notably Forbes-Robertson and Gielgud—and yet with more excitement. With Copey I also met Robert Benchley (in Copey's classroom) and, for a greater thrill, his old flame Mrs. Fiske, in her dressing room in the theater.

Item. George Orwell was but fourteen years old in 1917— too young to prophesy what none of us would have then believed. Let's just remember today that, when President Eliot took office in 1869, Harvard's total endowment was $2.5 million; when President Lowell succeeded him forty years later, the figure was $22 million. In 1980 it cost more than $22 million just to heat, light, power, and physically run the University.

Item. All this would be incomplete without a word in remembrance of proctoring college board examinations in which I once wrote down a blind student's answers to the questions in every subject involved. With what a sense of awe, let alone respect for my candidate did I literally sweat through those summer sessions in Austin Hall! It was an exercise in—actually a *lesson* in—agonized restraint, for I dared not betray in my tone of voice or in any hesitancy whatsoever, my personal knowledge that the examinee was in error. This proved most difficult, quite naturally, in algebra (one of my better tools in physics). When the student said "$a + b$" for "$a - b$," was this but a blind boy's natural slip, or did he really *mean* what he dictated, totally unaware he was totally wrong? Never once did I say: Do you want to think that one over? To help him here would be a truly wicked disservice. He passed, went through college, on through law school, married, had children, and has led a successful life. What courage!

This same student once told me a story, the genesis of which was his own idea. During Prohibition his several roommates bought some bootleg gin. Without being asked, my blind student volunteered to try it. It *could* make him sick; it *couldn't* make him blind. Shades of J. B. S. Haldane, who wrote a ghastly essay "On Being One's Own Rabbit" in *Possible Worlds,* 1927.

Item. Looking back, it now seems to me that to enter Harvard is to superimpose upon one's tiny private landscape a very complicated map of strange hills, valleys, contours, and paths: a country of conflicting languages, disciplines, and often misleading signposts. Even with friendly help and advice, someone like myself will, at times, remain quite terribly alone. "So much to do,/ And not know how to do it;/ So much to true, and not know how to true it;/ So much to rue, and all one's life to rue it." I wrote those young man's lines in my journal shortly after leaving graduate school.

Entering Athens as a Spartan, you may one day discover, and gratefully understand, what the astronomer Harlow Shapley meant when he said that in opening a book of mathematics he was sometimes moved by the same emotion he had when he entered a great cathedral. Edward Thomas, the English poet killed in World War I, clung to his belief that "either a book feeds me or it doesn't." At college one learns to be fed.

Item. I still think that whereas in 1916–17 the college board examinations were difficult, Harvard as a college, even though (or perhaps because) the nation was at war, proved relatively easy to get into. No lowering of standards, mind you, just fewer customers at the ticket window. One did not worry about that ultimate job in the outer world. We *knew* there were jobs. *Eheu!* A vanished world! Today we live, to use a physics term in a psychological sense, within a force field of tremendous competition. Inflation frightens us; the future frightens us; life frightens us; death frightens us. Why, even though we were at war when I was a freshman, I don't recall being abysmally frightened by, or even openly apprehensive of, enlistment just ahead. We went about our business of the classroom, enjoyed foolish diversions, all in an atmosphere of complete God-given freedom. Harvard let you alone. And though we did not think it out, irrational as many of us were, we too could be excited by what Justice Holmes—distinguished son of a distinguished father, both of them no more than names to most of us—had referred to as "little decisions . . . which have in them . . . the germ of some wider theory." We were full of irritating little decisions which had to be made and *were* made. But certainly *not* made by many of us in any catenary fashion, with the farthermost end of the chain attached to any visible dividing cells of wider theory.

Item. My generation at Harvard came largely from unbroken families. We were, without a doubt, too docile, too obedient; we never dreamed the world's smoke signals were in code. The code now is broken, and we read the dreadful summary: use freedom to kill freedom.

John H. Finley, Jr. '25

John H. Finley, Jr., born in New York in 1904, entered Harvard from Exeter and graduated in 1925 in the combined field of Greek and English; he was editor of the Advocate *and president of the Signet. He went on to the American School of Classical Studies in Athens, to the University of Berlin, and to a third year at the University of Edinburgh and in France; a book of verse,* Thalia, *emerged from this period. Returned to Cambridge, he received his doctorate in 1933, the year of his marriage to Magdalena Greenslet. He began in 1942 his twenty-six years as Master of Eliot House, became Eliot Professor of Greek Literature in 1948, was vice-chairman of the committee that produced the widely read* General Education in a Free Society *(1945), and taught a course under the program until his retirement as Senior Professor in 1976. He was George Eastman Professor at Oxford in 1954–55 and received a Harvard L.H.D. in 1968. His writings include* Thucydides *(1942),* Pindar and Aeschylus *(1955),* Four Stages of Greek Thought *(1960), and* Homer's Odyssey *(1978).*

My college years passed into decades. Old friends in Cambridge or wider worlds remain who they always have been; how trace those bonds? Most lives fall into chapters but Cambridge flows on. Samuel Eliot Morison's *Four Centuries of Harvard* helps quiet the traffic of the Square, and bygone personages escort talkative high school students to the subway past Sever, the Widener, and Grays.

Older professors in the 1920s still attested to Mr. Eliot's epochal changes, though we hardly knew that. By superimposing on the ancient Anglo-Saxon college the risen structures of European learning—in the reconstituted Law and Medical Schools and the newly founded Graduate School of Arts and Sciences (1878)—he created the model of American higher education. Oxford and Cambridge lacked graduate schools; the continental universities lacked colleges; he made the American combination. President Gilman of Johns Hopkins was his only rival, but the Medical and Graduate Schools in Baltimore originally lacked a college. We took the change for granted as, seemingly, did our teachers. Though the era of Norton, William James, Farlow, Agassiz, and Santayana had passed, its mood persisted. Mr. Eliot's first graduating class, 1869, numbered some 170; on his retirement forty years later, the class had reached some

750. Our professors drew from those wide years, the period of new ties with Europe, of Henry James's novels, of travel, of the rise of museums (Mrs. Gardner's among them), of boarding schools of British cast, and generally of horizons other than Thoreau's. Henry James's traveled Americans commonly start from some elm-shaded town. The eminent editor of *The Divine Comedy*, Charles Grandgent, '85, among many others—not least Bliss Perry, Kittredge, Haskins, Rand, J. L. Lowes, Taussig—may exemplify those men. The son of a Boston schoolteacher, he describes in a late essay a boyhood job on a vendor's cart selling pots, pans, and sewing goods to lone housewives on remote farms. Yet he graduated when Richardson's Romanesque Sever rose opposite the Federalist clarity of Bulfinch's University Hall; the brick Gothic of Memorial Hall had stood for seven years; outreaching styles framed his Harvard. He went on to study in Europe but in late years sufficiently remembered the College of his youth to write me a kind note about a story in the *Advocate*. Legend held that he would occasionally brighten the *Lampoon*'s arid moments. Dante and the *Lampoon* remained touchingly compatible to him. We assumed that vernal union.

Professor Edward Forbes, '95, Emerson's grandson and with Professor Sachs the creator of the Fogg Museum, told of admiring after college the beauty of the Oxford quadrangles and of wishing something similar for Harvard. With the damming of the Charles River in the early 1900s, the formerly tidal, not fragrant flats, which oarsmen of the time had thought it worth their life to cross, became green and solid, and Mr. Forbes with friends began acquiring them for the University. When he approached Mr. Eliot, the great man judged that Harvard would never reach the river— even he did not foresee that—but Mr. Forbes took his ideas to important graduates from as far away as New York (he spoke of them almost as foreigners), and the president soon relented. Mr. Lowell's freshman dormitories rose there; we thought them, like our professors, native to Harvard. A

power plant with two mighty chimneys occupied the future
site of Eliot House; Mr. Lowell was later reputed to have
called assiduously on maiden ladies who inhabited the even-
tual site of Lowell House. A pillar of the Athletic Association
who grew up in Cambridge, Tom Getchell, told of watching
as a boy horse-trucks transporting the subway excavation to
fill the outer reaches of Soldiers Field. The vast growth of
the University in Mr. Eliot's time had in the 1890s produced
the Gold Coast, originally by private capital; it still faced
firetraps of rooming houses. We migrated from the freshman dormitories to one of these or to the Gold Coast's fading
grandeur, finally to reach the Yard as seniors.

The Houses of just after our time were Mr. Lowell's
crowning achievement. Mr. Eliot's heart had been with the
expanded university; its overflow reached the College by the
free-elective system; undergraduates were to respond as
best they could. But Mr. Lowell looked to the College.
Though the Business School and the Widener Library were
his further creations, by the system of concentration, tutorial, the freshman dormitories, and triumphantly and finally
by the Houses he gave shape to the greatly expanded College. Mr. Wilson had left Princeton after vainly trying to
replace the clubs with some version of the Oxford and
Cambridge colleges; Yale had initially demurred at its
alumnus Mr. Harkness's like proposal, but Mr. Lowell
promptly accepted his offer to Harvard. The Harvard
Houses have been called a Princeton idea done with Yale
money; they fulfilled Mr. Lowell's vision of the College. The
old unity of the Yard had long since scattered; the Houses
effectually multiplied it by seven; they became the setting of
the national College. A lone youth from a distant school now
found friends in the Yard and moved with them to a House.
Mr. Conant's national scholarships sped the change. Mr.
Eliot and Mr. Lowell jointly created the model of the new
American university-college. Harvard's eminence and, from
the point of view of the faculty, its demand both followed—
the former in its scope, the latter in the expectation that

teaching and scholarship belong together. College was no longer simply to crown youth; it was to suggest maturity. As American life grew more organized and undergraduates from remoter backgrounds joined the stream, the former repose quickened.

But for us in the middle 1920s, or for some of us, the repose lingered. The pre-House College was not hospitable to everyone. Fraternities elsewhere made people at home, though in absence from the faculty and by talk of athletics. The fraternity system reflects American middle-class marriage; professors stay home on their wives' garden-club afternoons; with all goodwill, they lack places to eat and talk with the young. The Oxford and Cambridge colleges, by contrast, assume wives' patience while husbands dine in hall. With the rise of the Houses, a few bachelors—the picturesque and erudite Arthur Darby Nock and the beloved, admired Jack Bate—would enliven meals; young tutors who had yet to achieve a departmental office but were personages in a House chiefly set the new tone. In our time Copey still held court in his upstairs southern wing of Hollis, and professors still afforded Cambridge. Psychiatrists who want their children in Shady Hill School and well-off admirers of culture have now so raised the rents that the faculty largely inhabit suburbs, sometimes to lunch in a House if the walk is not too far.

Clubs and societies, many of which are now gone, gave quasi-homes to some of us; others endured the lack of the old commons in Memorial Hall, which had united the classes of the late nineteenth century. Even so, the most intimate chapter of Morison's *Four Centuries,* that on his own college years before 1908, suggests the continuing tone. People of different tastes—the athletic, the literary, the fashionable, the radical (for instance, John Reed, '10, who lies in the Kremlin)—combined friendship with going their own way. Such bonds increasingly brightened our junior and senior years when life had settled down and college kept opening. World War I had receded, the era that took Cum-

mings to *The Enormous Room* and Eliot to *The Waste Land.*
The delusive American shine before the financial crash of
1929 marked our years, with bleak results for some glad
products of the bibulous age of Prohibition. But the lure
remained; even with the new system of concentration,
courses were a kind of home brew; a year of chemistry,
history, philosophy, and Greek resembled a mix of hops,
yeast, water, and raisins in producing unforeseen froth.
Purposeful people heading for a medical or legal or scientific
future were rarer then; the future was simply to arrive. The
Crimson, the *Lampoon,* the *Advocate,* and Lincoln Kirstein's just later *Hound and Horn* collected literary people;
teams gathered others; the Signet, the Liberal Club (with its
own building), and the theatricals of the Hasty Pudding and
Pi Eta wove further bonds, all somewhat haphazardly. This
was neither the old Harvard of the Yard nor the later Harvard of the Houses but something in between, a place of
discovered sympathies, of lights and shades, and of occasional sun-flecked shafts as from some high window.

My father urged me to the American School of Classical
Studies in Athens; he had been Red Cross commissioner to
Palestine in the first war, had walked to the storied places,
known T. E. Lawrence, and reached Damascus with Al-
lenby. It was the time of one of the first dire transfers of
national populations, of Greeks from Turkey and Turks from
Greece, after the Greek defeat at Smyrna, the rise of Mus-
tapha Kemal, and the Treaty of Trianon. Sad shacks filled
the once empty, now heavily built-up plain between Athens
and Piraeus; the modern crowding of Athens was under
way, but the outer country was unchanged. I had the luck of
helping the eminent Karl Blegen, later the discoverer of the
Linear-B tablets at Pylos, excavate on towering Acrocorin-
thus, but I proved no archaeologist, took distant walks with
friends, and read the authors. Marathon became as actual as
Bunker Hill. The fame of German scholarship then drew me
ignorantly to the University of Berlin in the hopeful interval
between reparations and Hitler, the period of Stresemann,

Briand, and the Locarno Pact. The Hellenist Werner Jaeger, later to adorn Harvard, then the author of a famous book on Aristotle and soon to write his widely known *Paideia,* as the new professor only thirty-eight years old added his luster to the prewar septuagenarians, including the great Wilamowitz-Moellendorff, suggestive of Wagner in his velvet jacket and string tie. Born a rare Protestant in Catholic Kempen on the lower Rhine, Thomas a Kempis's town, Jaeger had been early exposed to theology but forsook it for the idealizing Greek classic in the confident time before Hitler, then in that darkness reverted to the Christian authors; the long history of antiquity shone in his golden Harvard summer.

He kindly had me with other students—they in formal morning coats, I in my one blue suit—to his tree-surrounded, mansard-roofed, spacious house in a Berlin suburb; it resembled houses off Brattle Street; German architecture had apparently accompanied German learning to Mr. Eliot's Cambridge. In *The Leaning Tower* Katherine Anne Porter describes correct Berlin boarding places frequented by Privat Dozenten; I found my way to an upstairs establishment behind the Reichstag full of indigent Russian exiles and presided over by a massive counterpart of the Wife of Bath. I went to lectures, read Plato, met a few students, and began a poem about distant New Hampshire. Contemporary and later Harvardians who went on to Oxford or Cambridge gained as a lasting instruction the habit of 50 percent membership: they belonged, but not quite; spoke English, but with a difference; were on their own in vacations; they learned what escaped me, a way of joining in while keeping something back. The hepatitis that I acquired (probably) at a beautiful village spring near Sparta continued to haunt a next overseas year that started in Edinburgh; there followed what sealed my future, an invitation to return to Harvard. The kindly, graceful teacher and learned editor of Athenaeus, Professor Charles B. Gulick, '89, suddenly fell victim to what is now curable, detached retina, and teaching was needed. A New Hampshire character once asked me to speak at his distant Rotary Club: "It's awful late," he said, "and I'm put to it. I wouldn't ask you if I could think of anybody else." The department's plight was similar, and my lone Europe changed to crowded Cambridge. The book of verse was published; I did not imagine myself a professional Hellenist, but my not then but present wife was brilliantly dawning on my life, and it seemed that I should be settled. Years of tennis have prompted the comparison of verse and fiction to the forehand, scholarship to the backhand, which crosses the body, takes more care, but may less often hit over the backstop. Both kinds of writing ask immersion, but scholarship more temperedly because first ideas must be checked against others' ideas; the flame must survive heating and cooling.

Roger Merriman's transplanted Balliol in Eliot House— with his old oar above the study fireplace, his photographed crew listing him at a great sum of stones and pounds, and at one end of the room the replica of a carving of Henry VIII and Francis I on prancing horses and flanked by retainers, much in the confusingly impressive manner of History I— was then flourishing. The gifted young staff included F. O. Matthiessen from Yale; Theodore Spencer from Princeton via British Cambridge; the mathematicians Marston Morse and Hassler Witney, later of the Institute of Advanced Study; one of the future inventors of atomic energy, Kenneth Bainbridge; and the Senior Tutor J. M. Potter, the lamentably short-lived future president of Hobart. Potter was as big as Mr. Merriman and, like him, had one bad eye; House discipline was simple in the presence of 400 pounds and two piercing eyes. The College, scattered for a half-century, here and in the six other Houses reknit former ties between rich and poor, purposeful and idle, literary and athletic, local and distant. Occasional House dinners for visiting celebrities and sparsely rehearsed but hilarious versions of Shakespeare or Ben Jonson at Christmas brightened the year. Of all these, none matched *Henry the Fourth, Part Two* at Christmas 1941 with Mr. Merriman, then in the

last year of his high mastership as the old king and with
Prince Hal, his friends, and most of the audience soon to be
off to war. The play has doubtless been better given but in
retrospect never more affectingly; it marked the end of a
brilliant first era.

This was my full start in teaching, tutoring, and writing. I
too wanted to leave for the service but had been named the
new Master; faith that scholarship and concern for the
College are compatible was usual then. Jim Conant, as early
as during his great war years in Washington, may already
have conceived his hopes for General Education, to be his
and Harvard's reply to Hutchins's innovations at Chicago,
the like changes at Columbia, and St. John's touted Hundred Books. The Provost Paul Buck became chairman of a
committee that included I. A. Richards, Raphael Demos,
Arthur Schlesinger, Sr., the Radcliffe President W. K. Jordan, and Ben Wright, later president of Smith. As things
worked out over the three years of meetings, I as vice-chairman had some responsibility for the writing. The resulting
book, *General Education in a Free Society,* surprisingly sold
seventy thousand copies, partly as phrasing the antiauthori-
tarian goals of the Second World War, but partly also as
setting the ever-increased demands of specialism within a
humane frame. It further unified Mr. Eliot's and Mr. Lowell's combined changes.

The scientific Mr. Conant proved astonishingly conscious
of the College; after his war service in Washington and his
ambassadorship to Germany, he even became by his late
writings a founding spirit of the comprehensive American
high school. Professor Whitehead, on expressing surprise at
Conant's appointment as president and on being reminded
that Mr. Eliot too was a chemist, is said to have replied, "Ah,
but he was a bad chemist." But the philosopher for once was
wrong; Mr. Conant was indeed more Mr. Eliot's than Mr.
Lowell's successor; he was jealous for Harvard's eminence
but, descendant of Puritans that he was, equally wanted a
socially and intellectually responsible Harvard. Something

of Jefferson and Franklin persisted beneath his twentieth-century specialized acuteness; he was both an old and a new American; appreciation of his faith will keep growing.

My fortunate association with him carried from the original committee to teaching one of the new courses, The Epic and the Novel, with a first term on Homer, Virgil, Dante (all in translation), and Milton and a second term—initially by Harry Levin (the course was his idea), then by Ivor Richards, then in their Cambridge years by Thornton Wilder and Vladimir Nabokov—on novels from *Don Quixote* to *Moby Dick* and *War and Peace*. Among its great moments was the appearance of a bat in Sanders Theater when Richards was holding forth on witches; also the five-minute comic strip with which Wilder would start his lectures, sometimes jolting on a chair with an imaginary lasso. Graduate students held sections of twenty on the third day of the week, with enlistment far beyond the call of duty; one of the few sections to which I was lured leaves memories of freshmen and upperclass concentrators in physics or economics cheerfully arguing. That seemed college at its freest.

Our term in the Master's house lasted twenty-six years; our children grew up there, and our non-Oedipal son went on to Eliot House. The sole break was an Oxford year on the Eastman Visiting Professorship, which rotates among fields. The generous MacLeishes then characteristically brought their light to the House. Hellenists abound at Oxford, but their hospitality was not annually taxed; I went from college to college like a sailor on leave. My chief friend, who had been at Harvard, was the unrivaled conversationalist and outpouring writer, C. M. Bowra, the Warden of Wadham College and then the vice-chancellor. Surprise is a key to joy, and his surprise was to have reached Oxford from a Shanghai boyhood and the trenches of the first war; people thought him chiefly a wit, but he was rather a journeyer in the wide world, grateful to have found and adorned his bright haven.

Varied backgrounds and less pressing schools initially

differentiate Harvard from Oxford undergraduates, but the four years bring them out much the same. A Master's chief pleasure is to watch the change, in people individually and toward one another. Some had sought Harvard as a university, others as a college; the ones looked to the more complex professions, the others enjoyed the present; they would start respectively with A's and with C's. But time had its effect: initially ardent chemists would come late to the Mallincrodt after lingering over luncheon and would even sink to a B; popular and athletic souls would tire of gregariousness, rouse to friends' talk, and sometimes as juniors reach a B. Male destinies are shaped like a diamond: the egotist at the bottom, the saint at the top, the theorist at one edge, the responsible man at the other. Gifts seem less decisive than temperaments; education shrinks egotism, and few show signs of sainthood, but it makes a difference whether Albert Einstein or George Washington is the model—whether ideas or people and institutions set the goal. Few people seem wholly of the one or the other side, but the Socratic "know thyself" commends finding which is chiefly one's own. As *King Lear* and *Hamlet* suggest, Shakespeare seems on the side of Einstein.

Hints of this choice emerged in people's House years. A Master or professor stands halfway between a father and nobody; he knows about you but not with the static electricity that family love gives off. Life slopes downhill; parents are more concerned for their children than children for their parents; a Master similarly counts little to the young relatively to friends, girls, sport, and the joys of youth. But he must be there; he is a kind of tree, an oak of Dodona the swaying branches of which gave shade and were thought to utter dim truths. Under our American system of college, then graduate school, a fellowship, or (what does not greatly differ) a training course in the State Department or in a bank or on a newspaper, one function of a Master was central: the letter of recommendation. One had known people for three years, knew their friends and roommates, read parents' letters and tutors' and others' reports in their folders, and chiefly had talked with them and taken notes. An attempt at a kind of prophecy followed, partly but not largely academic, as far as possible of the unique person, never complete but important under our system, a shoehorn to the next step. A role of the mature is to speed the rising generation. Professors are not merely to write books. With the rising American competitiveness, more members of a senior class of nearly 150 in the House would need such letters; those who left for the service or a temporary job would often return. But in those glad years nearly everyone got what he wanted; there were twenty-eight Rhodes Scholars, three in one fortunate year. No one envied others' successes; they would be successful too; that mood was a delight of the House. Did they all deserve what they got? Surely so, since the gifts and charms of the young are real, whether or not fortune would give full future scope. Youth leaves a lasting mythology, and college notably so: the brilliant Achilles, the inward Hamlet, the towering guard or tackle Ajax, old Nestor or Polonius, loyal Horatio. A Master's fortune is to be conscious of such myths forming.

But search for important answers, if not for others' benefit at least for one's own, remains the motive of academic life. Writing and teaching involve exposition less than discovery. One starts a page or even a lecture thinking to say A and B, suddenly to realize that a more crucial C and D lurk somewhere beneath; writing is a kind of well-digging. Fugitive sight of a still further E and F commonly dawns at the end, but they must wait until next time. Gifted undergraduates and graduate students give welcome help, but the lone search remains. Young and old must equally find order among the myriad facts of history and experience; the facts are all true, but ordering them, reaching priorities, is the final demand. One wants to merge the closeted self with the enlarging world, but like a janitor in the cellar the self keeps giving notice that he is there; the ultimate hope is to get him upstairs to a window. That is to say that students, for all the privilege of their company, are only part of academic life; search for clarification is the other part; one would otherwise have nothing to give, even to oneself. Harvard's double existence as both university and college, Mr. Eliot's legacy, phrases the continuing demand. The Widener Library has a nearly lifelong circulation; decades waft one from a low desk in the stacks to a top-floor study, a kind of Ithaca, not least among the privileges of the Harvard journey. Odysseus at least in Ithaca and Prospero in Milan surely relived their travels, and with new meaning; distance still accompanied them, not quite as it was but freshly instructive. Later academic life does that.

Thomas Boylston Adams '33

Thomas Boylston Adams, class of 1933, left Harvard before graduation and attempted to earn his living during the Great Depression as a newspaper writer on the Boston Herald. *Failing at that, he got a job with the Waltham Watch Company. In 1942 he entered the U.S. Army Air Forces and served as a gunnery officer. After the war he joined the youthful Sheraton Corporation and grew up with it. He left in 1963 to return to literary work and soon found himself in politics, running for the U.S. Senate and U.S. Congress in opposition to the Vietnam War. He was honored by the Nixon administration by inclusion on the White House Enemies List.*

He also became president of the Massachusetts Historical Society, treasurer of the American Academy of Arts and Sciences, a member of the faculty of the Peabody Museum of Archaeology and Ethnology at Harvard and an associate of Adams House. He was elected an honorary member of Phi Beta Kappa in 1958 and became its president in 1977. He married Ramelle Cochrane in 1940. They have five children, three of whom are Harvard graduates. He writes a column "History Looks Ahead" for the Boston Globe.

All children, born into a world of others' making, accept its geological formations as a matter of fact. For the child born in 1910 the shape of New England society had not changed since the Civil War. That had been a great upheaval. The mountains had come tumbling down, and the rivers had overwhelmed the earth. But the floods had receded, order had been restored, once more the fields brought forth crops. The earth smiled. There were great meadows and quiet woods, sweet smelling always. Cows and horses grazed in the pastures. There was no sound but the occasional whistle of a locomotive and the rattle as a train passed on the distant railroad track. Then the quiet returned, and out of the quiet was heard the singing of birds.

The child did not inhabit this world alone. There were brothers and sisters and, of course, parents. At either end of the poles of existence there were grandfathers. From these, in what way he did not know and never afterwards could detect, came the knowledge that once there had been a great upheaval. Then things had been straightened out. Courses had been set. The world had moved steadily along those courses ever since.

There was something called the War. It was very far away and was being fought against the Germans by the Allies, who were friends of ours. There were maps in the grandfathers' houses with colored pins that were moved at teatime, after a good deal of earnest talk. The War was important, but its outcome was never in doubt. All that had been settled long ago. The Union was a settled thing. America could not fail. Behind and beyond all was a vague presence, a certainty, Abraham Lincoln.

The old soldiers disappeared, the grandfathers, they who had fought for Abraham Lincoln, who had carried out his plans. They had white hair and white moustaches. They were magnificent. One grandfather was very tall, a little stooped when he got up from his chair. He moved slowly. Then he straightened and stood very erect. The other grandfather was always on an immense horse called Red Oak. The child amused himself by turning his jack-o'-lantern, cut from a pumpkin, towards him. He was very frightened and leaned far out from his saddle. Red Oak was unperturbed.

The uncles came back from the War. They were not impressive. Except they were dressed in ugly khaki uniforms with puttees they were indistinguishable from parents. They soon put on ordinary clothes and the whole business was forgotten. But first there was the Yankee Division parade. The children watched it for hours and hours from a window of a house on Commonwealth Avenue. The people in the street and in the bleachers built along the mall were cold and wrapped newspapers around their feet and under their coats. The wind blew the papers about the dirty streets. The parade of khaki men marched endlessly by. But the bands were fun. You could hear them a long way off, coming up the avenue playing Sousa's marches. They wore blue uniforms with gold braid and their instruments were shining brass. It took two men to carry the big drums. The whole thing was some sort of enormous picnic.

The parade over, everyone went back to the job of running the country. There was a lot of talk of the League of Nations and the parents went to hear Clemenceau, the Tiger of France, speak in Symphony Hall. But things calmed down.

Everyone but an occasional aunt, who seriously taught a nephew French, forgot about Europe. Books came into the house, thick, heavy, written by grandfathers and a presence even more vague, great uncles. They were about the Civil War. The child, or boy that now he was, discovered a fascination in history. The photograph, always on his mother's dressing table, of the boy in the Civil War uniform with the odd-looking visor cap, who seemed not much older than an elder brother, had written those letters home he was now reading. The other grandfather had been there too—that is, at the Battle of Gettysburg. They had not known each other then. But business ventures in the West had brought them together after the War.

There were volumes of Nicolay and Hay in the house. There was talk at the dinner table. His father, who went every day to the Office, much preferred the Athenaeum and brought home books about the Napoleonic wars. The boy came to realize that there were two major events in modern history, the Battle of Waterloo and the Battle of Gettysburg. The Battle of Waterloo had resulted in the Waterloo generation, always spoken of at the dinner table with a slight turning down of the corner of the mouth. The Waterloo generation had done its level best to bury us during the Civil War. His father liked to tell how his grandfather had sat silent at a fashionable dinner table at the height of the London season of '63. The talk was all of Lee's triumphal march on Washington and the flight of President Lincoln. Suddenly through the open windows came the newsboy's shout, "Great Union victory!"

The arrogance of the English had never again been quite the same after the victory of Gettysburg. There was the Boer war, and now the Great War. Europe was going to smash. So, for that matter, was the country. But it might get on its feet again now that the Republicans were back. Except that the Republicans were just about as bad. "Cabot" was the limit. "Cabot" was Senator Lodge, and he was all wrong about the League of Nations. Politics were rotten. Politicians were not respectable, like body lice. Society ignored them, except for occasional scratching.

The Gettysburg generation had delivered politics to the ashcan. They had gone West, built railroads, built cities, developed water power and irrigated deserts, speculated in mines and ranches. They owned the country and, up to a certain point, the politicians; beyond that point they ignored them. These Civil War men and women, this Gettysburg generation, had supreme contempt for the crowd of sutlers, camp followers, hucksters, and immigrants that poured into the vacuum created by their victory. For theirs had been no sordid victory of empire-seeking Spaniards or French or Britishers. It was the victory of right, of freedom, of emancipation of the slave, and of Abraham Lincoln. The politicians had betrayed it. So the politicians be damned. Society would build without them and hire them as its servants.

The volunteers of 1861, those who survived the war, mostly married the sisters of other volunteers. In one grandmother's house hung the heavily framed portrait of her brother killed in battle. In Memorial Hall, which the boy passed through with his mother on the way to see Harvard's glass flowers, he read the first and middle name of one of her brothers, given to him in memory of her father's companion in arms, killed in the charge of the 2nd Massachusetts Regiment at Gettysburg. The dusty stained glass, the dim lighted tablets pleased him. The place had a curious musty smell. Thereafter, in any state of the Union, in foreign countries, a whiff of that curious mustiness evoked intact the early vision.

He climbed Beacon Hill to see Robert Gould Shaw forever advancing beside his black troops who could never break step. This was what it was all about. He stared at the figures in bronze for a long time. Then he wanted to look at General Hooker mounted on a very handsome horse at the steps of the State House. But his mother drew him away. The horse was all right, she said, but General Hooker was a disgrace. He had been put there by the politicians. They went to the

Public Library to see the great murals. They paused on the stairs to read under a stone lion the list of the battles of the 2nd Massachusetts.

Harvard, the Civil War, Massachusetts! They were one and inseparable. The boy was part of them as surely as a true believer is part of the Trinity. Since the rather vague and excessively attenuated Unitarianism of his family had never brought him inside a church, they proved a perfectly adequate substitute. As Saint Thomas Aquinas suggested, they were in all, above all, and through all. The boy and his mother went to the Club for lunch. The extreme gravity of the elderly gentlemen who waited on table impressed him. Even more impressive were their striped waistcoats.

It seemed to him not strange, but perfectly natural, that his name had been put down at the Club at birth, to come up in twenty-five years. Likewise his name had been put down for the School. He did not want to leave home, the almost complete freedom he enjoyed there, and go to boarding school. But it was so written, and go he must. His elder brother was already there. In the last spring of an undisturbed childhood the wives and children of '98, in two or three large buses, came to spend the day with his family in the country. He took all the boys swimming in the pond. The next day he won a swimming race in the Charles, off the Weld boat house. The germ theory of disease did not then trouble simple enjoyments. In the afternoon he saw Harvard beat Yale in the ninth inning. That was dramatic enough, but it was funny to see the spectators, most of whom had disappointedly been drifting away, come running back, chagrin on their faces because they had missed the big moment.

The plan of education was Mandarin. Harvard was, of course, open to all comers. But the chances of admission were enormously improved if a boy went to a Mandarin School. All that was required for entrance to the School was elementary Latin, some acquaintance with English literature, arithmetic, and the ability to write a page without too many egregious mistakes of spelling. Of course it helped if the boy's father had gone to the School, too, and gone to Harvard. But the School would do the rest and do its best. Part of its method of doing its best was to sift out, as rapidly as possible, all those, whether or not the sons of graduates, who appeared likely to fail, after six years of training, the requirements of the college board examinations. The School had no hesitation at all in dropping a boy, even after five years of work, if the prospect of his passing the boards was in doubt.

Therefore the standards of the School were considered high. Much emphasis was placed on grades. Grades were achieved by rigorous preparation for classes; acres of figures, long division, and square root; pages and pages of Latin vocabulary memorized, pidgin French and the dreadful dissection of some English novels, plays, and poems. And spelling. Endless exercises in spelling. "You are allowed just three mistakes in spelling on the boards. One more and you're out!" The first few years were not too bad. Towards the end the boredom became intolerable.

Whether it was the boredom, some shifting currents in the world's thinking, or the mere violent reaction of the too willing horse too long fed oats and too tightly restrained, the boy animal reared up, pawed the air, and was in danger of breaking his traces. He decided he did not want to go to College. College meant Harvard. There was no other. Vague-scented breezes were coming from across the sea. There were Americans in Paris: Hemingway, Eliot, younger men like MacLeish. There was freedom there, a world to discover. And the living was cheap. A dollar would buy hundreds, thousands of francs.

He knew he did not want to be a lawyer. No professional career appealed to him. If he had any scientific bent he would never discover it. Neither he nor his teachers could escape from the tangle of the multiplication tables. The world of business was simply unattractive. Too many of his classmates at the School were tainted with new money. The

brokers and bankers were rolling in the stuff, so filthy rich
they gave their sons new Packards on graduation. Neither
their conversation nor their behavior encouraged emula-
tion. One at least was thought to be a bootlegger. The Mandarin ideal was depreciating so fast as to lose all value. The
world that had been bought was hardly worth throwing
away.

The education that had been interrupted for six years,
squeezed almost to extinction, was abruptly resumed on
graduation from the School. He discovered with dismay the
very real dismay of his parents on learning of his desire not
to enter the College. His parents had always treated him
with kindness, and he had no desire to distress them. He
simply could see no point in going to the College. He was
born a Harvard man, so why go there? He was already the
type, so firmly molded that no education could ever change
the shape or deceive for half a minute the most casual
observer. His parents, very sensibly, agreed with everything
he said. They only reserved the right to continue to believe,
in their own quiet and persistent way, that Harvard might
still have something to teach a Harvard man. They gave him
a little money and bid him Godspeed.

Before he sailed for France, he had made up his mind to
return in the fall and enter Harvard. Fortune gave him a
more than even break. He was asked to join a family party
for the summer. The mother of a devoted friend had recently
married, after long years of widowhood, a Frenchman. She
had taken a house in the Basses-Pyrénées, which she intended to inhabit with her new husband and his three
sisters. The two boys would be welcome there, to learn
French if they could, to absorb a little civilization if they
might. They sailed on the *Aquitania* and promptly got
drunk. That was the clear duty of Americans in the days of
Prohibition. It was also a useful preparation for Harvard. A
freshman unfamiliar with liquor stood in some danger of
being killed on his first contact with the bootleg stuff.

The trip had only one unfortunate consequence. He did

learn French. That made his course in freshman French an
agony almost unbearable. The dreary business of learning
over again what one had already learned before confirmed
his worst suspicions of the folly of a college education. But
he also learned a good deal about the art of French cooking,
a subject which Harvard did not teach, and the taste of
French wines, which, if happiness is a legitimate pursuit,
Harvard ought to teach.

He saw one day on a French road, along which he was
bicycling with his friend, a sight that made him glad he was
an American. It was a sight common enough, he would
learn, nothing but a company of conscripts marching along
in fatigue uniform. What made this sight poignant was the
halting of the company and the falling out and the falling
down of a boy, apparently younger than himself, frail as a
reed, in an agony of pain, by the roadside. He seemed very
far from home, farther even than the Americans. The idea of
military service seemed extraordinary to the Americans,
free to go to Harvard or not to go to Harvard, as they pleased.
Did Locarno mean nothing? It had been hailed at the School
with prayers of thanksgiving. The masters, with no dissent-
ing voice, believed in it, believed it was the beginning of the
end of war. And just now—the French papers were full of
it—Kellogg and Briand had signed their pact in Paris. There
was no more war.

Paris was very gay. Even the few dollars the boys had in
their pockets would buy hundreds, thousands of francs. The
money looked like toilet paper and had to be carried in
bundles in a specially designed portfolio marked with the
various denominations and sizes. All the Americans in Paris
were in the Ritz bar drinking champagne cocktails and
peeling off bundles of francs. The boy returned to America
confirmed in three vices: French cooking, French wines,
and French architecture. For the rest of his life he would
crawl through cathedrals whenever he could. He would
have liked to continue to ride his bicycle in America. But his
friends laughed at him. He was almost alone in not possess-

ing a motorcar to drive to Cambridge. Even his parents dissuaded him. The roads were too dangerous, too crowded with cars going too fast, even to ride a bicycle in safety to the railroad station.

The day of his registration as a student at Harvard was gloomy. The heavy foliage of summer clung to the trees, made doubly heavy by their coating of gray dust. It was hot. The boy was a young gentleman now and wore a rumpled suit of clothes or, at most casual, gray flannel trousers and an odd coat. He always wore a necktie. He would have liked to wear his French beret. But he knew perfectly well, even if his best friend had not told him, that if he had he would have been positively jeered at. All men wore hats of some kind when they stepped into the street. The hat of a gentleman was felt, gray or brown.

The trees were heavy with dust. The air was heavy to breathe. The clouds hung heavy in the sky, great billows of dirty felt like the billowing dirty quilts he had seen in cheap French hotels. He met a few acquaintances from the School. They had picked up some strangers from other schools. They wandered aimlessly about for a while in the dusk. There was a feeling of doom in the air. The laughter was hollow. All were strangers. He came into the quadrangle of Gore Hall early at evening. A few heavy drops of rain were plopping down. He crept up the institutional stairs to his room. There was an odd, unpleasant smell. He had not thought about the place for years. The stairs up into the Town Hall where he used to go to dancing school.

The next days were not much better. Corn flakes or some such trash for breakfast in a room much too grand for breakfast. The table was an ugly varnished yellow. Then a ceaseless wandering about unfamiliar streets, into the familiar Yard, into unfamiliar, yet generically familiar classrooms with the forever familiar writing-arm chairs. The class was French in the cellar of Boylston Hall. At his right sat a heavily built young gentleman who spoke to him politely. His name began with *A-y*. Alphabetical still. Just like

School. *"Bonjour, messieurs. Aujourd'hui nous sommes à Paris. Il fait beau . . ."* Oh, my God!

There was worse to come. In the New Lecture Hall he was introduced to geology and Professor Mather. Years later he would know Kirtley Mather well, work with him closely and with great pleasure in the affairs of the American Academy of Arts and Sciences. He could not understand then, as he could neither understand nor bear as a freshman, how such an interesting man could make geology so uninteresting. It was the greater blow because his Father had taught him from childhood the lore of Professor Shaler, shown him the glacial scratches on the South Shore rocks, and he had learned to believe that the study of geology at Harvard was one of the turning points of life. Professor Merriman in History I was merely funny. He had a bald head that seemed to come to a point and glowed on the lecture platform like a tall candle. He was a family friend, and he had attractive daughters and a son, a good friend of an elder brother. His idiosyncrasies rather fitted in with inherited prejudices. He would occasionally knock the hat off some young gentleman walking covered under the tablets in Memorial Hall. Moreover, the reading in his course never failed to interest, though the lectures seemed sometimes a little stagey and dull.

There were other courses. He had to take four. He took no more than four because he wanted at least two full days with nothing to do but read. In Widener, or an occasional trip to Boston and the Athenaeum, he drank deeply of the pure joy of uninterrupted time. He read. He read with no time out for lunch. What, he could not remember. And in November he was put on probation. He had pulled down a B, two C's and a D, a respectable showing for a gentleman, so he thought. The gentlemen he knew all got C's. Surely a B and a D equaled two C's?

His Father wrote him a note and asked him to come into the Office. The Office was on State Street. There were rolltop desks, a mahogany counter with a gate, an ancient clerk, an ancient secretary pounding a typewriter even more ancient than herself and a dusty bookkeeper even dustier than her books. Nothing had happened in the Office for at least fifty years. The Oriental rugs on the floor, black with dust, were all that remained of the great days of railroading.

His Father's face was sad. His Father, all too prone to bursts of Proud Tower temper in ordinary life, never showed temper when things were really bad. The young gentleman had merely to say that he would get into no more trouble. He never did. He just stopped reading so much. His Father was satisfied. But also his Father's face looked thin and old. Was anything the matter at home? No. The Market was in bad shape. That was all. Things would no doubt get better.

Perhaps for the first time since he had entered the College the young gentleman glanced at a newspaper. On the way out to Cambridge in the subway he bought the *Boston Transcript* for three cents. The wide, eight-column sheet, printed in almost illegible type, was about as interesting as usual. President Hoover had made a speech. There had been some debutante parties. The governor was on an automobile tour of the state. There had been a further decline in prices on the stock exchange. Mr. Mellon was not concerned. The fundamental business of the country was sound.

In Harvard Square he picked up the *Boston Herald*. Compared with the *Transcript* the *Herald* was yellow journalism. There was talk of a crash. There was a cartoon of a man in a Pilgrim suit wearing a plug hat, pointing a blunderbuss at some ducks that were tumbling out of the sky. The gun was labeled "call money"; the ducks, "stocks." It seemed to be some kind of Thanksgiving Day joke.

He went back to College and did some work. Not much, but enough. And in his room there was a certain education. He had bought an inexpensive Victrola that operated on a spring and wound with a crank. An unexpected roommate, also from the School, had filled much of the space with a small grand piano. This valuable friend taught him to follow a musical score, after a fashion. It did not occur to him to take any course in music Harvard might have to offer. He feared his own ignorance. But he went fairly often to Symphony Hall to hear Koussevitzky and his famous orchestra. He was in the hall when the *Sacre du Printemps* was first played, and the audience fled, banging down their seats as they fled. He sat through, with the same audience, a solid week of Brahms, afternoon and evening.

Unfortunately the musical friend and his Cord roadster with the French horn disappeared forever one spring day. As he had gone to no classes he did not trouble to take any examinations. Another friend, the companion in France, came to the rescue. A group was being formed to rent 59 Plympton Street, a three- or four-story firetrap with a reputation for liberty. He joined the group.

For the summer he got a job, through an elderly historian, a family friend, writing editorials for the *Boston Herald*. He was paid by the line and began taking home small checks, of which he was very proud. In charge of the Page was a very great gentleman; solidly Republican, like the paper, and a personal friend of Calvin Coolidge. The summer nights were short and hot, and each morning it seemed that snow had fallen. Boston Common was completely covered with newspapers on which the homeless had slept. In his parents' house the atmosphere was tense. There were long silences at table. At night he would occasionally wake to hear his parents talking in low voices. The cook left and was not replaced. Only this seemed to cheer his father, who moved into the kitchen and at least during preparation of dinner could get his mind off the awful things happening at the Office.

There would be money for College. His allowance would be continued exactly as it had been. Actual expenses at the College were not a problem. In that closed world a young man trained from childhood in frugality could live very cheaply, with plenty of money left over for bootleg liquor and the necessary clothes to attend parties in Boston, even though his allowance was a quarter that of his friends. Nevertheless, the elder brother made the decision to leave Harvard and save a year by entering immediately the Columbia Architectural School.

The young gentleman returned to College and entered the world which was supposed to prepare him for Life. It was an extraordinary world. There were classes, of course. Some time had to be given to them. But the object of coming to Harvard was suddenly apparent. It was to get into a Club. A gentleman who was very shy and had no friends except a few left over from the School had no recourse but to retreat to the library by day and come out only at night to attend parties. These took place in Boston, three or four a week. They comprised cocktails, often violent, a dinner, and a dance, usually at some large hotel ballroom. The girls were pretty, and the young gentlemen were all more or less drunk. Often the ballroom was magnificently decorated. Money seemed to be no problem. Evidently there was lots of it if you knew where to go to get it.

The rest was waiting. In due course he was elected to a Club, for no reason except that his brother had been a member and some of his friends from the School were going into it. The Club was as pleasant a place as he would ever know. Companionship was there always and mild ways of wasting a little money and a great deal of time, such as backgammon. There were more vicious ways of gambling for those who had a taste for it. There were delicious meals and as much liquor as anyone cared to drink. And it was all very inexpensive. It was Circe's isle set down in a sea of confusion.

From the Club, gentlemen went to classes, always wearing coat, tie, and hat. Some of the classes were really interesting. Professor Kittredge was a very great teacher. Those who had read Shakespeare from infancy, who thought they knew him by heart, found they knew him hardly at all. The discovery of real scholarship was a revelation, as on the road to Damascus. And there was a course in Tennyson by Bliss

Perry, who had written a book about poetry. The examination was on Tennyson and the book. The examination paper was returned marked B+ with a note in the professor's handwriting: "I see you know Tennyson but have not read my book."

The only professor the young gentleman ever knew well was Augustus Maynadier, a kindly old bachelor who had known his father, and who invited him from time to time to come to his rooms to talk about the Arthurian legend or the short story. From Fritz Robinson he learned something about Chaucer. It would be yet twenty years before he learned anything about Robinson and the real charm of his mind, in his study insulated with books. And then there was a course called The Philosophy of the State. The real hatred which he developed toward this course, the antipathy which it inspired, was explained a few years later when the class of 1933 found itself in uniform fighting the Nazis.

It all ended in a blaze of glory, like an explosion of rockets, at the boat races at New London. There were club cars pulled out on the sidings. There were yachts in the harbor decorated with innumerable flags. The Club was invited for lunch on an enormous steam yacht. The observation cars pulled out through a haze of gin made that afternoon in a bucket. Presumably there were races. And there was no money. There was nothing left but to go to work. If you could find work. Better men than you had lost the job you were trying to get.

Neither Harvard nor anyone else understood the Great Crash. The Gettysburg Generation had rebuilt the world, bought it and paid for it and delivered it over to their sons; made them the Lords of Creation. These sons had sons, and time ran away with their inheritance. Part of that inheritance was Harvard. They thought not to earn it. They lost it, and Harvard was the better for their loss.

It was interesting for the working man to return to the familiar Yard long after. Crash, Depression, Hitler were history, subjects for discussion in courses. The overpowering event, which would serve his generation as topic of conversation for the rest of their lives, was one with Gettysburg and Waterloo. There were sons, who had worked hard to get into Harvard, working hard to stay there. They were mixed in with a great variety of races seeming to bear but one characteristic in common, intelligence. There were no Mandarins visible. He walked by the door of the Club. He felt no desire to go in. He would never enter that door again. Fifty-nine Plympton Street had disappeared, covered by one of the new houses. Within the houses young men and women seemed to be on good terms with each other, with tutors, professors, and the Master. In the new Democracy, learning seemed not only to be available but to be encouraged.

The arrogance of wealth had disappeared. As yet no new arrogance was visible, not even the arrogance of superior intelligence sharpened to too fine a point.

Robert Stuart Fitzgerald '33

Robert Stuart Fitzgerald, born in Geneva, New York, in 1910, grew up in Springfield, Illinois. He attended the Choate School for a year before entering Harvard in 1929. His junior year he spent at Trinity College, Cambridge, studying classics and philosophy. After earning his A.B. degree at Harvard in 1933 (he gave the commencement Latin oration), he worked for two years as a reporter on the New York Herald-Tribune. He spent the summer of 1935 at the MacDowell Colony. His first book, Poems, was published in New York that fall. So was The Alcestis of Euripides, the first of several translations done with Dudley Fitts. From 1936 to 1943 he worked as a writer and editor for Time. He served three years in the U.S. Naval Reserve. After the war he wrote book reviews for Time for three years and taught, first at Sarah Lawrence College, then at Princeton and at the Indiana University School of Letters. He lived in Italy with his family from 1953 to 1964, completing there his translation of the Odyssey. In 1964 he returned to teach at Harvard, where in 1965 he was appointed Boylston Professor of Rhetoric and Oratory. In 1971 Spring Shade, a collection of his poems, appeared, and in 1974 his Iliad. He became Emeritus at Harvard in 1981.

During my sophomore year at Harvard I dared enroll in a course in the history of French criticism given mainly for graduate students by Professor Irving Babbitt. On the Harvard faculty and in the quarterlies at the time, Babbitt was known for his independence as a proponent of a cause he called Humanism with a capital *H*, as opposed to Romanticism with a capital *R*—an evil that he believed had beset the world especially since Rousseau. He had written to this effect severe and learned studies of ideas. T. S. Eliot, calling himself a classicist, had professed sympathy for Babbitt's Humanism, but the sympathy was not returned. Babbitt had no ear for Eliot's verse or perhaps for any other after Racine. He was a big bent old man with no nonsense about him who used to come into his dusty classroom and upend his green book bag over the desk, letting a dozen books tumble out, books old and new of all shapes and sizes. He never needed to refer to them, but there they were. He would hunch at the desk and talk, quoting effortlessly from Malherbe and Boileau, rubbing and seeming to scratch or even lightly to pick his distinguished nose, while he glared over his low spectacles at the handful of incipient romanticists before him. The day came when he referred without tenderness to the work of Eliot and said, with a grumpy gesture, "He used to sit right there. We called him Tommy."

Outside rustled the moderately spacious Yard, criss-crossed by paths under elms, with vistas of brickwork, choice and Georgian to the west. Sever Hall, where Babbitt's half-dozen gathered, was and is a mammoth old-fashioned building like an early gym, bulging, however, with class-rooms. Young book-carriers in crowds at every class bell clattered up or down the wide well of stairs. In another Sever classroom three mornings a week with a dozen other la-borers I construed Plato for Professor Gulick, whose best remembered utterance concerned neither the *Apology* nor the *Crito* but the Greek language, how to learn it. Ap-proached after class on the subject of there being "so many new words in each assignment," the gray-browed old ram-rod with his eagle look said helpfully, "Memorize them," as he stuffed text and notes into his bag, inviting no further queries. Horace and Plautus were the texts in yet another class over which presided a stooped young man in hard Donegal tweed who had piercing black eyes and a thin bony face with a slight mustache and goatee. My lesson from this man, Parry, came one day when I thought I could make my rendering of Horace more racy with slang. Parry usually spared himself at least the spectacle of recitations by keep-ing his gaze out the window. This time he let me finish and then swung around to fix his eyes fully on me while smiling a relishing smile. "An ignoble translation," he said to me with precision. I knew the word but had not in my time heard anyone use it; now I had had that privilege.

For these courses I could claim the expected background, but Babbitt's graduate course presumed wide reading in French literature, and mine had not been wide. I probably felt up to it because two summers before I had briefly steeped myself in the land of France. Riding my bike out of Dieppe one cool August morning I met a fine figure of a mustached man striding behind a plow in a roadside field, who sang out, *"Salut!"* as though the whole human race were manly and free. At sundown that day the sliding gray-green Seine, the stone quays and quayside trees, the Ile de la

Cité, and the balanced exaltation of the cathedral in with-
ered yellow-rose light, all before me for the first time, quiet-
ened me with memory of life greater far than my own. The
tall, tinted, ancient houses at my back with their crazed
chimney pots might have looked down on Henri Quatre. My
school roommate and I got a room in a cheap hotel, Rue
Vaugirard, and found Le Dôme, where at a sidewalk table we
sat long with our beer and peanuts, as Arab rug sellers and
other figures of the boulevard went by. A week later we sold
our bicycles and took a slow train, third class (*"Ne Laissez
Pas les Enfants Jouer avec la Serrure"*), southward through
the country to Dijon and then to Genèva, sometimes using
pages from my cheap copy of Voltaire's *Dictionnaire philo-
sophique* in impoverished station W.C.'s. The rich, sad countryside, the *mutilés de la guerre,* the blue-bloused trainmen,
the bottled Vichy, the Gaulois taste, the odors of France and
the French then entered our sense of the world. So much
the better if I had now, at Harvard, to embrace their literature. I relied heavily on my trusty yellow volumes of Fa-
guet's History, supplemented in the library by hours of
Sainte-Beuve. For my term paper I chose the skeptical early
encyclopedist, Pierre Bayle. Since Bayle did not represent
what the instructor approved, this choice may have been a
trifle refractory.

Babbitt's learning, crust, and drive impressed and appealed to me, but I listened to him on poetry and particularly
on Eliot with mulish reserve. In the matter of poetry, I
considered that I knew what I knew, and the power of *The
Waste Land* surpassed that of *Phèdre,* at least in my lifetime.

At eighteen, on a spring evening at a New England
school, I had sat in a low-ceilinged room in shadow while
under a lamp amid books a young high-strung teacher with
distinct articulation read it all aloud to me—the strangest
and most disturbing thing I had ever heard. A number of
voices spoke for distant lives and civilizations; the central
voice spoke from some point or mood beyond us, pained and
profound. Echoes came through of poems in other lan-

guages and in our own. Dramatic scenes were suggested and broken off. There were furious ironies. The rhythms shifted. Luxurious imagery gave way to scriptural desolation. At times one felt oneself directly and devastatingly addressed. I was entranced and frightened, speechless at the end. A year afterward I drifted into the Dunster Bookshop, in a neat, small frame house in Cambridge, and picked up a new book, thin and fine, in tan cloth with a gold title, *Ash Wednesday*. As warm spring air stirred in from an open window, a new music came to me in hesitancies and suspensions and resolutions, and from another page a new, lovely, impudent invention in style. I took the book away to my room. No more than in the case of *The Waste Land* could I put to myself clearly the nature of the work or its effect. I simply knew that it was utterly surprising, utterly superior:

> Beyond the hawthorn blossom and a pasture scene
> The broadbacked figure drest in blue and green
> Enchanted the Maytime with an antique flute . . .

Had anything more ravishing than that ever been printed? His other verse and essays had to be read and all writing judged by reference to them, my own included.

Now and then phrases and lines took form in my head, and I found myself, usually late at night when I had tired of trying to read Latin or Greek, making an inky chaos of a sheet of paper—for an illegible mess seemed the only medium or broth in which a poem might be cultivated. The trance of exhaustion and the trance of conception seemed one. In the small hours when the rumor of other life had subsided and only the wind over the glow of the avenue gave an occasional buffet to my panes, I sat under my goosenecked lamp, incapable of anything but this work of the ear and the sixth sense—queerly most fully alive when most nearly dead. What could be done with books and tasks had been done; one could do no more, being now stilled for this void into which flooded the knowledge of the heart: loss and grief, loneliness and longing, fear and desire. Love of shape and cadence resembled love of places and persons; the emotions were distinct but one entangled the other, so the artifact came from experience and reached back into experience:

> Whenas in suit of light this lady goes
> And network of the morning on her hair . . .

So began one mannered song because a girl and I had gone for a ride one Saturday in sunny October woods, having borrowed two saddle horses from her sporty cousins. All that year I had this girl as much on my mind as I had Plato or Plautus, Boileau or Bayle.

First admired at Charlevoix in July, sitting near a diving board at the end of a pier, tan and smooth and deep-breasted in a sky blue swimsuit, she gave me a satiric look and then a grin or two. She had rather close-set golden-flecked gray eyes. I offered my only dive, a jackknife. Her repertory was larger and much more beautiful. Almost at once I found myself in my white linen suit at a dance in the boat house with a band from Petoskey and Japanese lanterns. She wore her straw-colored hair pulled back across the ears to a solid coil behind. Broad, well-made shoulders and unflawed arms gave her ease in her "formal," and with her good carriage, her clean-cut profile and slightly hooked nose, she had a young empress air. This went to pieces when you saw her face in animation, as it most often was, freely crinkling in prolonged mischievous amusement: what came across then included an endearing whiff of the hayseed. We left the dance floor after "Three Little Words," going hand in hand along the dark beach until we found a skiff to sit in, and she lay back against something while I devoted myself to her lips, then in time to her throat and the other rondures that her party dress left bare. Even in the dark I sensed her all-pervading flush, a rosiness in the tan that later on would charm and move me. It did not necessarily wait upon being touched. She was a junior at Wellesley, and in the fall we sat together in the stadium and jumped and hugged when the

long-shanked, long-armed Harvard quarterback saved the
day against Army with a last-ditch, daringly delayed, perfectly cool, sixty-yard forward pass for touchdown from
behind the Harvard goal line. Whenever I took anyone anywhere that year, it was Emily Morrier, whom I may now
summon up, a little pigeon-toed in her high heels, cold-
nosed in her fur collar, drawn into the shadow of Hollis entry
on a winter night to kiss. One could not have a girl at night in
one's room.

Being twenty and vain or social enough to go in for full
evening dress, I had got, besides my tuxedo, a tailcoat with
white tie and waistcoat. I owned a chesterfield overcoat.
Repressing my misgivings, I bought a derby. Home with all
this for the Christmas holidays in Springfield, I not only
went to the country club dances but at Emily's invitation
took a train to St. Louis for the Belle Rive New Year's Eve
ball. Charlevoix, Saint Louis, Belle Rive . . . only a century
after French had been heard on the big river and no more
than half a century after the epithet "Frenchy" had been
heard (you could imagine) by her forbears, Emily seemed
oblivious of all that, as of the exploring soldiers, Jesuits, and
coureurs de bois who had left the place names. No one heard
her name, or thought of it, as French.

The derby I had bought, all wrong for the head it sat on,
appeared in St. Louis for the last time. During the day about
town I thought I carried it off, but I knew better in the
evening when my girl asked in passing if I really needed to
wear that. Hatless we went to the dancing, of which there
was a great deal. Reentering her house on the quiet between
two and three, we found one lamp lit in the living room and
in the grate a dying fire. We sat on the floor in the warmth.
Nothing stirred in the sleeping house. After a while both her
shoulders flexed as her strong hands reached back to un-
hook her bra. She had done this for me before, in the dark on
a back seat amid her furs, on a cold drive from New Haven to
Northampton after the Yale game. Now she gave into my
hand the visible wealth of her body, looking at me in some-

thing like sorrow before she closed her eyes. I thought we would marry. It was a theory that we sometimes held, and we jested about it, as well we might.

On the fourth or top floor of Hollis Hall my room at the rear looked out through three square windows at western sky, into which across the way poked the narrow, eight-sided steeple of the Unitarian church. To the right as you entered stood a rented Ivers & Pond against the wall, across from it an unused fireplace and a desk, and the bed was placed between, under the windows. Drafts came in through the ill-fitting and flaking old sashes, but I had not the wit to move the bed away; all winter I sneezed and sniffled, rinsing out handkerchiefs in my washbowl and plastering them to dry on the mirror. Near a window in one corner a coil of heavy rope, secured by a ringbolt, had been sitting for generations, awaiting use as a lifeline in a fire. The room next door on the Yard side had been occupied once by Thoreau, H. D., according to a printed list in the entry. In late morning every day but Sunday appeared the cleaning biddy to make up the room: gray but rosy Mrs. O'Shaughnessy, whose buxom upper body seemed stacked a bit too far forward on her hips, as though she were about to topple. In restlessness, on evenings alone, I could cross the room from desk to piano as from the Old to the New World, freeing my spirit in Beethoven as Chateaubriand did his in the wilderness. *The Well-Tempered Clavier* on the rack served a steadier mood with the two or three preludes and fugues I had learned to play. Here again pure form, in this case that of music, for a while relieved and ordered the formless wavering and suffering of existence. Alone, at times I lived in horror.

What was the nub of that early misery but a conscious-ness of self as an irreducible burden? The pale thick-headed face in the bathroom mirror gave the lie to any skill or sangfroid enacted in the world; weak and defective forever the self knew itself to be. And there were other things. From time to time for years without much warning I felt the

familiar world lose continuity until the mere being of anything seemed fearsomely odd. Precious in a way this might
be, but when it happened I could be at a loss for any sane
response to quite ordinary situations and persons. Then at
my father's death a bad light on mortality had taken me by
the hair. No pleasure in study or girls or friendships or
athletics could make me forget for long the great terror at
the heart of life, while at the same time I refused on principle
to fear anything. On my own I had incurred an ill clairvoy-
ance, like that fixed in *The Waste Land* and in the air during
and after the Great War.

Sometimes around midnight a hail from below would get
me into my coat or sweater and down for a walk. This friend
and I shared boyhoods in central Illinois—nothing to sneeze
at as a bond at Harvard. We also shared a literary obsession
and a certain learning with respect to death. White-faced
and slight, with a forelock and large wide-open brown eyes,
he carried his head a trifle cocked to one side in consequence of a nearly final carotid incision once made by his
own hand. He therefore feared nothing, like me. He would
be waiting below in pea jacket and watch cap, and we would
be off along the river where the lights burned and rippled all
night. After Urbana he had come East for a master's and
now had Anglo-Saxon and German on his hands. He lived in
no dormitory but on Cambridge Street in a graduate student's old-fashioned apartment with gas jets. Here at midyear he, Bill, and I sat up together from midnight to eight
cramming for exams—his in German, mine in Tudor history, the choice in my case being between knowing what I
could hold on to from the night's reading and being totally at
a loss. Our nocturnal rambles often ended up at the all-night
Georgian Cafeteria on Boylston Street for onion omelet
sandwiches, known as Westerns, at the expense of whoever
had some money. Each borrowed, jotting nothing down. We
were so nearly equally poor that without trying to keep track
we knew we'd come out even, that is, no poorer than before.

At my door on a weekend afternoon might appear the

most exacting of my friends, the teacher who had read *The Waste Land* to me two years before and changed my conception of poetry. Lank, tall, and mettlesome in scarf and greatcoat, collar turned up, but always bareheaded in any snow or rain, his glasses glinting over distant gray eyes under his extremely high, narrow forehead, he would come in swinging his green book bag and would be into it before you knew it, with his very long, very light, dancing fingers, to fish out the latest funny or exciting page he had found in prose or verse. No one I knew or was to know in the world ever had such style as Dudley Fitts. Now and then I got a letter from him in Latin, a typed page headed *"Dudleius Roberto Salutem,"* fluent, crisp, and full of wit, to which I would sweat for hours to reply. When I had been about to register at the university one September day, after lunch at the Harvard Club in Boston, Dudley took me up to the library, then empty except for a mild old bearded figure whom he recognized, recumbent on a couch. Professor Kirsopp Lake, convalescent after surgery, had an academic tale for his former student and for me if I could follow it. It seemed that at his old university, Leyden, a degree committee at one time had seen fit to introduce just below the ordinary passing degree the exquisite distinction of the degree *VIX*—"barely"—(solemn glee on the part of raconteur and auditor), a formality that remained unchallenged for years until a later committee in one prodigious case invented the still more subtle gradation (gentle pause for maximum effect) *VIX ET NE VIX QUIDEM*—"barely and not even barely"—(whole-souled laughter, with some wincing on the part of Professor Lake). He was a great patristic scholar, and I saw him again later when he lectured to a survey course, recommending in inscrutable tones the Hittites to anyone who wanted a future in scholarship. I did not leap to take up the Hittites. What I wanted if I wanted anything was quality in my writing, and I trusted Dudley to tell me if and when it showed up. In poems of his own, as in "Priam," quality had been audible: "The stars marched down with lightning to the sea . . ." and I trusted him, too, when without ever quite saying so he made me think I must have Greek as well as Latin, hard going though it turned out to be.

If anyone presided over my young life in those years, this buoyant and meticulous spirit did. On occasion I revisited my old school and his dormitory room there—books and books and two portraits: his sardonically beautiful dark-eyed sister and his hale and noble wind-blown girl. Over the legend *Nil Sine Magno Labore* his bookplate showed a ton-sured monk at an organ, rightly enough since his own performances on this instrument, which he played for chapel, in the case of difficult fugues became perfect mar-vels of nerve, dexterity, and attention—his long fingers flying, his lean face rapt. Once or twice his cheeks were wet. Seven years older and far ahead of me, he let me see how the structural arts of language and music could tingle with strenuous life. But beyond that, and beyond everything, were the shared presciences of a poetry for which he thought I too had an aptitude, a poetry that should be free of dead form but as formal as you chose, under Eliot's shadow, certainly, but bringing notes of one's own from the broken world.

A High Church childhood accounted for some of his La-tinity; his father had been a pastor in Ipswich; Dudley used the saints' calendar in dating letters; he once deplored, in Latin, the desperate state of my faith. But his own was a sentiment, a fondness for liturgy. When his sister asked if there was any historical truth in the New Testament, he answered sharply, as became Kirsopp Lake's best student, "Not a word." But he didn't believe that, either. Possibly Harvard made a church for him, as in a sense it did for his Cambridge friends, reading or writing people: young tutors in English and classics; a girl who edited for *The Atlantic;* Lincoln Kirstein to whose gallant *Hound and Horn* Dudley contributed; Robert Hillyer, who taught verse making; the benign Virgilian, Professor Rand. When he called on these people he sometimes towed me along, and on some of them I called in my turn. The Yard contained in apparent homeliness and peace the heart of the University, beating in the hourly bell, but just outside moved the traffic of the Square, actually triangular, with its eating places and stores and lights, and beyond that the streets of boardinghouses and professors' houses, Garden and Brattle and Mount Auburn. The latter led to the cemetery, favored for walks, and there at pause in the shallow snow one winter day I looked down to find at my feet the two small stones of William James and Henry James. Of the country setting I knew mainly Concord, where I rode a few times with Kirstein. Tall and superb with crew cut and beak, a delighted connoisseur of style, he liked taking the jumps on the woodland trails and afterward plastering cream cheese on hot toast for a sumptuous tea. On other occasions I meditated on the small pond of Thoreau or paced on the gentle hill where Hawthorne had paced behind the frame house where he lived. No one then paid much attention to these places. In the other direction a nickel would take you by subway to Boston for scallops amid the sawdust of the Oyster House or venison and corn bread at Durgin Park. But of aristocratic Boston I had only the faintest notion and of social Boston a thin ration. I got into my white or black tie only for a few dances at the Somerset, where I knew a face or two and felt drawn to one, snub-nosed and quizzical, attached to a long body that handsomely warmed the chest. This might be called my closest contact with a Bostonian family in the best tradition: they had a country house in Milton, her vivacious mother had lived in an embassy, her massive father practiced on State Street and collected Greek coins.

The setting had plenty of other aspects, but these were what I knew, and the institution at the center took peculiar savor from them all. While professing no dogma and no deposit of revelation, Holy Mother Harvard, if the irreverence may be forgiven, had engaged in teaching all nations, and her savor as well as her puritan soul entered into everything she taught. As to the soul, I will recount one event. Taking a train on a weekday evening in February and using what remained of the light for my Plato, I became aware only at Wellesley Station that snow had begun to fall. Through a light coating I made tracks up the hill to Cazenove Hall. Emily and I were going to study together in the parlor. The parlor remained empty except for us. Through the windows we saw the snow windlessly coming down. After a while Social Thought joined Plato on the floor and with no more conversation we resorted to one another. By the time I made my way down the hill to take the train back to Boston, I sank in snow over my shoe tops and drenched my feet. A few days later my fever became so parching that I took a taxi to the infirmary and bedded down. Stillman in those years was a small brick building up the river. During this, my only sojourn, I read Cocteau's *Thomas the Impostor* and found a sentence that I would never forget: of a corpse in a trench in 1916, "The soul had left this body in haste and without a backward look." Emily sent me a commiserating letter in her closely set, curly writing, enclosing some aromatic candies, red drops, bitingly pungent when crunched. There were four or five other students in the single big ward. The event I speak of was the arrival one afternoon of a slightly portly gentleman with walrus mustaches in chesterfield and homburg, with a small black Scotty on a leash. He inquired into our condition and passed the time of day. It was Abbott Lawrence Lowell, president of the University, out for his constitutional and visiting the sick. Visiting *his* sick. That kind of thing, soon enough to go out, still happened.

E. J. Kahn, Jr. '37

E. J. Kahn, Jr., sold his first piece to The New Yorker *while he was a Harvard senior, in the spring of 1937, and he has been contributing to that magazine ever since. His most recent book—*Far-flung and Footloose: Pieces from "The New Yorker" 1937–1978—*contains fewer than one-tenth of the more than two million words he has written for that magazine. In addition to many articles for other magazines, he is the author of more than a score of books, among them* Harvard: Through Change and Through Storm, The Big Drink, The China Hands, *and a 1978 memoir,* About "The New Yorker" and Me. *He has served on the governing boards of The Authors League of America, The Authors Guild, and P.E.N. He was an elected director of the Associated Harvard Alumni from 1969 to 1972 and has served as chairman of the board of trustees of the Scarborough School. He lives in New York City and Truro, Massachusetts, and is married to Eleanor Munro, the author of, among other works,* Originals: American Women Artists. *Among his sons are two Harvard graduates, E. J. Kahn III, '69, and Joseph P. Kahn, '71. He is a member of the Century Association and the Harvard Club of New York.*

I have returned to Harvard many times in the forty-odd years since my graduation, formally and informally. Informally, as a father of two Harvard College sons, as a spectator at football games, and as a reporter gathering material for a book about the ivied old place. (I learned more from auditing courses during the 1967–68 academic year than I did in four years as a tuition-paying student.) Formally, as a quondam director of the Associated Harvard Alumni and a member of the Overseer's committee to visit the English department. Whenever I found myself back in Cambridge in one of these latter capacities, it seemed to be de rigueur for all us homecoming alumni to have a meeting—at dinner, at lunch, even at breakfast—with undergraduates. These rituals were supposed to be important, and maybe they were; the idea appeared to be that such confrontations with live students would give us old grads a sense of what was really going on.

How the undergraduates we VIPs broke bread with were chosen for our get-togethers, and how they felt about them, I never quite could determine. The students were all nice enough, but wary. Sometimes also sleepy. I could not help reflecting that they were well ahead of where I'd been at their stage of development: I don't recall ever having had anything to do with Harvard alumni—except those who had joined the faculty—when I was an undergraduate. If I had, I might have been a worthier student. There were good enough reasons for my lack of communication. For one, my father had gone to Columbia. For another, although I went to a number of Ivy League football games when I was a child, growing up in New York City, they were mostly in the Yale Bowl, and I always sat on the Yale side. The Old Eli who was usually my host never invited me to the Yale–Harvard game—he saved important occasions like that for his adult friends—so the alien fans I bumped into at New Haven were largely people from far-off places like Dartmouth and West Point. It was different, of course, with my own children; they were dragged to Harvard–Yale games almost as soon as they were weaned. I should perhaps add that when I was courting my present wife the highlight of our first weekend tryst was the epochal 29–29 tie with which Harvard stunned Yale in the fall of 1968. She has never been much of a football fan and doesn't understand to this day what it was that Saturday afternoon that infected me with bad cases of both hysteria and hoarseness. It is a tribute to the other sterling aspects of her character that I married her notwithstanding.

I was young when I entered Harvard—not yet seventeen, and a sixteen-year-old, at that, of monumental innocence. I was about the equivalent, I should say, of a 1980 twelve-year-old. I was assigned to a fourth-floor room in Stoughton, and that was an educational experience that strongly influenced my later life; I have hated climbing stairs ever since. The unquestioned leader of the quadrumvirate residing on that floor was a sophisticated eighteen-year-old who had gone to a prep school and who handled all vexing freshman situations with such consummate sangfroid that I rather hoped he would guide me all the way through the labyrinth of college. He vanished from the scene at the end of that year and hasn't resurfaced since. So much for appearances. The most important decision I recall having had to make as a freshman—aside from momentarily debating whether I should attempt to finish the compulsory 100-yard swimming test or should simply drown—was to pick a field of concentration. That turned out to be easier than natation. The venerable don who was assigned to discuss this weighty matter with me—he was probably a first-year graduate student—asked me what I had studied in high school, and when it came out that I had taken rather a good deal of both Latin and Greek, he urged me to continue on that exemplary course and to embrace literature. Literature, which stopped being a field of concentration at about the time that two-platoon football was born, then consisted of any combination of a modern and a classical language. I could have selected, say, French and Latin. I went for English and Greek. I was lucky; one of my Greek courses was taught by John H. Finley, Jr., whom, some thirty years later, I finally dared address as "John." To my delight and amazement, he was unperturbed. I had closed a generation gap. That gets easier, of course, as one gets older, but not, evidently, for everybody. There are tenured Harvard professors today who, to my dismay, sometimes address me as "sir."

Despite Professor Finley's gracious and gifted efforts, my Greek deteriorated, while I was at Harvard, almost to the point of nonexistence. I had worked hard at high school and had received generally good grades. (The student there with whom I competed most sedulously to be Number One in our class turned out, years later, to be the father-in-law of a book editor of mine.) If I learned little in college, I did learn, alas, that it was possible to get through Harvard almost without doing any work at all. I had one classmate who never attended a single lecture in the Old Testament course we both took. The night before the final exam, he borrowed my notes, which were skimpy at best. That was all the studying he did. He got an A in the course. I got a B. After that tour de force, he never could bring himself to take academic requirements seriously, and indeed he didn't bother to finish college, which did not prevent him from ultimately becom-

ing the chairman of the board of a large global corporation.
That A he got in Bible was a primary factor in motivating me
not to study, either. (I knew I could never comprehend
physics and economics anyway, no matter how hard I might
have tried.) I confess all this without pride; also, probably,
with insufficient remorse.

In any event, by the end of my senior year, I was supposed
to be an expert in Greek. After all, I had had three years of
the subject in school and four more at Harvard. One of the
final requirements in my field of concentration was a three-
hour sight translation, Greek to English. My tutor, who had
watched despairingly as my command of the ancient language eroded, did not think I had a prayer of achieving a
passing grade of 60 on that marathon quiz. Neither did I.
Fortunately for me, the tutor informed me—no doubt un-
ethically—he was going to be one of the two faculty members who would grade my translation. After I struggled
through it, he concluded that any honest arbiter would give
me a 52. So he gave me a 68, to get my average up to par. The
other grader, a stranger, irrationally gave me a 72. My tutor
was outraged and not long afterward committed suicide. I
hope there were other reasons, too.

Toward the end of my freshman year, my academic sloth-
fulness intensified. I had been editor of my high school
weekly paper—it was a job available to just about anybody
who could spell—and so I naturally tried out for a spot on the
staff of *The Harvard Crimson*. I thought I was doing all right
in the competition—that I would probably make the staff
and thus be allowed to climb the stairs to the second story of
the *Crimson* building, an aerie to which mere fledgling
heelers were denied admittance—until the managing editor
took me aside late one night, after the paper had gone to
press with one of my efforts hearteningly featured on the
front page, and told me that he was sorry, but the *Crimson*
had already filled its Jewish quota for that term.

Babe in the woods that I was, I didn't even know about
Jewish quotas. (Years later, I was invited to be a speaker at

the *Crimson*'s annual banquet, held upstairs in its building; the latter-day editors had forgotten about quotas, if indeed they had ever heard of them, and had evidently also forgotten that I was not one of *their* alumni. I accepted; I have a forgiving nature, and, besides, I wanted to see what the second floor looked like.) So after that rebuff I was understandably eager to enlist in the ranks of a rival daily that was spawned in the spring of 1934, under the leadership of two senior defectors from the august *Crimson:* Joseph J. Thorndike, Jr., who went on to become the editor of *Life;* and John U. Monro, who attained the only slightly less prestigious post of dean of Harvard College.

The new paper was the Harvard *Journal,* a feisty daily that kept those of us happily associated with it on the go, day and night, often all night, for thirteen heady weeks, until the academic year terminated and the *Journal* ended, too, deep in debt. The *Crimson* let it be known in blunt, unconditional-surrender terms that no one who had fought for the enemy could ever aspire to join its ranks. So my undergraduate journalistic career was abruptly over even before I became an upperclassman. It never occurred to me to try out for the *Lampoon* or the *Advocate.* Membership in those august institutions, I had somehow got the impression, was reserved for students who had a real gift for writing and might someday even make a living at it.

As a sophomore, I landed in Eliot House. That was long before John Finley became its Master. Roger Bigelow Merriman—"Frisky" of History I fame—was in charge then, one of the authentic giants of a faculty that also starred John Livingston Lowes and George Lyman Kittredge. Everyone of consequence back then seemed to have three names (James Bryant Conant was our president and Franklin Delano Roosevelt, the outside world's), and it would have been hard to conceive of endowing with authority anyone so leanly lettered as a Derek Bok. I was lucky enough to take Kittredge's Shakespeare course. I quickly forgot most of what Kitty attempted to teach me, but years later, when I became acquainted with a scholar who had devoted much of his life to trying to prove that Shakespeare's plays had actually been written by Christopher Marlowe, I would always remember the story of how Professor Kittredge, who clung stubbornly to the belief that Shakespeare ·had written Shakespeare, once rose to his feet at some banquet or other and declared, "Gentlemen, I shall now prove that this menu was written by John Keats," and proceeded deftly to so do.

Eliot House was a congenial home away from home. We had biddies to tidy up our rooms. We had waitresses to serve our meals—one of whom served extracurricularly as a singer with a very amateur jazz band some of us organized, to the distress of the occupants of nearby chambers. (If our cacophony ever reached Master Merriman's ears, he did nothing to shut us up.) Probably most of the members of our band wanted to sleep with our vocalist, but I, at least, was far too shy ever to pop the question. I played the drums, poorly, as was made more than manifest when Chick Webb and his band came to play at an Eliot House spring dance. That talented percussionist brought along a singer who, similarly, was better than ours, a young woman named Ella Fitzgerald.

We cared about the outside world. The depression was lingering on while we were undergraduates, and for the parents of many of us the annual Harvard tuition of four hundred dollars must have represented a substantial outlay, if not a genuine sacrifice. Hitler was coming into power in Germany—he staged his 1936 Olympics just after our junior year—and war clouds were thick over Europe. Many of us responded to that by standing on the steps of Widener and solemnly reciting the Oxford Pledge, according to which we were adamantly opposed to taking up arms to defend the king of England or anybody else. A few years later, most of us were in uniform, having reneged on that unequivocal oath without a twinge of guilt. Harvard had taught us, if nothing else, to be flexible and to adapt to change. How much Harvard has ever truly changed is moot. In the spring of 1969, after the campus riots, my publishers urged me to rewrite a history of Harvard I had finished; they couldn't believe the validity of my basic premise, which was that, after three hundred and thirty-three years of existence, Harvard would probably weather a storm of even that turbulence. So I made some changes in the text. I should have stood my ground. Harvard did survive. Survived better and longer, come to think of it, than my book.

We cared about domestic politics, too, in the thirties. A lot of us, even those from staunch Republican backgrounds, assumed that sooner or later we would have special entrée to the White House, because surely that establishment would sooner or later be presided over by our classmate, Franklin Delano Roosevelt, Jr. We had another classmate who more steadfastly ran the political course. He would bang on our doors in the middle of the night, when we were undergraduates, demanding that we rouse ourselves and dash off telegrams to the governor of Alabama about the Scottsboro boys; in the class album published to celebrate our twenty-fifth reunion, our herald of the dark, demonstrating admirable consistency and persistency, identified himself proudly as secretary of the Communist party of Vermont.

Many of the ultimate successes in our class (corporation presidents, corporation lawyers, that sort) were achieved by men who attracted little attention as undergraduates, though as seniors we did presciently choose as our first marshal a fellow who later rose to become dean of students at Harvard and in that capacity was responsible for throwing Teddy Kennedy out of the place, which in the context of twentieth-century American history was perhaps no small feat. Our dean was Robert B. Watson, who afterward also became Harvard's director of athletics. It was illustrative of Booze Watson's high ethical standards—he acquired his nickname, it went without saying, because he never drank—that in spite of his privileged status, when his classmates were more than forty years out of college they had never yet received seats for the Harvard–Yale football game any closer to midfield than the ten-yard line.

One of the odd things about Harvard and me is that—not counting football games—I really had very little to do with the place until I'd been out of it for a quarter of a century. I never went to any reunion before our twenty-fifth. I didn't even join the Harvard Club of New York, although it was right across the street from my office, until nearly twenty years after graduation; since then, I have been one of its most faithful patrons and have staggering monthly bills to prove it. Why? I was a late Harvard bloomer, I guess. It was the twenty-fifth reunion, probably, that turned me on. Practically none of the classmates I'd known well as a student went to that reunion. Today, when I meet classmates at subsequent reunions or elsewhere, we pretend that we knew one another in our undergraduate days, but we didn't. Many of my closest friends from my Harvard class are men I never talked to until they were nearly grandfathers. It is all very puzzling. Why do I have this genuine affinity for Harvard when in fact it so little touched my life for so long? Something must have been instilled in me at Cambridge during those four undergraduate years—a germ, a seed, a chance remark maybe by John Finley, the precise wording of which, like my Greek, I have long since forgotten—something that persuaded me, consciously or unconsciously, that the Harvard connection would become and would remain an integral and cherished part of my life. As indeed it is.

Arthur Schlesinger, Jr. '38

Harvard dominated my first forty years. I was seven years old in 1924 when my father came east from Iowa to join the Harvard history department, and I was forty-three years old in 1961 when, by that time in the department myself, I took leave to join the Kennedy administration. Except for boarding school, a year at Cambridge University, and the war years, I lived most of my early life within a mile of Harvard Square.

Entering the College as a freshman in the autumn of 1934 was not therefore a major culture shock. I moved from the family house in Gray Gardens East to Thayer Hall in the Yard. But I was already a habitué of Widener Library and the stadium, I had friends on the faculty, and Cambridge and Boston were familiar territory. Exeter, moreover, had given me such a rough time intellectually that the transition to Harvard proved far less agonizing than the transition had been in 1931 from the Cambridge Latin School to Exeter.

My room in Thayer Hall was on the second floor facing Harvard Hall and the Square. My roommate turned out to be a decent, reticent, forbearing young man from Chicago, Edward T. James, later known for his work on the *Dictionary of American Biography* and on *Notable American Women*. We roomed together throughout our college days.

The Thayer Hall boys were a good, robust lot, many from the Middle West, most from public schools.

In sophomore year we dispersed to the Houses. These were the early years of the revolution in Harvard living wrought by A. Lawrence Lowell and Edward Harkness. The sensitive and Dos Passosish Harvard novel by George Weller, '29, *Not to Eat, Not for Love*, came out in 1933 and we all read it. But the pre-House College so poignantly portrayed by Weller already seemed another age.

Ed James and I decided to go to Adams House, partly because of the swimming pool and the allegedly superior kitchen, also because my father was a fellow of the House and consequently I had some acquaintance with it. The master was James Phinney Baxter, historian and later president of Williams, a hearty, shrewd, rubicund, twinkling man, who radiated a certain practical Yankee downrightness amid the preciosities of Harvard intellectualism. Raphael Demos, a Greek who taught philosophy with charm and candor, was senior tutor, followed by S. Everett Gleason, a witty medieval historian.

Our rooms were on the top floor of C-entry. We each had a bedroom and shared a spacious living room and a narrow balcony looking over the *Crimson* building toward the Yard. (After the war four or five students occupied the same suite.) The dining hall lived up to its culinary reputation, but we had not anticipated how pretty some of the waitresses would be. America was deep in depression. Yet Harvard Houses had table service and even printed menus. Coming back after the war was a great letdown: waitresses and menus gone, and students lining up as if in army mess lines to receive food shoveled into indented trays.

Which House was one vital decision. The other was which field of concentration. I chose History and Literature. History and Lit was then in its early glory. The number of students accepted each year was limited, and this, combined with the pleasure that both faculty and students so plainly found in their work and each other, gave the field a we-happy-few atmosphere that one sometimes found exasperating. Still the attempt, then in its infancy, to make connections between history and literature was exciting; the professors were stimulating; and I never regretted the choice.

I was especially lucky in tutors—Perry Miller in my sophomore year, F. O. Matthiessen in my junior year, then back to Miller in senior year for my honors essay. Miller and Matthiessen were close if sometimes prickly friends but very contrasting teachers. Miller, the historian of ideas, was gruff, vigorous, direct, always happy to shake up and shock his students. He also often referred to a mysterious early career as a hobo and as a seaman on tramp steamers; this made him a romantic figure in the eyes of the young. Matty, the literary critic, was courteous, intense, sensitive, soft-spoken, intellectually insinuating rather than contentious. Miller was an atheist, Matty a devout Anglican; Miller a New Dealer, Matty a Stalinist fellow traveler. Miller was, in addition, an ardent heterosexual, Matty a devoted homosexual, but I was aware of neither proclivity at the time.

Both were generous in the expenditure of time and concern, and I learned more than I can say in rugged, shouting discussions with Miller at Leverett House and in taut, quiet sessions with Matty in his darkened (as I recall it) Eliot House study. Miller was a man of rigorous standards, and he early gave me to understand that glibness was not enough, a valuable lesson if one imperfectly learned. He also left me with a lasting appreciation of the power of Calvinism. He was an atheist who believed in original sin—a position congenial to one who had recently been impressed by Leslie Stephen's *An Agnostic's Apology*. I first heard from Miller about Reinhold Niebuhr, who later became such an influence on my life.

Because I was temperamentally more akin to Miller, I perhaps learned even more from Matthiessen. He made me read *The Waste Land*; I remember, in a juvenile fit of inverse snobbery, putting another jacket on the book lest people think I was succumbing to aesthetic fashion. We went over the poem line by line, uncovering deeper resonances and reverberations. It was an exciting experience, and I owe to Matty a fondness for poetry that has never lapsed. Though politics later divided us and for a time after the war he even stopped speaking to me, his Stalinism was not obtrusive then. One night I was invited to meet Harry Bridges in his rooms and was struck by the deference the literary scholar paid to the tough, sharp labor leader. But I was not aware how deep our political disagreements were till I returned in the fall of 1939 from a year at Cambridge. Stalin had signed his pact with Hitler; Great Britain was mired in the ambiguities of the Phony War. I said to Matty one day that Winston Churchill was the only hope. Matty said with great intensity, "Winston Churchill is the epitome of everything I have hated all my life."

A third member of the faculty who had great impact was Bernard De Voto. He had been a good friend of my parents. My first memory of him was in Prohibition days when, after forays across the border into Canada, he used to drive up to our back door and deliver carefully wrapped packages that turned out to contain bottles of whisky and gin. For a time I supposed that Benny De Voto was the family bootlegger. At Harvard he offered courses on composition and contemporary literature. The second was lively and opinionated, but the first was a genuine revelation.

"Verbs and nouns are the guts of a sentence," he told his students. "Adjectives and adverbs are the water. A writer is as strong as his verbs." I began by writing dramatic criticism for him. George Jean Nathan was my model—a bad model because, like Mencken, he had a style that worked for him but for no one else. I had even thought wistfully of becoming a drama critic, but De Voto soon persuaded me that this was a waste of life. He was quite right too, I often reflect, as I sit through (or walk out of) our contemporary drama. De Voto read one's *jejuneries* with meticulous care, exposed pretentiousness and falsity with pitiless eye, scrawled insulting

but unanswerable comments in the margin, and goaded his
students to think through what they were trying to say and
to say it plainly, concisely, and concretely.

He was a great teacher. But James B. Conant, a generally
admirable president, did not consider teaching students
how to write a scholarly endeavor, and De Voto was refused a
permanent appointment. In the fall of 1936 he went off to
New York to edit the *Saturday Review of Literature*. It was a
grave loss to Harvard.

Then there were the historians. From Samuel Eliot Morison I gained a tremendous sense of the role of *style* both in
writing history and in being a historian. From Frederick
Merk I gained a tremendous sense of what fastidious, scru-
pulous, passionate scholarship was all about. I need not
mention my father, to whom my debt was incalculable.
Harvard had a notable history department then, and I recall
also Charles H. Taylor's thoughtful and superbly organized
course in medieval history; Crane Brinton's exasperatingly
casual lectures on modern intellectual history—casual at
least in manner but surprisingly effective in inculcating a
set of attitudes by the end of year; and Paul Buck's judicious
rendition of the history of the American South.

There were many distinguished professors whom I
missed. When I got to know them in later years, I wished
that I had heard Joseph Schumpeter and Alvin Hansen, but
I was not much interested in economics at the time. Nor did
I take C. H. McIlwain's famous course in political thought. I
did see a little of the most generally revered man in those
days at Harvard—Alfred North Whitehead. Whitehead, I
take it, is not much read today and is regarded, when read at
all, rather as a sage than as a technical philosopher. But he
was a glowing presence in Cambridge in the 1930s.

I attended Whitehead's last lecture. He concluded by
saying, "Civilizations die only of boredom." On occasion, his
very able son Thomas North Whitehead, a professor at the
Business School, asked students over for an evening with
his father and mother. These were taxing but fascinating

occasions, greatly relieved by the lively presence of young Whitehead's stepdaughter Sheila Dehn, who later married the historian Myron Gilmore. One was at once terrified and beguiled by the old philosopher, so courteous in manner, unaffected in speech, imperturbable benevolence almost concealing his capacity for stabbing insight. Perry Miller once told me that Whitehead was another Emerson, "only harder headed and cleverer." I doubt that anyone was harder headed and cleverer than Emerson, but I can see Miller's point. Whitehead was one of those whose insights were far more penetrating than his system.

Academically this was a rich time. But the academic was only a small part of undergraduate life. Looking now at a journal I kept intermittently during those years, I find, not only comment on tutors and professors, on lectures heard and books read, but page after page on girls, parties, plays, movies, late-night bull sessions. How we talked then, and how seriously we took those talks! One is educated as much, it is said, by contemporaries as by teachers. Yet probably the most lasting education comes from recollection of one's own folly.

My friend and classmate Theodore H. White—having first met as freshmen in 1934, we now, half a century later, live across the street from each other in New York—gives a vivid and generous account of the class of 1938 in his splendid *In Search of History*. I had only a passing acquaintance then with John Roosevelt, Joseph P. Kennedy, Jr., Marshall Field, Jr., Kermit Roosevelt, and other sons of the famous. The exciting figure in Adams House in those years, at least for the young intellectuals, was Chadbourne Gilpatric, '37, a philosophy student of flashing charm and audacity; in later years I enjoyed working with his older brother Roswell in the Kennedy administration. I also learned much from two foreign students assigned to the House while they pursued postgraduate study in economics: Robert Triffin of Belgium and Shigeto Tsuru of Japan. They were a little older and combined intellectual cosmopolitanism with a genuine zest for things American. Triffin decided to become an American citizen, and I had the honor of standing up with him before the authorities, but he has never ceased to apply his high intelligence to the reconstruction of the monetary system of his native Europe. Tsuru returned to Japan where he is now the elder statesman of the economic profession.

Gilpatric was the energizer of the group. Living as he did on a gospel of spontaneity, he would burst into our rooms and say, "Let's get out of here," and off we would go, whether to the Wellesley campus to call on tolerant girls, or off for a weekend to small towns in New Hampshire or the Berkshires. Once we went with Triffin and a Belgian friend of his on a brilliant fall day to the village of Monterey in western Massachusetts. We spent the night at the house of an old man—Princeton, '79—who regaled us with anecdotes about his classmate "Tommy" Wilson and memories of the Bad Lands in the eighties.

On another occasion I went with Ed James and John O'Keefe, who had been my Exeter roommate and later became an eminent government scientist, on a jaunt to the Cape. There an old man entertained us with stories of Grover Cleveland and his friend Joseph Jefferson, the actor, getting a little high and chasing each other around the Sandwich railroad station. Such incidents reminded one of the brevity of American history. At the Signet Society, A. Lawrence Lowell would recall the election of 1860 and the shame he felt because his father favored Lincoln while the fathers of the other little boys were all for Bell and Everett. We could not escape history. When we graduated in 1938, the fiftieth reunion class was the class of 1888. How ancient they looked!—a chastening thought to be borne in mind in June 1988 when we gather in the Yard, those of us still extant, for our fiftieth reunion.

The Signet Society was in those days a most agreeable refuge. It served the best luncheons in Cambridge, prided itself, sometimes justifiably, on the quality of its table talk and laid hold of visiting dignitaries, like H. G. Wells, for special parties. I was chosen in the first sophomore seven; some of the others were Benjamin Welles, later foreign correspondent for *The New York Times*; Frank Keppel, commissioner of education under Kennedy; Morris Earle, now a federal judge; Hans Zinsser, who became like his father an eminent doctor; and Alfonso Ossorio, the artist. The initiation was an ordeal with the candidates frozen with nervousness under a bright light and stupefying questions issuing out of the dark, several in the unmistakable accents of A. Lawrence Lowell. Later I discovered that this was a triumph of mimicry performed by George Lee Haskins, '35.

The *Harvard Advocate* was my main formal extracurricular activity. James Laughlin IV, beginning his distinguished career as literary entrepreneur, and John Slocum, later of USIA and Newport, were the dominating figures, both joining personal urbanity with elevated taste. I wrote on the theater, politics, jazz, Harvard, and other subjects, on all with a certitude far exceeding my knowledge. But it was great fun.

Looking at my journals, I discover that an inordinate amount of concern went to girls. The nature of this concern would prove, I daresay, incomprehensible to the present generation, for we spent more time trying to figure out how to kiss girls than undergraduates today appear to spend getting them into bed. Whether this represents a gain for progress, I do not know. We were an innocent generation. But cheerful memories remain: trips to the countryside in the dazzling fall, skating down the Charles on moonlit winter nights, strolling about Fresh Pond or the Wellesley campus in the spring, dashes to Revere Beach for a swim and a ride on the roller coaster. And the house dances in those days, with Fletcher Henderson and his band and the Dorsey brothers not seldom appearing and *in person*, were memorable events.

I am struck, in contrast to the preoccupation with girls, by the lack of preoccupation with politics. The Great Depres-

sion was all around us, but for me, at least, it seems to have
been largely a succession of offstage noises. Harvard was a
cocoon. I was, it is true, an ardent New Dealer. I was thrilled
when Franklin D. Roosevelt spoke at the tercentenary celebration in 1936, and I was among the few students to cheer
when FDR drove along Massachusetts Avenue amid a
chorus of boos during the election campaign later that year.
But I was not an activist.

The great student peace strike of 1935 seemed to me
misdirected—why strike against universities, which were
hardly the causes of war?—and silly. I was interested by
Marxism but hostile to Stalinism and indifferent to undergraduate political activity. When Harvard students organized a chapter of the American Student Union in 1936, I
wrote somewhat sententiously in my journal: "I am not
joining because of a firm conviction that any spare time I
have in college should be spent in enlarging my intellectual
horizons rather than in messing about with pseudo-political
organizations that will never do anything very effective."
When a group was formed to repeal a teacher's oath imposed
by the Massachusetts legislature, I wrote, "It made me feel
more than ever that I shall recognize no general obligation
to turn my theories and ideas from the abstract to the concrete. . . . I shall never consider it my duty to fight vigorously
for a program merely because I believe in the program; it
will take some further inducement to lure me from my ivory
tower. Those who want the barricades can have them; but I
don't, and I admit no mystical obligations which drive me
there."

There were moments of unease. One day I fell to talking
with a couple of striking seamen who gave a graphic account of the conditions on board the American merchant
marine. "This episode," I noted, "made me feel acutely uncomfortable because of the contrast between, on the one
hand, the very evident courage of these men and their very
real devotion to a cause whose success would help many
besides themselves, and, on the other, my own (unspoken)

wish that they had not intruded their gallantry and their suffering into my orbit." Such intrusions eventually led me to join the Student Union. Still I was far from being an activist.

The next highly politicized student generation came in the 1960s. One then was struck by the differences with the 1930s. In the thirties undergraduate agitation was addressed to national and international issues. The most revolutionary radicals of my day obediently wore the jackets and ties required in the dining halls and observed without protest parietal rules of inconceivable stringency and absurdity. Questions of student participation in the self-government of academic institutions were never raised. Even those Young Communists who met conspiratorially to overthrow the capitalist system apparently never dreamed of doing anything to revolutionize their immediate environment.

It is always said at the time that the voices of student protest will be the spokesmen of their generation for years to come. This is rarely true. Of the radical student movement of the thirties one recalls few enough who have had public influence since, and most of these—Edward R. Murrow, James Wechsler, Eric Sevareid, Joseph P. Lash (none Harvard men)—more in the end as commentators than as participants. I have no idea what happened to the student activists in my day at Harvard.

One almost detects a tendency among those who engage too fiercely in agitation when young to succumb to premature fatigue or disillusion and to withdraw from public concerns thereafter. Perhaps it may be that there is some rhythm of life by which people exhaust themselves too quickly, become disenchanted too soon, and that mature political commitment requires wider and different concerns in one's youth. Certainly the one man in my Harvard years who had the greatest public impact in later life—John F. Kennedy, '40—was wholly uninvolved then in political action. In retrospect, I consider it a lucky instinct that led me to protect myself as an undergraduate against politics

and to concentrate rather on enlarging intellectual horizons. My guess is that most people do most of their reading
before the age of twenty-five and live off that reading for the
rest of their lives. So read when one can. There is plenty of
time for political action later.

Yet a tension remains between cerebration and experience—a tension that hit me hard in my third undergraduate
year. I had started in the autumn of 1936—or so at least I
remembered the following May—with "an unprecedented
sense of anticipation. I felt overflowing with potency, with a
capacity to accomplish things. What things, I did not know;
but the conviction that they were just around the corner was
pretty firm." I now concluded in the spring that I had accomplished nothing, learned nothing: "I have exhausted after
two years most of what Harvard has to give me at this time." I
wished that this were my last year.

I speculated, with full undergraduate gravity, on the relationship between knowledge and experience. "The only
knowledge worth anything," I thought, "is grounded in
experience. . . . Intelligence, it seems to me, has much more
to do with the proper handling of experience than with the
proper handling of reason." The trouble with universities
was their efficacy in restricting experience. "The ivory
tower," I now decided, "is a pretty adequate metaphor. A
college professor is rather well insulated from most of the
currents which electrify vital life. . . . The range of experience here in Cambridge is too confined to increase my
knowledge very much more, except in a purely tape-mea-
sure sense. I need a different life, experience of a different
character, if I am to grow." I recalled Thoreau explaining
that he finally left Walden because "it seemed to me that I
had several more lives to live, and could not spare any more
time for that one."

My senior year turned out not to be so bad, because it gave
me the opportunity to write the honors essay that later
became my first book. Had it not been for Orestes A. Brown-
son, however, Harvard by the fourth year would have be-

come intolerably redundant. If Cambridge and Oxford can educate students in three years, so surely can Harvard. Still, if four years is an unbreakable rule, then the senior honors essay is the way to take the curse off it.

Larger questions remained for me. I had no doubt that I wished to make my career as an American historian. "But the only institutions which would pay me to study American civilization," I reflected, "are the universities; and, in sealing myself in them, I am cutting myself off from the only way of life that would give my work any particular depth." One learned, as I believed, then and now, from people who had more experience than oneself. Yet life as a teacher is life spent among people with far less experience than one has had oneself. Living among those who know less than you do, I thought, only encourages parochialism and complacency. "No man, however strong," as Henry Adams said, "can serve ten years as schoolmaster, priest, or Senator, and remain fit for anything else. All the dogmatic stations in life have the effect of fixing a certain stiffness of attitude forever, as though they mesmerized the subject."

For the class of '38, the war came along to disrupt expectations and give people the chance to live new lives. I next encountered Everett Gleason, my old senior tutor; Allan Evans, another medievalist; and Philip Horton, who had been curator of Widener's poetry room, in the Office of Strategic Services. None returned to academic life after the war. I did come back to Harvard in 1947 and do not regret the next dozen years. But the words, long forgotten, that I had written in the spring of my junior year defined my dilemma at Harvard in the late 1950s. I now remembered Henry Adams's assessment of Cambridge in the 1870s after some years in the Harvard history department: "Several score of the best-educated, most agreeable and personally the most sociable people in America united in Cambridge to make a social desert that would have starved a polar bear. ... Society was a faculty-meeting without business." He knew, Adams added, both congressmen and professors, and he preferred congressmen. So he left for Washington where he and George Bancroft, my putative ancestor, watched the scene and wrote (in Bancroft's case rewrote) their history.

I did not return to Harvard after I left in 1961. An academic community, like any other company town, makes for a highly constricted way of life. Forty years of Cambridge were enough. Yet one owed much to Harvard College. For Henry Adams, remembering his undergraduate days in the 1850s, Harvard College was in the end "a negative force." While Adams allowed that negative forces had value, he considered his college years, for his purposes, "wasted." In the 1930s Harvard College, for me at least, was a positive force. Though one had several more lives to live and could spare no more for that one, the College remains in memory a grand and indispensable prologue.

Thornton F. Bradshaw '40

Thornton F. Bradshaw was born in Washington, D.C., in 1917. He was educated at Phillips Exeter, Harvard College, and the Harvard Business School. Following service in the U.S. Navy during World War II, he taught at the Harvard Business School where he became an associate professor. After a few years as a partner in a New York consulting firm, he joined the Atlantic Refining Company, which is now the Atlantic Richfield Company. He was president of the Atlantic Richfield Company from 1964 through June, 1981. Effective July 1, 1981, he became chairman and chief executive officer of RCA.

Mr. Bradshaw is an overseer of Harvard, director of several major companies, and trustee of a number of educational and cultural organizations.

Harvard has touched my life at so many times and in so many ways that it is difficult for me to cordon off the undergraduate days as a discrete experience. After Harvard College I went on to the Harvard School of Business Administration (known then as *The* Business School); taught there for six years after World War II (known then as *The* War), had my first Washington experience under Harvard's aegis during the Korean War. Later I became president of the Business School Alumni Association and then for seven years was a member of the school's visiting committee. Now I am an overseer and a member of the Committee to Visit the Kennedy School of Government. Interspersed among those formal alignments were, of course, many other Harvard contacts, in Cambridge and elsewhere.

How then to isolate four years of life as an undergraduate without blurring the lines and without confusing the remembrances with the visions and perceptions of later days?

I know when it started. It began on a rainy day in 1936 when President Conant provided me, as a member of the favored entering class in that favored year, with a precious seat to the greatest academic show on earth—the Tercentenary Celebration. Of all the students of Harvard, the only ones invited to attend were members of the entering fresh-

man class. What an extraordinary introduction for a freshman! I knew it was only by the luck of the numbers that my
class had been invited, yet I never did quite overcome the
feeling of being specially chosen to review the glittering
ranks of academics from the world over, come to do homage
to Harvard. The President of the United States was there, of
course, both as head of state and as a prominent Harvard
alumnus.

The pelting rain did not dampen the celebration—for
me—but I could see the ermine capes, worn by some of the
visitors, wilting and the multicolored robes sagging and the
academic plumes drooping. My roommate, Paul
Cherington, who had been at Exeter with me, and I were
both properly impressed that we had indeed put childish
things behind us and were now of the company of scholars.

The mood was not dispelled that night when a group of
classmates, mostly from Exeter, gathered in our room—
Matthews 51—for our own celebration. We drank far too
much beer (my first alcohol), toasted each other, Harvard,
scholarship, and the glowing future of the world now that
we had been admitted to it. Near dawn the party ended and
after a few hours of sleep so did the euphoric mood of the
fellowship of man.

The day was gray, the room a shambles. I had a throbbing
headache. Shaving was out of the question. Dimly I remembered I had a series of appointments with department heads
that morning, hoping to convince them I was qualified for
advanced standing and thus able to take courses not generally open to freshmen. So I gingerly picked my way to
Holyoke House and began my rounds to the beat of a drummer I had never heard before. Fortunately, the offices were
dark; the professors were not at all interested in me and
were quite prepared to admit any student with an appropriate record—providing he would leave the office quickly.

So in the course of a day or two I was introduced to a
brilliant panoply of the world of scholars, a good solid bout of
student drinking, friendships that would last the years, the

indifference of senior professors to students, and the idea that Harvard has everything for the asking, but one must choose.

The remainder of the four years were variations and extensions of the themes struck in the first few days.

I think things were simpler in those days, the pace slower, the pressures far fewer, although the pain and pleasure of growing up are very likely the same in most circumstances.

There certainly was time for talk. Meals were unhurried, even at the Freshman Union. Later, at Lowell House, with its printed menus, its waitresses, its tone set by the black tie and dinner jacket invitees to high table, dinner was the kind of civilizing experience that it has not often been since. The Master of Lowell House, Julian Lowell Coolidge, by his own example, saw to it that certain standards were kept.

Lunches at the Signet Society, the literary and "intellectual" club, were opportunities to be fed by Archie, the steward, and to converse, tentatively, awkwardly, with Albert Bushnell Hart, Ted Spencer, Robert Hillyer, John Livingston Lowes, and others. Formal dinners at the Signet, attended by prominent alumni, were wonders of wit and the light touch provided by toastmasters such as David McCord and John Finley.

We undergraduates tried to emulate what we perceived as the insouciant approach to wit and learning. Initiation to the Signet consisted of each new member entertaining the old members with a display of his ability as a raconteur. My group included Blair Clark who became president of the *Crimson*, E. C. K. Reed who became president of the *Lampoon*, and Elliot Richardson who went on to eclipse us all with the variety and importance of his accomplishments. In spite of this star-studded cast, the evening was heavy handed and must have been tedious to the audience, which expressed its disapproval loudly.

Outside the college walls the talk went on. Saturday night meant a trip to Boston on the MTA (5¢)—few students had cars: a meal at Durgin Park—clam chowder, steak, Indian

pudding with ice cream ($1.05), and then possibly a movie
(25¢). For dinner Madame Bourget's on St. Botolph Street
was also a favorite—one dollar for what seemed to us to be
superb French cuisine, the tab payable to Madame herself
in the kitchen. After the movie or, on rare occasions, the
concert, there was Jake Wirth's with the long mahogany bar
and sawdust on the tile floor. Again there was talk, elevated
by beer and sandwiches or—for the more adventuresome—
pigs' feet. The Union Oyster House, in business since 1826,
served seafood dinners from 75¢ to $1.35. For more formal
occasions, there was the Lafayette on Commonwealth Avenue—a roast squab dinner for $2.00. Locke Ober at $4.00 a
head was considered out of the question, except perhaps at
graduation time.

I have no way of knowing whether talk, particularly at
dinner, continues as the thread that connects all the different and separate experiences at Harvard. Then it was the
pot into which we poured our separate ingredients and
shared a common stew.

Each of us did go his own way. After the freshman year
when the bonds of friendships formed at prep school had
remained strong in the face of the uncertainties of a larger
world, some of us became more "literary," others more political, others more social, others more athletic. In any event,
the scene and particularly the cast changed.

I undertook to storm the *Advocate* fortress, the old lady of
Bow Street, at that time in her seventy-fifth year of publishing the best of undergraduate literary efforts. Having occupied the editor's chair at the Exeter *Review*—the literary
magazine at Exeter—I naturally assumed the same position
was being held for me at the *Advocate*. Although I did
eventually become president of the *Advocate*, the path led
not through literary excellence, but through social resilience, political tenacity, and a wish to have the job, this
latter not being shared by many.

The first test of resilience came at my induction to the
board of the *Advocate* during my sophomore year. The "neo-

phytes" were expected to stage a play, written for the occasion, which would be witty, literate, and bawdy. The first two I am sure it was not. I remember very little of it—the printed program fortunately has been lost. Some of the props I do remember—a sheep and a pail of eels, although the purpose to which these were put I do not recall, or do not care to. I do remember—or at least I was told—that I left at a late hour with a prominent alumnus, who at that time was head of one of the largest publishing empires in the country, and that we both crashed through the railing on the narrow staircase leading down from the second floor of the *Advocate* house. I attended my nine o'clock history class the next morning. So much for social resilience.

The politics of the matter were solved by packing the board with friends who shared my view that the *Advocate* had to be saved from the preciosity of a small group who affected capes and walking sticks and wrote short poems about childhood. We—my friends and I—believed that the objective of our administration should be to put the *Advocate* on a sound, business-like basis so that we would not have to skulk about avoiding creditors. This was a bit like trying to balance the federal budget, although we did not know it at the time. Another objective was to bring the *Advocate* into the mainstream of the vast forces that were shaping the University and unshaping the world at the time. Many a dull and earnest editorial was written along these lines.

Perhaps the major reformist thrust of the *Advocate* was the campaign to destroy the power of the tutoring schools that ringed Harvard Square. There was a sizable population at Harvard that was unable to attend classes consistently or do the reading because of the pressure of other activities. Debutante parties in New York and Philadelphia, in particular, competed for limited time. Tutoring schools promised that anyone so distracted could obtain the gentleman's three C's and a D. Keeping his name out of the newspaper was another and more personal matter.

In general, the tutoring schools delivered on their promises, due in some measure to the low level of teaching at Harvard at the time. Most senior professors spent their time either researching and writing or working with those students who were truly gifted. A good deal of the teaching was done by graduate students who struggled to keep one lesson ahead of the class.

We felt that the tutoring schools detracted from the seriousness of intellectual life at Harvard and permitted some students to remain at Harvard who would perhaps have been more at home at Yale or Princeton. So after exhaustive research—which included infiltration into the tutoring schools, in which I personally participated—a number of blasts were leveled at these iniquitous institutions. That the schools continued and prospered we attributed to our woefully small circulation. Besides, several of our staff who attended review sessions for the purpose of unmasking the tutoring schools continued as clients.

On the literary side, I decided to write the music column myself. I had learned that the major record companies sent the new releases to the reviewer and that he was entitled to keep the records. My own record collection was small and needed building. The music critic at the time was Leonard Bernstein, so I wrote a "Dear Leonard" letter.

Years later when I became president of the Los Angeles Symphony Orchestra and met many conductors, I did what I could to avoid meeting Leonard Bernstein. For a mess of records—78 rpm, at that—I sold my integrity.

The *Advocate* never did escape from the constructive tension of constant exposure to bankruptcy. We even put out a bond issue—somewhat successfully—after learning about indentures, sinking funds and the like from Professor William Leonard Crum. These bonds must surely rank pari passu with Russian imperial bonds. Both bear a proud insignia.

In spite of this interregnum of the philistines, the *Advocate* continued, and perhaps even advanced, the tradition of publishing the best of undergraduate literary efforts. The

Advocate published stories by Robert Clurman, Nelson Gidding, Cavish Lewis, and Robert Markewich, which can be read today without undue embarrassment to the authors. We were greatly helped in this literary effort by the presence of Harry Brown as Pegasus, or editor, a truly talented poet and writer. Whenever we ran short of material, Harry Brown would sit up for a night and fill out the issue, an effort that raised the literary standards considerably.

Shortage of material, like shortage of cash, was endemic to the magazine. Three other magazines were competing with the *Advocate*—four if one counted the *Lampoon*: the *Harvard Monthly*, then edited by Cranston Jones; the *Guardian*, edited by Ward Hussy; and the *Progressive*, under the leadership of Irwin Ross. The in-basket was entirely empty at the end of the summer of 1939 when I returned to Cambridge to put together the September issue, which had to be ready to entice the unwary freshman into subscribing. Furthermore, my entire staff—including the unsinkable Harry Brown—was still on vacation. I did what every editor does—riffled through the pages of back numbers of the *Advocate* and republished not the best of writing, but pieces by the best-known authors.

The issue contained a piece by Theodore Roosevelt decrying the pacifists of the class of 1880 whom he accused of standing "on an exact level with the poltroon" and further stated that "his appropriate place is with the college sissy who disapproves of football or boxing because it is rough." Others who contributed, without royalty payment, were Witter Bynner, H. V. Kaltenborn, Van Wyck Brooks, John Reed, Conrad Aiken, Oliver La Farge and Walter D. Edmonds. In his undergraduate days, Witter Bynner was already writing odes; H. V. Kaltenborn, essays about the press; Oliver La Farge, stories about Indians; and Walter D. Edmonds, tales of adventure. Conrad Aiken's 1911 short story about a murder not committed presaged his novel *King Coffin* published in 1935. The crystal ball for the others was not quite so clear.

The issue was a success, by which I mean it was pub-

lished in time for our circulation manager to wave fresh
copies at freshmen.

The *Advocate* was something of a club then, and no doubt
its quality and acceptance both suffered from this fact. On
the other hand, Harvard had not yet changed, and the clubs
were still a discernible part of Harvard life. More than half
the entering class in the late 1930s came from private
schools, and about a quarter of each class joined the clubs.
Furthermore, according to D. M. D. Thurber's survey of the
class of 1940, when asked what aspect of four years at
Harvard had done most for them, 40 percent responded
social life and clubs; about 45 percent said courses and
tutorial; and 15 percent, activities, which included drama,
publications, athletics, and so forth. Intense concentration
on preparing for graduate school had not yet elbowed aside
all other contenders for the student's time.

The Porcellian, Delphic, A.D., and Fly were still spoken of
with awe by those of us who were in the lesser clubs. After
all, did not President Roosevelt regularly attend dinners at
the Fly? And did not J. P. Morgan found the Delphic Club
because he and his crowd were unable to get into the Porcellian? Or so the rumor went.

Later we learned that most Harvard students did not
know the names and locations of any of the clubs and that
their lives had not been blighted by this appalling ignorance.
My own club is now the home of the Harvard Hillel Society,
undoubtedly its highest and best use.

But this knowledge came later. The social credentials of
Harvard were considered to be important, but not so important as in the days when the Harvard registration list could
be used interchangeably with the Boston social register.
The Boston debutante scene still required a Harvard. Although it was considered unforgivable to appear in class
without a jacket and tie, it was quite acceptable to appear at
Professor Merriman's nine o'clock History I class in white
tie and tails.

Also the Harvard connection ensured an unimpeded road

to success, with no distances too far to reach, no heights too precipitous to climb. It was considered in the normal order of things that John Roosevelt's father was President of the United States and that Jack Kennedy's father was ambassador to the Court of St. James's, and that many of the great jurists, publishers, cabinet members should be Harvard men.

The world was changing and Harvard with it, but not yet.

It might appear from my description of Harvard life in the late thirties that studies and classes were somewhere in the background, a necessary excuse for more important activities, that extracurricular activities were at the core, and the curriculum at the periphery. Not so. The classroom and library experience was central for most undergraduates and, of course, the ivied walls did not blank out the world, which was moving toward changes that would affect us all.

The curriculum at that time was fashioned on the smorgasbord approach: let the student choose. The catalog of courses was massive and included a tantalizing and frustrating array from Icelandic sagas to Indic philology to history divided into ten-year periods. Students were permitted to choose from this groaning board, subject only to the modest restrictions imposed by selection of a field of concentration. This was, of course, before the days of President Conant's "General Education" and long before President Bok's "Core Curriculum."

The freshman adviser was supposed to help and guide the student through this vast menu, to ensure that he did not choose all herring or all ice cream. Early in my freshman year a cartoon appeared in the *Lampoon* which achieved increasing significance as time went on. It showed an imposing figure of an adviser with his hand on the head of a small, cowering freshman, and the adviser is saying, "Come back and see me—next May, for instance."

It was too much to expect the student to choose wisely— and I did not. Yet there were great moments, enough of them so that I was convinced at the time that I was being educated, enough of them so that I have been an avid reader and eager learner all my life and have never lost faith that education would someday solve most of the world's ills.

I was introduced to Plato and Aristotle by Raphael Demos. Arthur Holcombe gave me—and Jack Kennedy—a continuing interest in the process of government (Jack learned more than I did). Carl Friedrich alerted me to the galloping apocalypse of the totalitarian state, which would threaten free men throughout my life. Kenneth Kempton tried to make a writer out of me and failed—but I know one when I read one. Professor Morize began my continuing struggle to learn the French language and understand the French people. Both I admire, but I have not mastered the language or, at times, understood the people.

Professor Allard, in his French Literature of the Eighteenth Century, continued the struggle. Near the end of each hour, without pausing in his lecture, he would begin the process of dressing for the unfriendly New England winter—first one galosh, then the other, then the scarf and the overcoat, the hat, then the walk down the aisle—all the while lecturing—until he opened the door and disappeared at the sound of the bell and the echo of the last finely chiseled sentence. An example of Gallic precision, which I admired but did not understand.

Professor Sam Cross taught Slavic literature to a wide variety of students, many drawn by the reputation of a "pipe course," which meant a C with little effort, a B with luck, and an A if one became interested. Many became interested.

Pitirim Sorokin taught a fascinating introductory course in sociology, a subject barely admitted to the company of educational courses. I have since learned that sociology is one of the great integrative disciplines and suffers now, as it did then, because it tries to draw patterns that can be understood from a world far too complex for the principles of economics or the theories of history.

Sometimes the memorable moments came from fleeting contact with a great teacher or a world figure, or ideas, that seemed important then and seem so now. I attended the last lecture given by Alfred North Whitehead. I do not remember what he said, but I remember the man. I listened to Heinrich Bruening, the last chancellor of the German Republic, as he described the twilight of democracy in Germany.

Roscoe Pound, then a former dean of the law school, gave a series of lectures, open to undergraduates, which traced the growth of English common law independent of social and economic pressures. He illustrated his lectures with nineteenth-century cases that severely limited the rights of private property, and he showed that in each instance the presiding judge was a large landowner, a "man of property." I have never forgotten the lesson or the man.

The epitome of the teacher as actor was, of course, Roger Bigelow Merriman. His History I, from the fall of the Roman Empire to the present day, was a *tour d'horizon*, a sweeping view of history. It was said that if a student sneezed he might miss the entire twelfth-century renaissance. No one who took History I will forget that life in the Middle Ages was "slow, slow, inconceivably slow!"

Had I had my wits about me I would have responded to the urges that Professor Merriman aroused and concentrated in history. But I wanted to be a business tycoon, and so I selected economics. I was disappointed then and am now—not in business but in economics.

Perhaps Harvard's economics department did not have a sense of direction during the late thirties. Perhaps economics did not. In any event, it appeared that Keynesian economics had failed, although the bells were not tolled until many years later. A great depression hung over the land, to be lifted only by the war, which brought on a level of spending never envisaged by Keynes.

Macroeconomics—input-output models—was in its infancy. Leontief was not, I think, an important factor at the time. Professor Edward Chamberlin provided a holding action with his *Theory of Monopolistic Competition*. But no one, it seemed, faced squarely the issues of a mixed economic society—the relationships of the private and public sectors—which were to dominate my lifetime and more to come. In the meantime, Alfred Marshall and Frank Taussig were the prophets of the true god—the unfettered marketplace. The hidden hand ruled supreme.

Perhaps I would not have this harsh view of economics at Harvard in the late thirties if I had known Joseph Schumpeter, Sumner Slichter, and Gottfried Habeler at the time, but I did not. Later I was much influenced by Schumpeter and Slichter.

Economics did not seem irrelevant to me then—nothing did—but it does now. Some of my inability to sort out what was important in economics and what was not was undoubtedly due to my own lack of sophistication in political matters and therefore in economic matters. I really did not understand Joan Robinson, and she—it turned out—was relevant.

I don't know why I was politically and economically underdeveloped as an undergraduate. My family had been hard hit by the depression or, more accurately, had never gotten off the ground because of the depression. A dime was not to be spared. We lived a life of quiet, respectable poverty with the white collar frayed around the edges. I lived that life too, until a fairy godmother appeared who sent me to Exeter and then to Harvard.

The Horatio Alger instinct was strong, and I felt what made America strong in the past would renew its strength in the future. There would indeed be two chickens in every pot, and I would help put them there and would be rewarded for my efforts. Perhaps this was the twilight of innocence in the University, although I am sure that many of my classmates did not share my perception of the present and my optimistic view of the future.

In fact, some of my classmates thought mine was the view from the terrace. This view was reinforced by an article I wrote for the *Advocate* with the unfortunate title "Education for the Masses," in which I advocated educating most people in how to survive in a hostile world, reserving the traffic in ideas to me and others worthy of carrying the burden. It is too late to withdraw the article, but not too late to disavow it.

I thought it a waste of good classroom and reading time to join the picket lines in Boston. Many of my classmates did not. I thought the struggle in Spain was far away and not our affair. If fascist Germany and Italy and communist Russia were involved, then "a pox on both your houses" reflected my view. Many of my classmates raised funds to provide an ambulance for the loyalist forces. None, to my knowledge, left to join the Lincoln Brigade.

The interminable discussions at the rathskeller between the Leninists and the Trotskyites seemed irrelevant to me. I reserved my special scorn for those who returned from debutante parties in white tie and tails and sat up all night arguing the case for the socialist state. (I was exposed to only one such instance, but was much disturbed by the incident and have amplified it in my mind into many.)

The country was isolationist then, and so was Harvard. I should like to be able to look back and say, "Because we were a favored few—with access to the great library, the teachers, the academic traditions of Harvard—we saw that the totalitarian states threatened the freedom and dignity of man throughout the world, and free men everywhere must rise." But I cannot say that. We did not see. We knew John Donne's words but not their meanings.

Class Day exercises for the graduating class of 1940 were held on a beautiful day in June in the stadium at Soldiers Field. My classmates and I were happy and excited. The girls were lovely in their gayest summer dresses. Kodak box cameras were everywhere.

Graduating from Harvard meant the world was before us to be savored, tasted, enjoyed. We had entered into the company of Harvard graduates: any one of us could become a President or an ambassador or a justice of the Supreme

Court. Of my roommates, one was going on to graduate studies in economics at Columbia, another to the Harvard Medical School, another to the law school, and another directly into newspaper work.

President Conant had invited a Harvard alumnus, head of the American Legion, to address the class. He proved to be an effective speaker. He talked about the war in Europe, the threat to free nations, and somewhere in his speech he said, "My class did not hesitate to ride the tanks to defend liberty and defeat oppressors, and I don't think you will either."

The entire class rose. The stadium resounded with noise of catcalls and boos. The speaker was never able to finish his speech. My guest, a Boston gentleman who had fought in the First World War and was a proud graduate of Harvard, shook his head sadly.

And yet, at the twenty-fifth reunion of the class of 1940 when the bell at Memorial Chapel tolled once for each class member killed in the war, the tolling—it seemed—went on forever.

John Simon '46

John Simon was born in Yugoslavia in 1925 and came to the United States in 1941. He received his A.B. in English and Ph.D. in comparative literature from Harvard. After some teaching, he switched to criticism. Currently, he is drama critic for New York *and* The Hudson Review, *film critic for* National Review, *cultural critic for* The New Leader, *contributing editor to* Esquire, *and a free-lance book reviewer. Among his books are* Ingmar Bergman Directs, Singularities, Uneasy Stages, Paradigms Lost, *and* Reverse Angles.

I came to Harvard in the fall of 1942 as a relative barbarian in search of refinement. But Harvard, under the impact of war (and, later, of peace) was losing its aristocratic gentility and sliding into comparative barbarism. On opposite courses, we more or less passed each other by. During my first term in Eliot House (I was one of those happy few freshmen who did not have to do time in the Yard, but were directly assigned to a house), there was still table service in the dining halls; by the next semester, or shortly thereafter, one had to stand in a chow line as if one were in the army. There could have been no greater blow to the elitism I was, as yet unconsciously, searching for. Still, if Harvard was becoming more democratic, one needed only to proceed in the opposite direction to become an old-style gentleman. Or so I thought.

Socially, I began as a pariah. My parents very generously paid for a single suite because I insisted that I would find roommates intolerable. As a result my clothing allowance was minuscule and I had no furniture except what the college provided, so that my suits looked unsuitable and my suite bitterly impoverished. A fellow Horace Mann graduate who came to Harvard with me remarked, when I dropped in on him as he entertained out-of-town visitors, that, even by

Harvard's notoriously sloppy standards, I was beyond the sartorial pale. I did, however, get to be friendly with the Eliot House intelligentsia: John Russell (son of Bertrand), Vincent Cronin (son of A. J.), Greg Henderson (related in a way I no longer remember to Admiral Samuel Eliot Morison), and one or two others, all of whom I regrettably lost track of in short order.

I started as a psychology major with the (for me) totally quixotic notion of going on to medical school and becoming a psychiatrist to please my parents. But in my very first biology lab it became apparent that I was not cut out to cut up frogs, let alone miss because of such activities a Radcliffe jolly-up where I could have met girls. So I switched to English, which had no afternoon lab sessions, and never regretted it. Except, perhaps, when Douglas Bush flunked me in his Milton course, thus theoretically disqualifying me from entering Harvard Graduate School. But some of my other professors persuaded Bush that I was graduate-school material despite my regrettable blind spot about Milton. So I went to Canossa, or Bush's house, where I did some recanting and cleared my way to graduate school.

But I am anticipating. Harvard in wartime was a curious place. All those students in navy uniforms (the V-12) snatching the best girls from the rest of us, and one minor sport after another being discontinued because intercollegiate football, which paid for the upkeep of the other sports, had been dropped for the duration. I went out for rugby, which I had learned in my English public school, and actually became some sort of letter man; luckily for me, I guess, rugby was discontinued before I had to show my stuff. I switched to fencing and enjoyed the foil without being very good at it; but I did have regular bouts with Charles Duits, whom the French surrealists in their New York exile had proclaimed the new Rimbaud. Later, Duits was to fall in love with Victor Hugo and go classical on them; still later, he published prose works of some notoriety from his perch in Montmartre. Fencing was abolished too; foiled again, I went out for crew, at which I was truly wretched. I then sank to the lowest form of athletic—or nonathletic—activity: gym classes, from which one could not wash out.

Living in the shadow of the draft, one tended to bite off more courses than one could chew. I always took five or six of them (four was normal) despite my extracurricular activities, which were many. I realized that my destination was comparative literature, but that existed only as a graduate field, so I stayed on in English as an undergraduate and took as many courses in French and German as I possibly could. My most inspiring teachers were Karl Viëtor, Harry Levin, and, later, Jean Seznec and Renato Poggioli. Here I should add the name of Hyder Rollins, whom I once requested for my tutor. This fine textual editor and southern gentleman was amazed and amused that an undergraduate should appreciate his austere scholarship and dry wit. He found that he appealed most to graduate students and had never had to give tutorial to an undergraduate. He wasn't about to do so now: why didn't I do it on my own, and at the end of the term he would automatically approve it. I wonder whether Harvard still harbors such generous, trusting souls as Hyder E. Rollins.

The real problem for me was distribution: finding a painless way of getting the necessary credits outside my field, in the sciences and social sciences. I had taken some geography, but that department bit the dust before I could fully avail myself of its mansuetude (it had been a veritable refuge for no-talents in science). So, for the rest of my science requirement, I struggled with a course in physiological psychology and somehow scraped through. Things were no better for me in the social sciences. Here I hit upon a course in economics given by the celebrated Joseph Schumpeter of Weimar Republic fame. I could hardly grasp a word of what I heard or read, and I wrote a final examination based almost exclusively on Oscar Wilde's *The Soul of Man under Socialism,* which, needless to say, was not assigned reading, but Schumpeter, another perfect gentleman, gave me what was then known as the "gentleman's C," and I scraped through again.

My greatest fiasco was in philosophy, in a course in aesthetics. It was my sixth course that semester, and I had done none of the reading. Henry Aiken, who assisted Irwin Edman (a visiting professor from Columbia that term), had included T. S. Eliot on the reading list, which annoyed me, because I then considered him a dreary poet and critic, and certainly no philosopher. On the finals, I went directly to the question on Eliot and wrote: "When Anatole France died, an editorial in *Le Temps* began, 'We mourn the death of Anatole who was France.' I look forward to an editorial announcing the death of Eliot who was T. S." One actually said T. S. for tough shit in those days, even at Harvard, even outside blue books. *Sic transit*—or S. T., I handed in my blue book five minutes after the exam began and flunked the course with relish.

Then there was the course in Aristotle's *Physics* I took with the renowned Harry Wolfson, who was as learned as a couple of dozen medieval monks, Renaissance humanists, Cabala and Talmud scholars rolled into one, and who spoke countless dead languages fluently but belabored English with the accent of a Jewish tailor from the Bronx. When Wolfson asked the class what, in Aristotle's hierarchy, came above stones, I answered, "Plants," which I pronounced with the broad *a* (plahnts) I had learned in my British public school. Wolfson stared at me blankly. An obnoxious girl behind me was bouncing up and down in her seat with her arm extended ceilingward. Wolfson called on her, and she shrilled, "Plants!" with a middle-American accent. "Yes," beamed Wolfson endorsingly, "plents."

I had my ups and downs in English classes, too. In a course in Victorian literature (taught by Samuel Chew of Bryn Mawr and graded by Richard Wilbur) I got a D for not answering enough questions. In an Elizabethan poetry course with Robert Hillyer, however, I got an A + on a midterm paper and was excused from the rest of the classes;

F. O. Matthiessen said (ironically, I believe) that I knew too much for a certain course of his, but I audited it anyway. Hillyer, incidentally, was a graceful minor poet who later distinguished himself by being bounced from Harvard for drunkenness and, still later, by ferociously attacking in the midcult pages of the *Saturday Review* the awarding of the Bollingen Prize to Ezra Pound; he did, however, teach the most advanced and prestigious of the creative-writing courses, English A5, for seniors and graduate students. I was the only sophomore ever to gain admittance to it, in what was, I think, the last year of its existence. I managed this by submitting some anodyne poetry of mine so much in Hillyer's style that I had to be taken on.

This may have been the only course in those days that met in the instructor's residence—specifically in Hillyer's digs in Adams House. One sat in armchairs and was actually permitted to read one's work out loud oneself, rather than having it droned out by the professor. The discussion afterward was quite ruthless, some pretty amazing characters being ensconced in those armchairs. I recall Gray Burr, who became a very minor academic poet, but who seemed to me then enormously accomplished; Bruce Phemister, who looked like a late Roman emperor and wrote decadent poetry (or was it decadent prose?); Mauricio Obregón, an urbane and sardonic South American, who, I gather, has become a major figure in the cultural and political life of his country (Colombia, was it?); and Norman Mailer. I remember my first sense of the excitement of the literary life when the phone rang during one of those classes and Hillyer delegated me to answer it; I came back to announce breathlessly that John Dos Passos was on the wire. I still haven't read a single one of his books.

Two incidents from this course I recall clearly. Once Mailer was reading a long, rambling, prose-poemlike stream-of-consciousness piece about a woman giving birth—to a bastard, of course—in which a tree image kept recurring. Hillyer, somnolent behind his desk, nodded approvingly each time this bucolic trope was invoked. But he nearly fell out of his chair when, at the very end, the woman (in Mailer's voice) identified this thing that only God can make as "John's tree," the penis of the bastard's father. Another time, I was reading a play that I had somehow contrived to get produced outside the framework of any Harvard drama group, with the help of United War Relief. It dealt with ten Yugoslav girls in a Nazi concentration camp who were being taken, one by one, to the officers' mess to be raped. One of them manages to shoot a couple of officers, whereupon she and the remaining girls are shot, but at least are spared a fate worse than death. The scene was the girls' detention room, and one could merely hear the offstage cries and gunshots. After I finished my impassioned reading, Mauricio Obregón remarked, "It would be greatly improved if the offstage were the onstage and vice versa." A typescript of this work, entitled *Death There Is None,* was still to be found recently in one of the darkest recesses of Widener, cataloged not with my other books but under "Simon, John I., playwright," a fellow who, if he ever existed, certainly doesn't exist any more.

Theatricals at Harvard! There was, for instance, the Eliot House Christmas play, which that particular year was *Eastward Ho!* by Chapman, Jonson, and Marston. In the all-star cast were John Finley, Harry Levin, F. O. Matthiessen, and other distinguished faculty members, as well as my humble self in the role of Security the usurer. After the performance, the greatest of our imported English eccentrics, Arthur Darby Nock, professor of classics and religion, ran up to me to congratulate me in a tremulous voice (come to think of it, it was always tremulous) on a piece of acting that took him back to the beloved melodramas of his youth. I was crestfallen at being hammed with such quaint praise.

Or take the Harvard Dramatic Club's production of *Winterset,* in which I played the old rabbi, Esdras, who is left holding the bag by being compelled to deliver Maxwell Anderson's ghastly blank-verse soliloquy over the bodies of the dead lovers. On opening night, the lighting man, think-ing that the play was over, cut every single light just as I was girding my loins for the soliloquy, dismal under the best circumstances. The director was tearing his hair out in the wings as I calmly launched into that funeral oration in pitch darkness. It was my one genuine stage triumph (when the lights were on, I was always a terrible ham): I held the audience transfixed and nobody stirred. The director and the company practically loved me to pieces, but my exulta-tion was short-lived. I, who had used my most Gielgudian Old Vic English, was presently congratulated by a spectator on the subtlety of my understated Jewish accent!

In my graduate days, after the war, I almost got to play Prince Bougrelas in Jarry's *Ubu Roi*, which the French Club was all set to put on with Pierre Schneider, the future art critic, as Ubu. But Professor André Morize banned the play as indecent! During the war, college officialdom was still remarkably puritanical; some Radcliffe dean forbade the broadcasting over Radio Radcliffe of my play about Richard Lovelace, the Cavalier poet, because I had named a some-what amorous character Lady Cynthia Codrington, after an actual Radcliffe student. But Theodore Spencer, my then tutor, did not mind at all that a turnkey in the play bore his name. I had become president and main director of the Harvard Radio Workshop, and one of our productions was an adaptation of *The Women*, whose large cast could not easily be corralled for rehearsals. I finally had to call a dress rehearsal for the crack of dawn on the Charles banks, the only place open at that hour. My narrator, Liam Sullivan, the girls in the cast, and I convened there on a balmy spring morning. We brought along bottles of cheap white wine and had a rehearsal that was one of the sweetest experiences of our student lives.

I was supremely unpopular with the smart set and never made Signet or Hasty Pudding, let alone one of the real clubs. I had only one significant love affair with a Radcliffe girl (none at Wellesley—I had no car!) before going into the

service during my junior year. When I came up for the draft
the year before that, I managed to get myself deferred. At
that time, I convinced the draft board that I was too neurotic
to serve. The following year, I hoped to pull off the same act,
but this time, besides various psychiatric interviews, I was
also given a Rorschach test, which I flunked. Or, rather, did
not flunk, and so was drafted. I told a couple of my friends
(Brad Murphey and Jim Damaskos) who were psych majors
about what outrageous monstrosities I had claimed to per-
ceive in the ink blots. They informed me that a true psycho-
path sees nothing in the blots. I had a hard time controlling
myself from becoming genuinely psychopathic and killing
them for not telling me sooner.

Once again, I am anticipating. The war provided a good
opportunity to play practical jokes. For example, there was a
fellow majoring in German—let's call him Z., which sounds
more Teutonic than X.—whom everybody despised. One
day I wrote a postcard in German addressed to Baldur von
Schirach, the wretched poetaster whom Hitler had made his
minister of youth. I expressed admiration for Schirach's
poetry and inquired how I might get hold of more such
marvels, signed Z.'s name followed by his return address,
and dropped the card in a Harvard Square mailbox. For a
while nothing happened. Then, unannounced, an FBI man
called on me in Lowell House for the unlikely purpose of
discussing German poetry with me. I rewarded his subtle
deviousness by boring him as long as possible with a lengthy
disquisition on German lyricism, with special emphasis on
the "still undervalued" talents of Mörike and Eichendorff.

After listening with quasi-attentive excrucuation for a
good while, the fed inquired whether I could show him my
books of German poetry, and I eagerly obliged. Visibly disappointed, he asked in the most speculative tone available to
an honors graduate of the bureau whether I did not possess
more contemporary poetry—say, the works of Baldur von
Schirach? I feigned consternation: how could a true lover of
the German lyric mention that propagandist and hack in the

same breath with even such minor talents as, for example, Heyse and Geibel? If he was looking for trash like that, he might as well go directly to Mr. Z., who would stock up on such things. Now, Heyse and Geibel at least . . . The fed fled.

It was the redounding of such exploits to my ultimately no longer anonymous glory that may have prompted the remark of Elliot Perkins, the magnanimous Master of Lowell House, upon hearing of my being drafted: "Good riddance to that Hungarian horse thief!" I am only half Hungarian (and half Yugoslav), but had I gone into thievery, I would have specialized not in horses but in the books of the "X cage," as it was known: that sanctum of erotica in the bowels of Widener Library, into which one got only with faculty permission and whose books, their call numbers prefaced with an X, did not circulate. One's status as an undergraduate depended in no small measure on familiarity with the treasures of the X cage. A favorite among these was Rochester's *Sodom*, esoteric indeed in an era before the Olympia Press made it available to less Olympian readers. I can still recall from those days certain heroic couplets I would quote to stunning effect, such as the apostrophe to the female genitalia: "This is the warehouse of the world's chief trade,/ On this soft anvil all mankind was made."

In those pre-sexual-revolutionary days, the war had only just begun to loosen the old morality. Radcliffe, for instance, had a group called the Dirty Thirty, composed of girls famous for putting out, albeit mostly for servicemen. In my gang, however, one was a long way from having encountered for the millionth time the reality of experience (to paraphrase Joyce) and forging much of anything in the smithy of the flesh. One did, however, go to the Old Howard and other burlesque houses and compare the ecdysiastic talents of Sally Keith and Lily St.-Cyr as learnedly as one debated the relative literary merits of Ruskin and Carlyle. Still, there was some genuine sex in our lives, whether by the river, in our rooms at awkward hours and under tricky circumstances, or in more exotic places. I remember getting hold of the key to the old *Crimson* Network building for a tryst with my then girl friend, and having to risk both the night watchman and pregnancy: condoms were frowned on and diaphragms far from current (vide Mary McCarthy). "There must be a way out," I said.

"What you should be looking for is a way in," said my ladylove.

Night watchmen were to prove a bigger problem in quite a different context. Free tickets were being distributed for an unidentified academic ceremony in the Yard, but it was considered highly uncouth to apply for tickets to some routine academic ceremony. After the tickets were gone, however, it emerged that Winston Churchill was receiving an honorary degree, and getting in became mandatory. Three of us—the Welshman Timothy Hallinan, the Missourian Lee Stoutz, and I—resolved to scale the wall the night before, hide out in some Yard building overnight, and simply mingle with the crowd in the morning. It seemed easy and pleasant enough; we even found one gate left unlocked by oversight and didn't have to do any climbing. We hid in a second-floor classroom of Emerson Hall and did not sleep, not so much for the discomfort as for the excitement of it all. I managed, at dawn, to read a few poems in the *Oxford Book of German Verse* that I had stuffed into my pocket: a slim volume printed on India paper, it was the most compact book I could find. It proved to be a mistake.

As the Yard started filling up with people, the three of us walked, ever so casually, out of the classroom, only to bump smack into what must have been a graduate student signed up as night watchman. He asked to see our passes, whereupon we ran: Tim Hallinan in one direction, Lee Stoutz and I in another. The lucky Taffy escaped, melted into the multitude, and later taunted us with a recital of the pleasures of his day. We, however, were pursued and caught, handed over to the Yard cops and, by them, to the secret service men and city police. Somehow we had thought it prudent not to carry any identification in case we were caught, but even if we had had it, the results would probably have been the same: Churchill was a precious commodity, and the authorities weren't going to take any chances. I remember that, as I was being prodded into a police car, I tried in my best Alphonse-and-Gaston manner to let the detective get in first, for which I earned a more emphatic prod.

At the Central Square station, we were questioned, though not in great detail. Somehow the notion that we were just a couple of students trying to catch a glimpse of the Great Man did not seem at all perspicuous to these policemen who, in any case, were not overfond of Harvard boys. Lee was taunted: "So you're from Missouri, kid? You have to be shown?" Stoutz, to make matters worse, was a Germanic name. As for me, besides my foreign accent, I had that *Oxford Book of German Verse*. The evidence for our being Nazis was pretty nearly conclusive. We were locked into adjoining cells and told that the Harvard administration would, in any case, be notified. We may have been allowed a couple of phone calls, but, as everyone in authority seemed to be at the ceremonies, who was left to spring us?

It was a holiday weekend—very likely the Fourth of July—and there had been much carousing among my cellmates (some ten or twelve of them, I think), most of whom must have been picked up on charges of drunkenness. Rivulets of urine crisscrossed the floor; the air reeked mightily. Without being able to see each other, Lee and I pressed our faces to the bars and played word games, but I kept winning, so we subsided. I found a bit of bench that wasn't totally soiled, pulled my knees up under my chin, and waited. In midafternoon a dean of the law school showed up, vouched for us, and left. We had the choice of signing a waiver or spending the night in jail and pressing charges the following morning for unlawful arrest. You can guess which option we picked. The detective who drove us back to Harvard Square couldn't have been friendlier. Of course, we never saw Churchill.

When my days at Harvard were numbered and the war beckoned, my friend Peter, who was 4F, became distinctly intolerable. "Suppose you die," he said, "what does that really mean? A few more good meals not eaten, a few more trips abroad not taken, a few more girls (they're not all that different from one another) not shacked up with." And he added consolingly: "No big deal." I don't know how many girls Peter had shacked up with, but I had done so with far too few, I thought, to have to stop there. To make dying for democracy a little sweeter for me, Peter suggested that we jointly seduce Beth, the tall, dark, and (except for her legs) very pretty waitress from St. Clair's, where we used to hang out. If I remember correctly, she hoped to become an actress; surely then, she needed experience.

We made a date with her outside the MTA stop in Harvard Square and intended to take her to Peter's rooms, where supplies had been laid in. I felt rather uneasy about the cold-bloodedness of it all: Beth was so good-looking (even if her legs were not straight), and in the unlikely case that the thing might work, I did not at all relish the idea of sharing her with Peter. But he was older, more experienced, more likely to pull it off; and with war staring me in the face, this might be my last chance . . . So we waited at the appointed place and time, and waited, and waited. No Beth showed up, and we ended up drinking the wine of seduction ourselves. But life plays strange tricks. I survived the war—never even saw action. Poor Beth, however, did not survive Los Angeles, where she went shortly afterward. Brad Murphey sent me some clippings to one of my air force camps about the horrible murder of a young woman known as the Black Dahlia, who was held captive for days, tortured, mutilated, and killed. The details were so grisly that the police refused to give them out to the press. At first I couldn't figure out why Brad sent me these clippings; then I realized that the Black Dahlia was our Beth. The case was never solved.

In a roundabout way it was Harvard that got me out of the service after fourteen dreary but basically uneventful

months. I was then stationed in Macon, Georgia, and about
to be shipped out to San Antonio and thence to Japan. There
was, however, a teacher shortage in the nation in 1945, and
anyone with a teaching job lined up could get a discharge.
Donald Davidson—that underestimated agrarian poet, beloved teacher at Vanderbilt University, and superb gentleman—whom I had befriended while I was stationed in
Nashville, arranged through a friend of his at Mercer University in Macon to have me hired as an auxiliary instructor.
The salary was not quite good enough to be laughable, and
Mercer, a dubious college serving as an excuse for a Baptist
divinity school, was a joke. I called it a Baptist tabernacle
posing as a university. The real problem now was how to
follow up my air force discharge with a discharge from
Mercer. A Radcliffe girl I knew had sent me a copy of *Wake*,
a literary magazine Seymour Lawrence was editing at Harvard. In it was a vaguely lesbian poem she had written, and I
promptly assigned it to my freshman English class for expli-
cation. None of the kids got the point, so I rubbed their noses
in it. Word duly got back to the president, who fired me just
in time for the spring term at Harvard. But the Yard, to
which I was assigned, and an obligatory roommate—both
ominous-sounding firsts—had me worried. As it turned out,
George Isaac and I became good, contentious friends, and
he later married a Radcliffe member of our gang; we remained on the best of terms until his premature death.

Next term, George and I moved to a cozy suite in Leverett
House, overlooking a small, relaxed inner court. Oddly
enough, I remember little about those last semesters at
Harvard. My heart was in New York with a girl who broke off
with me and eventually married a Harvard professor. I loved
my courses with Karl Viëtor (who had kindly sent me a rare
volume of Max Dauthendey's poetry while I was in the
service) and was challenged most by Harry Levin's course
in Proust, Mann, and Joyce. The reading list in that one
included the full *A la Recherche*, which seemed a lot of
temps perdu for a slow reader like me, and I had to bluff a

good deal to pass. When, as a graduate student, I became Harry's assistant in that course, I finally managed—still with difficulty—to catch up with the reading. Jim Damaskos was the Lowell House librarian and was able to feed me the sumptuous, red-leather-bound volumes of the house library's Proust one by one. Reading them as fast as I could, I was always just one jump ahead of the students. My chief consolation (aside from Proust himself) was that I was reading gorgeous, slim French volumes in mint condition, whereas the members of the class had to make do with the two unwieldy doorstops (the Scott Moncrieff translation in the Random House edition) under which the reserve shelves at Lamont and the beleaguered students were alternately groaning.

I have named my favorite teachers, but I should mention some others, too, who also influenced me in various ways. I have mostly good memories of Theodore Spencer, Howard Mumford Jones, Albert Guerard, Jr., André Morize, Robert Gorham Davis, and dear old Professor Pease, my Latin prof, who was deeply impressed by the verse translations of Catullus I improvised in my blue books during finals. What he was too innocent to realize was that rhyme and poetic license allowed me to take certain liberties with the words whose meanings eluded me. There was also Howard Roman, a brilliant young professor in the German department, who later, to my chagrin, quit academia for the consular service and passionately urged me to do likewise and abandon a profession that, he insisted, was corroded with petty politics and vicious infighting. As someone who, in those days, hoped to combine the careers of professor and poet, I remained unconvinced. In the early sixties, traveling in Europe with an ex-Cliffie girl friend, I came across Howard: the American consul, or vice-consul, somewhere in Switzerland. Though not exactly in a state of Malcolm Lowryesque disrepair, he seemed nevertheless diminished from his dazzling Harvard days. Still, he assured me that he was happy and had done the right thing, as had I—for, by that time, I was eking out a less than lavish existence as a free-lance journalist and critic. (Geoffrey Tillotson, then visiting professor from London, had also counseled me to follow, as he put it, in the literary-journalistic footsteps of Théophile Gautier. I hope I am still following.) Leaving the university did eventually serve me in good stead; did it do so for Howard Roman? I wonder what became of him.

It would be unjust not to mention another figure, a not so grand but charming old man who was not my teacher, but whose lightly worn cosmopolitan erudition delighted me. This was Harry Wadsworth Longfellow Dana, a direct descendant of both Henry Wadsworth Longfellow and Richard Henry Dana, who had been dismissed under a cloud from both Columbia (for pacifism in wartime) and Harvard (for communism and pederasty in peacetime) and now lived fairly comfortably and quite graciously in his Brattle Street signory, Longfellow House, which, upon his death, became a museum. Harry Dana liked to invite bright freshmen to Longfellow House, where he was a stimulating host and nonstop talker. Anecdotes about his long sojourns in the USSR mingled with tales of his Boston Brahmin ancestors and also with horror stories about Nicholas Murray Butler, who had sacked him during World War I, and Harry Levin, who had more recently snatched away his invaluable Russian secretary and married her.

Late at night, Dana's mind would start wandering, and eventually a servant would put him to bed. But from armchair, through disrobing, to four-poster, he never stopped talking, and it would have been rude, if not impossible, to get in a good-bye. Dana's feeble hope was to entice some impressionable student into that massive bed of his, but, to give him his due, he never acted sour when his repeated invitations for an overnight stay (owing to the lateness of the hour!) were politely declined and one proceeded to clip-clop down necropolitan Brattle Street toward Harvard. There is surely some notion of the gentleman-scholar that I owe to blue-eyed, white-haired Harry Dana and his elegant remi-

niscences—a blue-blooded Marxist, way-past-menopausal
but still hopeful homosexual, and rambling raconteur who
could still rouse his octogenarian mind into delivering a
pungent recollection or prickly epigram with absolutely age-
less gusto.

But perhaps I myself have begun to ramble. I could keep
piling up recollections without adding substance and
definition to this already diffuse memoir. Yet I would like to
fix in my mind and yours the quiddity of that moment in the
history of Harvard College. What incident epitomized, I
wonder, what mood characterized the spirit of the time
preeminently? Was it a poetry reading by T. S. Eliot for
which the turnout was so enormous that the overwhelming
majority could not be fitted into Sanders Theater, but had to
listen to the sound piped into other parts of Memorial Hall?
If a comparable poet of today (assuming there is one) were to
appear at Harvard now, would he draw anywhere near so
large an audience—unless, of course, he were Bob Dylan?
Or was it the sense of mortality the war gave us—the
death's-head jeering, as it were: *Et in Academia ego*? I recall
a Harvard Radio Workshop production of Shaw's *Saint Joan*
in which Barney Bisgeier played the English soldier ac-
corded a yearly day off from hell for having improvised with
two sticks a cross for the burning saint. That same Barney
Bisgeier—a capital fellow—was soon to die in the war and
earn, alas, no reprieve from death.

Or was it simply the last period in Harvard's history when
one could still flunk out with relative ease and, knowing
this, had to be careful? The last period when it was easier to
get bounced than bedded? Learning and loving were thus at
a premium: there was still the fascination of what's difficult
clinging to good grades and good relationships. How are
things now in the mixed dormitories from which everyone
graduates?

Anton Myrer '47

P*romise*. That's the word that first leaps to mind, as I think back on that still, soft, golden September day in 1940 when I stood in front of Stoughton North Entry and looked off down the Yard, the sense of a profusion of entrancing possibilities. And the leisure to explore them. After the narrow severities of Boston Latin School, the inverted pride one drew from its martinetist demands (33 lines of Virgil every night, along with an act of Schiller's *Wilhelm Tell*, so many pages of Mérimée and chapters of George Eliot), Harvard was like being set loose in a huge bazaar crammed with adventure-some goodies, a kind of educational Arabian Nights. I never once worried about flunking out. Here it was—*the University* as I'd dreamed of it through a thousand afternoons, seat of that disinterested pursuit of truth that seemed to me the happiest of occupations. The Giants were here (that's how I thought of them, with a capital *G*—those legendary teachers whose names were on the texts I'd struggled with), and there, right over there beyond University Hall, rose mighty Widener, holding all that buried treasure. *Veritas!*

Well. It sounds sentimental, even a touch suspect, putting it like that in this far more skeptical and indifferent age, but that was exactly how I felt: excited, on fire, embarked on the Adventure of My Life. I remember a lot of us felt that

way, then. We enrolled in a wild gamut of subjects, swapped
enthusiasms during meals at the Union, audited one another's courses. Our tutors humored us good-naturedly
enough, let us wander at whim through the shimmering
bazaar; it was, after all, our freshman year. . . .

And what a glorious roll call! There was George Lyman
Kittredge, then I think in his final year of lecturing,
sprightly and impish, a kind of peppery Yankee G.B.S.; hale,
ruddy Carleton Coon, holding forth over in Fogg on the
food-gathering agonies of the Andaman Islanders; F. O.
Matthiessen, short, rotund, his eyes quick as light behind
his glasses, speaking with that crisp, astonishingly incisive
voice on the New England literati of a century before; Sid-
ney B. Fay, soft and measured, barely audible, dispassion-
ately dissecting the rise of Brandenburg Prussia; Crane
Brinton, sparkling and debonair, unveiling the dreams and
follies of the Jacobins . . . and up at New Lecture Hall there
was "Frisky" Merriman, leaning toward us over the lectern
like a great, benign bear, eyes slitted like a Mongol's, tapping
the absurdly long ivory-tipped pointer (the same pointer he
used with uncanny dexterity to flip the hats off the heads of
forgetful freshmen as they passed into class below him) and
thundering at us in that hollow, sonorous foghorn of a voice:
"You must understand that the fundamental theme of medieval Europe, gentlemen, is unity—unity—and again
unity!"

There was a very different kind of unity in the Europe of
1940: *Festung Europa* and beleaguered Britain; nothing
much in between. We talked a lot about the war; we'd grown
up with it, so to speak. We'd entered high school to the
German reoccupation of the Rhineland and the start of the
Spanish Civil War, we'd graduated on the day France had
fallen; we'd watched the beginning of the Battle of Britain
all that long, cloudless summer, waiting for the invasion
that strangely, miraculously never came. The war. We'd
grown accustomed to its presence.

There was an all-aid-to-Britain rally in the Yard that fall, which occasioned a good deal of wild rhetoric and half a dozen shouting matches bristling with "anglophile" and "isolationist" and other, less printable, epithets. I was one of a dwindling band of isolationists, even that late—but looking back I believe it was largely an intellectual stance, an effort of will; at heart I think I was as resigned as anyone else to the dismal prospect of our being drawn into it somehow, sooner or later. The next day President Conant, looking very old-Yankee and tart and no-nonsense, told us freshmen he hoped we wouldn't let world affairs interfere with our four years at Harvard.

Then, later in the winter, came the first really ominous note. The much-touted German film *Blitzkrieg im Westen* would be shown at Emerson Hall—I think it was Emerson.

"Well," the self-appointed spokesman for our little group said, "let's get on over there and see what we're up against." I remember that nobody laughed.

It *was* an intimidating film—exactly what the Third Reich intended, I suppose. Not the combat sequences. We'd read *Life* every week and followed the newsreels between the double features; we'd seen lost infants in Nanking, bereted volunteers crouching behind walls at Brihuega, the rest of it. It was the sure, cold perfection of this war machine—buildings reduced to rubble, rivers crossed, strong points enveloped, and above all the easy competence of the gunners and tankers and infantrymen. I still remember the close-ups: the men seemed unnaturally big in their snugly fitting, flaring black helmets and heavy black boots, moving toward their objectives with an almost amused professional disdain. (The French prisoners they kept rounding up, unshaven and hollow-eyed, looked like some inferior race of bipeds.) Would we someday actually find ourselves in battle against *them*? There was very little hilarity in the booths at Cronin's or McBride's that evening.

The group I fell in with at Harvard was drawn mainly from graduates of the more "democratic" preparatory schools of the Northeast, such as Andover or Choate or Deerfield, and the big, prestigious public high schools of New England and the Midwest. Like all healthy young people we were awash with prejudicial notions. We disliked the haughty Brahmin prep school products—"the St. Grotlesex crowd," we called them, using the portmanteau term derisively. And indeed, in their Brooks Brothers suits and white bucks, with their distinctive accents and their rather frosty, bemused air, their frantic preoccupation with being elected to (that is to say, punctiliously *selected by*) their exclusive final clubs, they did seem to constitute a college-within-the-college. *We* wore tweed or covert cloth jackets, flannel slacks, and loafers and didn't feel the least bit bemused.

We were mildly contemptuous of bookworms, whom we referred to as "greasy grinds"; we wanted to make good grades, most of us, but unostentatiously. Our attitude toward varsity athletics ran along much the same lines: we trained hard, we wanted to win—yet we didn't make too much of it. (We had our letters sewn on our white crew-neck sweaters—and then wore them inside out, so that only the stitched outlines showed.) The idea was to be unassumingly, casually brilliant. If possible. Ah, so long ago . . .

Our deepest scorn, though, was reserved for the "operators"—the men we felt had decided to use Harvard to further future careers. Curiously we exempted *Crimson* heelers—which was odd, because it was generally held that "Crime" editors on graduation stepped right on to *The New York Times* and from there to God knew what eminence. We all knew about FDR . . . and there *was* something almost awesome in the single-minded ferocity of the *Crimson* aspirants: they cut classes with reckless abandon, let huge reading assignments slide, skipped meals; they practically lived in the building, to creep back to their rooms at fantastic hours or appear at breakfast white-faced and with bloodshot eyes, nodding at one another with grim satisfaction. Each to his demon.

That was the glory of the Harvard of those years—its easy,

opulent diversity. The University was like some very rich, indulgent grandfather—an eminent Shakespearean actor, say, now retired—who might clap you on the shoulder and murmur, "That's it, my boy, go right ahead and be anything you like—aesthete or ringer, social butterfly or dilettante or politician—even a boozer or a bore, though I do hope you won't! But one thing I will insist on: that you decide for yourself what you will be. It's the first grand step toward growing up. . . ."

And so we plunged in all directions: the *Lampoon,* the *Advocate,* societies and *cercles* and *Vereine.* I chose swimming; I drifted into the sport almost by chance—and then seized on it with maniacal fervor. Some of this was due to Hal Ulen, lean, erect, his belly flat as a washboard, every kid's dream of a coach, calling down at us through his cupped hands, "Ride on your forearms, *ride* on them!" I was never very much as a swimmer—I lacked both strength and stamina—but those afternoons at the Indoor Athletic Building hover at the very heart of that golden time: the thunderous seethe of thrashed water, the bite of chlorine, the cavern echo of young voices against the empty stands; the time trials with their flash-caught glimpses of teammates capering along the pool's edge flailing towels, urging you on; walking up Holyoke Street in the chill dark, your hair still wet, eyes stinging, your whole body lulled in a heavy, pleasant weariness; above all the mesmeric rhythm of reaching, reaching, reaching through this buoyant substance that held you so effortlessly, that would never let you fall. . . . I can see now, too, that I was exorcising a ghost; for the greatest fear of a timid and often cowardly childhood was my boundless terror of the water. Here, beating my way laboriously up and down the lanes I made it friend and ally, talisman. Call it narcissism, return to the womb, anything you will, swimming held the ache of pure joy; forty years later it still does.

Ah, we generations of the Roaring Forties! We've been called so many harsh things (conformist, materialistic, apathetic, acquisitive—all those long, unkind modifiers); they were not true of us at all. Actually we were intensely romantic and committed . . . and incredibly, lamentably innocent. Take our love of the big bands; we would argue about them for hours. Tommy Dorsey (we called him "TD") had the smoothest orchestra. No, Glenn Miller's was the smoothest. No, Miller could be *too* smooth; at times he was almost saccharine. Count Basie had the greatest rhythm section, Jimmy Dorsey the best vocalists, Duke Ellington the most exciting sidemen. We could reel off the personnel of every band and tell who played what solo on which recording. There was Harry James, and Woody Herman, and let's not forget Jack Teagarden. And of course there was always Benny Goodman, king of all this dazzling nobility of downbeat. And when, oh, when was fabulous, temperamental Artie Shaw going to put together another great band?

They came through Boston in a glittering, brassy parade, well advertised, and we would go into an orgy of fiendishly elaborate planning. It sounds incredible these days, when nearly every high school senior cruises on his own wheels, but very few of us had cars of our own; my guess would be about one man in forty, though the ratio may well have been even higher than that. We loved to dance; with the possible exception of the class of '43 we were the dancingest class Harvard ever knew. Our favorite hangouts were Seiler's Ten Acres where Vaughn Monroe, not yet a national bobbysocks idol, held forth; the Bermuda Terrace at the Hotel Brunswick, where we caught Bunny Berigan, on the downhill side now, puffy with drink, but still displaying flashes of brilliance, or Ella Fitzgerald, who with Taft Jordan had taken over the band after the death of valiant little Chick Webb; and best of all the incomparable Totem Pole out at Norumbega Park, where the couches were deliciously Antoninian and the dance floor was as smooth as old horn. When the band began a set the tables emptied in a rush; everyone was on his feet. We prided ourselves on our versatility, gliding from fox trot to rumba to lindy to shag with ease; the very pinnacle of sophistication was "the dip"—in which you sank back on your flexed left leg and the girl, sinking with you, pressed against you enticingly.

And yes, the girls ... When it came to sex, the most charitable thing you could say about us is that we were a very, very mixed-up generation. The tortuous, involuted code we honored in those dear, dead days prescribed that the boy was expected to venture as far as he could until the girl invariably stopped him; then, protesting, he dutifully stayed within those bounds, whereupon the evening turned into a tortured, interminable ritual of kissing and groping about that left both parties dizzy, panting, half-stunned. Part of you was desperate to have sex; another more complicated part of you was not. Certain girls were known as "fast"—which was an exciting thought, but it was also disquieting. You could tell yourself that you certainly wouldn't think any less of a girl if she "went all the way" with you, and you would mean it ... but somewhere in the far, dim reaches of your mind you felt that some mystic societal tribunal you called "they" might well do so. We would sit up till all hours haranguing one another about which techniques rendered a girl most seducible and vowing that next time, by God, we were going to "cross home plate"—and then we would promptly double- or even triple-date in some borrowed car, which of course precluded any consummation at all.

Mainly we dated products of the Seven Sisters and the women's colleges in and around Boston. We loved to make outrageous Draconian generalizations—Smith girls were good-looking but arrogant, Vassar girls were belligerent tomboys, Sarah Lawrence girls were cold and affected, and so on—and then blithely scrap them all when some lovely, engaging creature came along. In all truth, geography dictated our choices more than anything else; Wellesley was conveniently near, Radcliffe was nearer still; there were plenty of girls who were "fun on a date," as we put it: quick, witty, good sports—and above all good dancers. . . .

The year hurried away, the spring came in warm and fair. We studied hard, for all our blasé deprecations, and did a lot better than we thought we would. Finals were enlivened no end when a notorious bon vivant whom I will call Falstaff kept surreptitiously ducking his round, curly head just inside the edge of his jacket. The proctors pounced on him, to uncover a Coke bottle filled with Southern Comfort and fitted out with a straw to which Falstaff, dazed with lack of sleep and the furious battering of the cram schools, had been resorting to keep himself conscious. The head proctor, a humorless, bony-headed type, began to lecture Falstaff, holding the bottle to the light; Falstaff snatched it back and refused to give it up, asserting loudly that it had nothing to do with cheating, that there was no University regulation against the possession of alcoholic beverages during examinations, and that in any case he needed it to get a passing grade. By this time the entire hall was in an uproar; I don't think any of us got back into the rhythm of the exam after that.

For our smoker we engaged a virtually unknown comedian by the name of Ed Sullivan. I remember he seemed embarrassingly unsure of himself, hitching his neck around inside his collar, hitching up one shoulder absurdly—mannerisms so soon to become a national institution. The dance committee betrayed us at the jubilee, furnishing a band without name, style or drive, but we had a good time anyway; most of us stayed up all night, ate breakfast at the Hayes Bickford in the Square and sauntered back through the morning sunlight to our rooms in our white jackets and maroon cummerbunds, feeling like wicked Riviera roués. Ah, the fragile, foolish innocence of those long-ago days . . .

The summer brought the German invasion of Russia—another thunderclap; I can remember that Sunday morning as though it were yesterday. The war had taken another huge, predatory step. But sophomore year began auspiciously enough. We came back from summer jobs or genial loafing and moved into the houses that rimmed the Charles River. There was very little intramural rivalry as I recall it. Oh, there were certain airy prejudices: the Eliot House crowd was socially snobberiferous, Lowell was prickly with sherry-sipping aesthetes, Kirkland held a preponderance of jocks, and so forth and so on; but as biases went they were vague and unfocused enough. The friendships forged in the Yard were what persisted. I remember that as upperclassmen we sought out old friends in other houses rather than make new friends in our own; but maybe it was only that our upperclass years were truncated so abruptly.

In any event we were informed that fall that we had a higher percentage of men on the dean's list than any other class in Harvard's long and illustrious history. (The dean's office added rather cavalierly that it could find no explanation whatever for this.) The news did nevertheless surprise a good many of us; now and then, sitting up late arguing about free will versus determinism, the inherent nature of man, or the origin of the universe (those formless nocturnal bull sessions that I remember more fondly than anything else during those fugitive, golden years), we began to think of ourselves as something rather special. And so we were— though not for any academic reasons. What was soon to be painfully clear was that the Double Four was to be the last class to enjoy a full year of the "old" Harvard, the leisurely, nonchalant Harvard of unlimited cuts, relatively relaxed fields of concentration, uncrowded dormitories . . . and the casual, disinterested pursuit of knowledge.

It was a great autumn to take your girl to the stadium: we beat Army, humbled Dartmouth, and capped it all with a glorious victory over Yale: one of the Crimson heroes, Don Forte, was surely the handsomest man ever to play football anywhere at any time. (To this day you can encounter old Harvardians who never knew that Forte was once sought out by the Hollywood brass and given a screen test.) The Yale dance was held at the Copley's Oval Room, perhaps our favorite hotel ballroom, where we roared our approval to

Gene Krupa's tom-tom pyrotechnics, Roy Eldridge's sky-scraping horn solos (it was an exhilarating rarity then to see a black man featured in an all-white band), and the saucy nuances of Anita O'Day. Her voice may have lacked the velvet shimmer of Dinah Shore's or the haunting, almost mesmeric plangency of Peggy Lee's, yet months later, brooding in Neapolitan *taverne* or Micronesian boondocks, it was Anita's brave little gamine face, her husky, defiant tones we recalled most fondly. . . .

In a few days it was all over: it was *that Sunday*. I was doing nothing at all, I remember—listlessly turning the pages of an old copy of *Collier's* and half-listening to some swing-band program—when the interruption came. After all these years the single thing I recall with absolute clarity is my roommate's face—an eerie mélange of shock, anger, dread, grim acceptance; expressions my own face probably reflected, and probably in the same order. Still—we had known it was coming; we'd followed that slow, malevolent parade of bombast, threat, invasion, absorption. . . . Why, then, this scooped-out, bottomless disquietude? Yet there it was. Actuality *is* shocking, we discovered for the first of many times. It had come, it was here. No more waiting or wondering. No one's life was ever going to be the same.

The clock began to tick more swiftly than we'd ever have thought it could. The phrase you heard everywhere on campus was "What are *you* going to do?" A few brave, impetuous natures went over to Boston and enlisted, a few prudent souls began inquiring into medical or religious alternatives; but most of us decided to finish out the term, to wait and see. It was going to go on for a very long time, this war—we knew it in our bones. They'd get around to us; they were going to get around to everybody before it was over.

We did try to attend classes, hit the books; we grappled with Bismarck's nefarious editing of the Ems telegram, the certainty of Descartes's external world, the whiteness of the whale—but it was no use; our hearts weren't in it. My tutor, Edward Fox, perceptive, sympathetic, with the sad, handsome face of a Gary Cooper, was very forbearing: I remember he chastised me gently for not being prepared on Sophocles' *Antigone;* gazing off at the river he talked about the future; one day this war would be behind me, and I would want to go on with my career. . . . He might as well have been discussing a voyage to Saturn. Perhaps another group of young men in another time could have driven on undeflected; for us, shaken early on by the Great Depression and reared on the gathering storm of world war, it was too much to ask. Our minds kept skittering away, to Plexiglas turrets and depth charges and automatic rifles. The war—in Singapore, Kharkov, Bir Hacheim—had taken over everything.

The Giants, too, were leaving, for government service—in seven-league strides, as Giants should. Langer, McKay, Brinton, so many others. We felt obscurely cheated and resentful (why? since there was no sense in studying, anyway). The first men began to depart, to the accompaniment of a series of impromptu parties, raucous and quarrelsome. One classmate, a man many of us respected highly, took the hardest road of all—refused even to register for the draft—and we had a grim foretaste of the future when two men in gray double-breasted suits and snap-brim hats came and whisked him away, with what we thought was unnecessary physical force, to God knew where. This was what Plato's republic demanded, then: everybody in step, no dissenters left hanging around.

Yet we remained at heart romantic, and incurably naive. If you doubt this, picture a large group of us running around gathering signatures and trying to organize a mammoth rally on the steps of Widener in support of a racially mixed regiment of volunteers that hectic, headlong spring. The dream died aborning, of course, a victim of individual fears, fierce opposition by the ROTC men, and finally sharp University disapproval. We were very bitter about this. The question of race seemed to us to lie at the very heart of this war. One ancient race had been declared inherently inferior, and (though we didn't yet know it) marked for extinction; memories of the Berlin games and Jesse Owens were still fresh. Why, then, didn't our government give the lie to that dark assertion, throw it back in the teeth of the master race? A preposterous hope in the face of the benighted military policies of those years. No, we were not conformist. . . .

Almost as though to mock that forlorn effort Margaret Webster's brilliant version of *Othello* came to Brattle Square, en route to Broadway—a production that may never be equaled in our collective lifetime: Paul Robeson, virile and credulous; José Ferrer the supreme Iago—feline, diabolically persuasive, the essence of gratuitous evil; Uta Hagen, lovely and trusting and demure. "Keep up your bright swords!" Othello had roared, vaulting up on the table to dominate the brawl. "For the dew will rust them." But all swords were drawn now. We crept back to our rooms and sat around, moved almost to tears, talking about nothing.

The University cranked up to summer session, filled the Yard with V-12 candidates, shifted to accelerated program. Everything was accelerated—classes, courses, meals, drinks, dates, love affairs. The old, contradictory code was faltering. We reached out for the girl now, clutching frantically at life, the supreme affirmation of life itself, as the angry cataract roar came on. Yet so deep was our romantic persuasion that physical consummation became its own grave, indissoluble commitment; many of us up and married the girl for that single reason as much as anything else.

More and more of us were leaving every day, the remainder were in a perfect fever to leave. There were chow lines and trays in the dining halls, there were hubba-hubba PT classes in the Indoor Athletic Building. So pervasive was the turmoil you felt that you could find yourself deciding to go over to Boston and sign up for the air force, apply for the Enlisted Reserve Corps, or enroll in a crash course in military Japanese—and then discarding all three plans, all in the space of half an hour. There were no longer any farewell parties; they had lost cachet—there would have had to be one nearly every evening.

My reading notes for Harry Levin's provocative Proust, Joyce, and Mann course break off in mid-sentence, as though I had slammed shut the big maroon and black law notebook and walked right off into the war. (What actually happened was that I was so enraged at learning I'd been rejected by the ERC that I took the subway over to Causeway Street and enlisted in the Marine Corps—an act of sheer impulse I was later to regret at long leisure. But then, as my roommate often said, I had a fatal tendency to rush to extremes.)

"In the duel Settembrini fires in the air. Naphta, furious that the rational humanist will not yield to his apocalyptic nihilism, commits suicide," my notes read, rather ponderously. "With his death the Magic Mountain's whole edifice of abstract theory comes crashing, and Castorp realizes. . ."

Realizes what? Did I simply drop my pen and head for Cronin's? Or did I suddenly realize that I was about to do what earnest, malleable young Hans Castorp had done—descend to the flat land and the war with the resolute fatalism of most of the rest of my generation? Keep up your bright swords. . . .

We were back, a lot of us, in 1946. We were the same—which is to say we wanted to be the same—but it was a very, very different Harvard. Compulsory attendance, roll calls—roll calls!—in class. No auditing.

"Fish or cut bait," a dean—a new, strange dean with a large square mouth, whose beady eyes glinted with unconcealed glee—told three of us. "We've got no time for that prewar folderol."

Fish or cut bait. There were double-decker bunks in the houses, chow lines, book lines at the Coop. There were even limited-access cards to the Widener stacks, which a girl guarded like Cerberus, primly and officiously ticking off the dwindling number of visits we were entitled to. (She was quite pretty too, which made it all the more infuriating.)

The accelerated schedule was still going full blast. Where before the war Harvard had seemed like that indulgent grandfather, this new University resembled nothing so much as an army supply six-striper—humorless, harassed, baleful, and grim. Get the lead out, move it, shape up or ship out. . . .

Given the propensities of the GI Bill, the tidal rush of ex-servicemen and high school graduates, the general crush and haste of that time, there probably wasn't much that even Harvard could have done about it. But we resented it all anyway. We did what the new powers that be wanted: narrowed our fields still further, compressed two years into one, one year into a frantic term, tramped lockstep along the treadmill; but we wouldn't pretend we liked it. We felt we had exclusive rights to the College—rights we'd earned on coral beachheads, in hedgerows. We wore our khaki or OD trousers to class, had our service coats cut down to hip length (the ex-officers of course had no need for this, theirs were already fashionably shortened), wore our old service shirts with the rank removed but with the divisional shoulder flashes blaring. We drank more than was good for us, got into fights with the postwar generation on Mount Auburn Street at odd hours, even got into arguments with our tutors, who were not as forbearing somehow as they had been. (*They* had been at the beaches and river crossings, too.) We were in a sullen fury to get out. "Save me a seat on the tailgate, Mac" was the prevailing phrase. This was not the Harvard we had known and loved.

Then just as we were leaving there was one final, redeeming, triumphant moment. At commencement (we'd already attended our class's third reunion the day before: still another goofy anachronism that seemed to us perfectly logical, perfectly typical of our fragmented, topsy-turvy Harvard lives) George Catlett Marshall, then secretary of state, came to speak. Over the years some of the University's honorary degrees have struck many of us as curious, bizarre, even suspect; but this one was preeminently fitting. There he stood—the man who had been right there behind us through the war years, the years of boredom and confusion and savagery and fear, running things with an uncommon selflessness and dedication, getting on with it while others goldbricked or wrangled or connived. He spoke quietly and firmly, as he always did, the homely-handsome face marked with purpose, compassion, high intelligence. His eyes seemed to reach each one of us—that steady, undeviating gaze that could behold the world in all its folly, its avarice and violence and self-deception, and still go forward resolute and undismayed: the last American gentleman. . . .

We applauded long after he had left, and then we strolled away out of the Yard, feeling vindicated, and a little contrite. Harvard had let herself be transformed, we felt, into a conveyor-belt diploma mill, had angered us beyond measure— and then with this invitation had caught up the old dreams and searches and sensibilities, made us all one again. It was, after all, the same *veritas*.

We could leave now, remembering.

Robert Coles '50

Robert Coles was born in Boston in 1929. A child psychiatrist and a writer, he has spent the last twenty years studying the ways different kinds of American children grow up (black and white, Chicano and Eskimo and Indian, rural and urban). He has also written books on such literary figures as William Carlos Williams, Walker Percy, and Flannery O'Connor. Now a professor of psychiatry and medical humanities at Harvard Medical School, he resides in Concord, Massachusetts with his wife and three sons.

As many college graduates settle into middle age they get rather wistful about those four years spent acquiring "an education." One hears from them (from oneself!) the not especially original observation that lectures and reading and, not least, the sheer expanse of time devoted to various kinds of intellectual inquiry are, in their important sum, far too valuable and unique to be set aside (occasionally the bitter word "wasted" is summoned) for young people of, say, eighteen or twenty. In my more sensible moments, however, I realize how utterly decisive the few years I spent at Harvard College turned out to be for my life. I realize, that is, how much I was given by certain teachers, and how long their lessons have stayed with me.

Most of all, Perry Miller; he taught me, starting in my sophomore year, about the Puritan Divines, those fiercely moral, God-obsessed, dour, driven (but also wonderfully energetic, willful, self-sacrificing) people who wanted to connect the prophets of Israel (Isaiah and Jeremiah and Amos), not to mention Jesus of Nazareth and his disciples, with the harsh, demanding social and economic realities of colonial America, its New England division. For Perry Miller those Puritans were constant companions—a source of edification, but also an ethical challenge of sorts, and one he never let us forget. He brought them to us alive. He gave us, without letup, their spiritual doubts and ambitions. (They were a decidedly determined lot, anxious not so much to obtain as to *win* God's favor!) And always, he asked us to make a leap, to wonder about ourselves through their eyes. I found him a compelling teacher all right, but he was something else: there was a manner about him that inspired continual attentiveness. Put differently, he was at once insistent and giving to us.

And who were "we"? In large measure, the Harvard College I knew as a student contained a thoroughly odd mix of undergraduates. The Second World War was over, but it lived in the minds of the considerable number of veterans who populated both the Yard (freshmen at twenty-five and over!) and the Houses. In contrast, I was a mere seventeen when I first got to hear Perry Miller, and eighteen when I dared go see him in his Widener study. I mention those statistics, I hope, not in narcissistic self-indulgence, an occupational hazard, I rather suspect, for those who choose to write essays such as the ones that make up this book. I bring up my age and the war veterans and Perry Miller and his room in a vast library because one afternoon those were the elements that suddenly came together—caused me to think long and hard about what I would, what I *ought* do with my life.

I was on my way to find Professor Miller's office, but not to see him—no, indeed. I was brought up to be shy, to keep a sharp eye out for my own presumptuousness, not to mention those "lusts of the spirit," as a grandfather of mine used to put it, which require constant surveillance: pride, ambition, self-importance, smugness—the "unreflecting egoism" George Eliot likes to confront us with, as she offers characters not unlike ourselves, whatever the differences that obtain between the middle nineteenth and late twentieth centuries. So, the nearer I got to Professor Miller's office, the more I knew I wanted to talk with him badly, and just as badly wanted to let him know how thoughtful and discerning and (very important) well read I was. I'd learned at least to notice that kind of egotism, to condemn myself with my grandfather's Calvinist broadsides—but then, strangely, to go about my business, content in the knowledge, I suppose, that I'd been self-critical. My plan, that day, was to locate a scene, then retire for a week or two of preparation. I'd read and read, then arrive well prepared for a discussion, if not self-presentation.

On the way, however, I met one of my classmates. I knew him from an English literature course we both had taken. He was in his middle to late twenties. He was from Minnesota. He'd fought in the Battle of Guadalcanal—a marine who decided, after the war, to go east and take on Harvard. Perry Miller had a touch of Hemingway in him—the intellectual who wants to be tough, even a bit brusque; the intellectual who can't abide a lot of the phoniness and pretentiousness and arrogance that one finds among some of one's own kind. The result—an obvious fondness on at least one Harvard professor's part for students such as the one I'd encountered by accident in the dark inside corridors of Widener Library, students who had fought in trenches and proved themselves in ways only a war provides—so I find myself plaintively saying, even today! The worst of it was that I couldn't be going anyplace but to see Perry Miller, as my classmate immediately surmised. He didn't even ask me where I was headed. He told me he had an appointment to see the man, and he invited me to join up. Oh, no, I wouldn't think of doing that. I'd come back later. Oh, yes, I should, I must. They had "bull sessions," I was told, every week or two, but there was "nothing personal," and sometimes they were joined by someone else, even several others—a friend of Miller's or of my classmate's. I persisted in begging off: I was "browsing"; I had other things to do. He persisted, too: come on—even if for only a few minutes. I now realize that he was shrewder by far about the psychology of at least some college students than I was then even remotely able to be; he saw the vanity in my mind's life and was uncannily confronting me with his perceptions.

Suddenly he stopped in his tracks, looked at his watch,

suggested that we go for a cup of coffee, since we were early
for Professor Miller. I was made anxious and annoyed by
that "we," but I was not one to quibble in the face of an
apparent stroke of good luck. I was delighted to move a
potential struggle to Massachusetts Avenue, to a place
called Hazen's, as I recall, one of those quick order places
that come and go over the generations, even as we, the
students, also do. There I could manufacture my alibi, and I
did. There he could tell me, gently but firmly, what he
thought I was up to—though his essential kindness allowed
him the indirection of group analysis rather than a series of
ad hominem remarks. It's too bad, he observed, that so many
of us are at such pains to impress, always impress our
teachers. Had I ever thought, moreover, how lonely some of
them are—how they ache for good talks with students ready
to speak their minds, rather than posture nervously to make
an impression? I was silent. If I may indulge the inevitable
nostalgia, it would be for *that*—the wonderful time, so terribly lost, when people didn't feel bound by the dreary, banal
constraints of psychology and psychiatry and so felt it ill
mannered to assault anyone and everyone with those endlessly self-satisfied and overbearing "interpretations" of psychological motive and psychological desire that characterize
the present discourse all too many of us have with one
another these days. I was, by implication, being *morally*
reprimanded.

We continued talking about Miller—and that was how we
often referred to him: no first name, no professional title. He
often did so himself—and with respect to us, as well: the
unadorned last name as a handy, summoning first name.
Wasn't Miller "great"? Yes! Was there anyone quite like
him? No! But all of a sudden there was a turnabout. My
coffee buddy said he thought Miller was a "wonderful
teacher" precisely because he was "like us." I didn't know
what to do with that comparison. For a second it wasn't
pursued by the one who launched it, and I made no effort at
amplification or qualification. I was disposed, naturally, to

immediate, outright disagreement, but was not open or honest enough for that, either. I wondered to myself in what respects Miller resembled the two of us, or other students. Professors are professors; students are students. Meanwhile, there was the convenience of that already half empty mug.

Eventually, the full-grown man opposite me (ironically, he possessed the status of a sophomore at the time) began to tell me what he'd been through fighting on behalf of this nation's freedom and how he viewed Harvard College after such a time spent. I know enough now, I hope and pray, to paraphrase his conclusions rather concisely. If one has faced death, one's own, again and again; if one has been asked to stand up and fight for something and on its behalf be willing to end one's life; if one has witnessed pain and suffering, anguish and doubt, fear and more fear; if one has experienced terrible loss—friends, acquaintances, and, not least, a battle or two, then, by God, one has been privy, by luck at once good and bad, by fate, by circumstance to exactly the kind of situation Miller's favorite writers (St. Augustine and Pascal and Kierkegaard and our Puritan forbears) knew to be critically important. That is, one has been compelled to ask questions. What is the meaning of life? How ought one try to live, day by day? Should we attempt to connect the pronouncements and formulations we hear in various classes or read in books to the particulars of our personal experience?

My friend went on to remind me that we were both fortunate to be alive, to be living in America, to be well fed and well clothed, to be able to speak freely to each other without fear of some dictatorial intrusion or worse, and, of course, to be at Harvard, where we could read the books Miller was pressing on us and thereby link arms with others who had fought their own kinds of battles. First I was bored. Then I became annoyed. Why do I need to hear all that? Why was he roaming all over the world, connecting Guadalcanal with Harvard Hall, where Miller lectured to us, and both places with the entire Judeo-Christian religious and cultural tradition? And why was he so talkative, so *emotional*? In "cool" (as we'd now say it) and not always humble Cambridge, in Hazen's, full then with a ceaseless parade of cleverly, showily dirty white bucks and colorfully striped ties (the price of our dining hall food in those years) and voices by no means tempered with self-doubt, never mind self-criticism, here was a tough former marine and one very smart student (I'd learned from the kind of observation one finds oneself doing in the course of the long intellectual haul) sitting and struggling without success to fight back tears, to break free of a choked voice.

I don't believe I'll ever forget those eyes, that voice. In time I would see the same clouding up take place in the eyes of Perry Miller, and I would hear his voice crack once or twice. He'd be talking about the ethical challenges Sören Kierkegaard hurled at us over a hundred years earlier, or he'd be mentioning those Puritans yet again—and then, in a flash, the lively, entrancing connections of a powerful, winning, always resourceful mind, a brave as well as prodigious mind, would for a moment vanish and be replaced by a human being who dared ask questions, rather than give answers to them, and ask them out of the heart as well as the head, and with respect to our future lives, rather than for the sake of a brilliant riposte, a stunning display of mental agility. Where do we come from? What are we to think of ourselves? Where are we going?

Those are, finally, the questions we are destined to ask as human beings. When I was a boy I would see exactly those questions written on a painting—the Tahiti triptych of Paul Gauguin's located in the Boston Museum of Fine Arts. My brother and I (he was a year behind me at Harvard) used to stare and stare at the French used by a great artist anxious to use words as well as unforgettable shapes and colors in the service of a universal disposition—the effort to fathom the purpose, if any, of this brief, precarious and so often confusing life we find (out of nowhere, it seems) to be ours to live, ours to realize as finite, and ours (through the distinguishing characteristic of consciousness) to try figuring out. The words were as mysterious as the Pacific island scene: *"D'où venons nous? Que sommes-nous? Où allons-nous?"* We were proud, my brother and I, when we got the English translation of Gauguin's existential French under our belts; proud when we'd learned about the symbols used in the painting. Our mother had to remind us, and not for the first time, that this painting, those questions, were not only aspects of an intellectual experience but a terribly important part of a lived life—an ethical outcry before the approach of death. And now, a few years later and in college, where abstract knowledge is necessarily wanted, offered, asked for, rewarded, here was a classmate who had, of all ironies, learned to ask the questions Gauguin had asked, and also on a Pacific island; and too, here was a professor who wanted to be sure that each and every one of us students would end up being, upon our graduations, no stranger to those questions. The tears, the tightened vocal cords were, I came to realize, uncontrollable expressions of a search: how to live a decent life.

I made my way, a week or two later, to Perry Miller's study—and arrived no smarter morally, I regret to say, than I was when I met my ex-marine classmate. Not that I was a crook or a cheat; I was "sincere," I suppose. I even think it fair to say I was a bit ethically sensitive, given the upbringing I had—parents ever mindful of both the Old and New Testaments, not to mention the morally aroused Victorian novelists (George Eliot and Dickens and Hardy). But I was also (and who can *ever* not to some extent be?) a self-centered, posturing, all too calculating young man, eager to be liked and thought intelligent and patted approvingly on the back and invited to return. The only trouble was that on those returns Miller, and sometimes that marine veteran with him, broke all the rules; they lost control of themselves, as I'm afraid I saw it then—by showing a good deal of passion and by making over and over again what was to me a strange and unnerving linkage between, on the one hand, their own ideas and ideals and hopes and fears and, on the other hand, the essays or treatises or short stories or novels we were reading. I remember going back to my room in Adams House and shoving aside resolutely Miller's essays or books (*Errand into the Wilderness*, say) in favor of *Organic Chemistry* by Fieser and Fieser, doing so with great relief and joy—a lot of facts to memorize, and that was that!

If the relentless detail of chemical equations offered a respite of sorts, I would soon enough, in the spring of that same second Harvard year, stumble into what, for a while, I am sure, must have been regarded by some unwitting part of my head (the so-called unconscious) as the second part of a double-barreled gun—a strange, unseemly and wrong-headed and unjust way of referring to Werner Jaeger, that gentle scholar so devoted to the language and philosophy and literature of ancient Greece. But then, the subterranean section of our mind is supposed to be arbitrary, capricious, frivolous, unreasonably truculent. I enrolled in Jaeger's course in Greek civilization because before I came to Harvard I'd had six years of Latin and four years of Greek, and I wanted to stay in touch—and I hasten to add, "do well," or so I thought would be the case. I squirm now as I draw nearer to those days—the combination (how is one to qualify it with percentages?) of moral earnestness and finely honed guile. But again I met up with a strangely irregular man—a professor who sang, as Homer did, as Sophocles and Euripides and Aristophanes did, and sang with unashamed baring of soul.

There was plenty of Greek to read, and one can get lost in the intricacies of translation as easily (sometimes, more showily, more snobbishly) as in the flow of chemical equations. But on each Monday and each Wednesday, when Professor Jaeger held forth, I had all I could do to withstand the moral and philosophical messages he sent our way in that Emerson Hall lecture room. Not that he was dramatic (and I don't use the word pejoratively). Unlike Perry Miller, he seemed (or so we wrongly believed for a while) vastly uninterested in the twentieth century—or for that matter, in the dozen or more that preceded it. He called us back to Athens and its great antagonist, Sparta. He called us back to men and women on journeys—trying to do justice to stoutly held ideals, in the face of those three fates who spin, forever and a day, the various cloths of our lives, then brusquely cut them short. He called us to the dreams and nightmares of playwrights and philosophers and warriors. (Yes, that one-time marine classmate of mine also sat there, a student of Jaeger as well as of Miller.) We left reminded of Areté, the virtue of the strong and the brave. We left reminded of moral principles and the tragic conflict (as in *Antigone*) they can generate: the law of the state and the rights of the family. We left connected to the entire span of Western civilization. And sometimes we left, a number of us, confused. Why? There were moments when Homer or Aeschylus nearly caused Jaeger to weep or made his voice tremble—and when, consequently, I wanted to flee. It would take time for me to be able to understand the reason I got uncomfortable, the reason I sometimes wanted "out," the faster the better.

I don't think I've ever rid my thoughts of those two teachers, nor do I expect I ever will. There are, already, too many instances of the use of the personal pronoun *I* in this essay—the egoism of the writer, compounded by the self-regard if not flattery that goes with even a limited memoir. But both Miller and Jaeger, if I may resort to both their names that way, took pains to ask of us that we suffer their subjectivity as well as their unbeatable scholarly lectures. For me, Harvard became, more than anything else, a matter of trying to come to some terms with what they offered— that blend of intellectual and moral passion they dared reveal to students in the late 1940s and early 1950s. I kept up with both of them after I graduated and went to medical school. I kept going back to their books, Miller's *Errand into the Wilderness, The New England Mind, Nature's Nation*, his wonderful anthology, *The Transcendentalists*, and Jaeger's volumes titled *Paideia*. I still have those books near my desk. Those two Harvard professors gave me their heroes. They helped me find a few for myself. When I read Flannery O'Connor, for instance, or Walker Percy, I think of Miller and Jaeger; and God knows, I think of them when I read Simone Weil. Kierkegaard is always there for me—Miller's gift to each of us in the course he taught, Classics of the Christian Tradition. And just as important, the spirits of Miller and Jaeger were there, whether I liked it or not, in the Adams House rooms and dining hall and in the time I spent doing work for Phillips Brooks House. A Harvard student can hear Gauguin's questions being asked anyplace, anytime—once he's been made to listen hard: by roommates, by fellow students, and just as often, maybe more so, by children who live across this or that pair of railroad tracks and for whom a volunteer's effort to be of help (to himself as well as others!) is an object of both continuing skepticism and eager gratitude. (As for the altogether human mixture of genuine charity, flagrant noblesse oblige, and all too confident self-regard that are collectively responsible for many kinds of youthful altruism, I have learned to stop worrying about apparent psychological incompatibilities and just be grateful that occasionally the whole "package" stays together.)

One struggles (perhaps unnecessarily and rather too insistently, too demonstratively) with the distance time has put between four full and active years and all the other years that have since passed. Since I came back, eventually, to face students in the same lecture halls where I once sat as a young listener, I find it almost a remonstrance to think again, through the effort of an essay, of Miller and Jaeger—the awesome depth, sincerity, integrity of their teaching. And that war veteran classmate of mine haunts me, too—the texture of moral experience he brought to Harvard and shared with a few of us callow if "eager-beaver" youths lucky enough to stumble onto his well-earned wisdom. Both Perry Miller and Werner Jaeger kept telling us, in their classes, that multiple-choice factuality and even the well-rounded and carefully eloquent exam essay were but a prelude to something else—to a moral life we must find for ourselves as we go slouching toward Jerusalem. To give us a boost for the long journey ahead they read and read to us. I am lucky to remember still some of the passages: from *The Republic* or *Timaeus*; from *Seven against Thebes* and *The Trojan Women*; from a sermon of Cotton Mather's that stuck and stuck; from the writings of George Ripley or Margaret Fuller or that wonderfully named nineteenth-century New England poet, Jones Very; and not least, from the isolated and forlorn Emily Dickinson, who traveled nowhere and knew no one, it seemed, and yet held the whole world in her mind's hands and gave it to us unforgettably.

Am I being conveniently rhetorical when I talk about those books, plays, writers—or am I remembering, really, through them, some fine moments in a particular college, when two professors wouldn't let up on us? They persisted, rather, in giving lectures that took on a life of their own—that is, one suspects, those lectures got worked into a number of lives. Miller kept insisting, for instance, that we live in a country meant by some of its founders to be not so much strong and rich as *exemplary*—before Almighty God. As for Jaeger, he couldn't let us forget for a minute, at least in his company, the luminous moment that was ancient Greece—an intricate, suggestive, commanding language, and minds utterly worthy of it. He begged us to see the repetitions of Greek thought in other tongues and times—always with the implicit or explicit demand that the past, however "ancient," be regarded as a necessary part of modernity. It was an extremely valuable message in its own right—and, I now realize, a rather appropriate and interesting one for us, students in America's oldest college, to be receiving week after week.

I went to memorials held for both of them—that last formal tribute, I guess, one can make. They were no saints; each had his faults. Why not, in today's psychiatric culture, go into them at length, as we put it in our pompous, clinical

way? Because, I have to make answer, and with it, conclude—because the issue is a kind of transcendence. Perry
Miller, who knew and taught the nineteenth-century New
England transcendentalists as well as their righteous colonial predecessors, was able to stretch himself wondrously—
for all his "problems," his personal or even professional
shortcomings, and none of us is without them aplenty; and I
know for sure that some of us who listened to him more
faithfully than we may have believed to be possible were also
stretched and stretched. That lecture hall crackled, at times,
with—what? Humanity for a second or two rather wonderfully realized: those fundamental questions Gauguin helped
my mother teach us were gone over yet again by a teacher
who reached for the very stars and sometimes, it seemed,
held a few in his intellectual hands. And the same with
Werner Jaeger; for all the world it seemed that those enig-
matic, bearded, stoic Greek faces, sculpted so many centuries ago and left to us by fate or accident in a remnant here
and there, were now near us, at last understandable and
part of our day-to-day existence.

I write, then, to acknowledge a privilege of my youth—to
have met those two teachers and the books they recommended in a certain place, Harvard by name. And I write in
the conviction that we are all part of a scheme of things,
compelled by what we are to try and try to answer those
questions that Gauguin knew shaped us. I am anxious to
salute two guides and, yes, to salute the place where they
worked and worked: in Cambridge, Massachusetts, and in
this particular century—well over three hundred years
since some of those who came here to a New World ended
up founding the first college in what would one day be a
nation of no small significance in the history of the West.

Peter S. Prescott '57

My Harvard: I am not sure that I ever had one—or, to be more precise, I had several, each incompatible with the others, each indelibly imprinted on the way I think and act today, which may be why I rarely think of Harvard now. My friends find this incredible. After all, I am one of few who have troubled to write a serious book about Harvard, or about a particular part of what was once one undergraduate's experience of Harvard. Reviewing this book, *The Harvard Crimson* said I should be locked up: "Not for the book he has written—which is not that bad. Rather, he should go for the life he has led." Well, that's clear enough, fair enough. I have written some negative book reviews myself and have told students in a course on criticism that they mustn't fudge around. The *Crimson* review reminded me of the last official communication I received from the University while still an undergraduate. It arrived, as I remember, printed in six-color letterpress on a scroll of parchment and suggested I turn over stocks and bonds to Harvard. Small contributions, this missive declared, were not welcome: they give no joy to the donor and are too expensive to process. Who could disagree? I had, at that time, $25 in capital funds available to Harvard, and Harvard had a president famous for his Christianity, so I wrote him a letter citing the story of the widow's mite, and got no answer, not even a secretary's acknowledgment. I rather admired that. Like the *Crimson* review so many years later, it demonstrated a flinty disdain that makes it quite possible for Harvard's alumni to reflect upon the place without any sentimentality at all.

And so, without sentiment, I look back on my years at Harvard, which were the years of the middle 1950s, not now remembered by anyone with affection, certainly not by me, although they seem now good enough years to have grown up in because they lacked the coercion of the years that followed. At that time I was courting the young woman I eventually married, trying to do well in my courses, attempting to cope with roommates who, for ill or good, consumed much of our mutual time. In spare hours, I worked as an editor of the *Advocate* and submerged myself in the diversions of Harvard's clubs. I also kept a journal. *Those* were my Harvards: my classes detracted from the attention the young woman required; my colleagues at the *Advocate* could not understand why I cared for the clubs. Few knew about my journal, in which I wrote: "I am also sympathetic to the Hegelian concept of the *Objective Geist.*" I also wrote: "I have been fascinated to find that Heidegger's *Sein und Zeit* fits in closely with, and greatly furthers, my ideas of ontology" and "the bourgeois mind is a comfortable thing for it is always in a state of repose, always in harmony with its environment." Rereading this journal, I have come to understand why the old alums I encounter today tend to talk about football.

Among my Harvards, only one has not been much remarked upon by other writers: the world of the final clubs. Secretive these clubs have always been, rejoicing in their anonymity behind chaste walls of Georgian brick. The Porcellian, doyen of all the others, predestined bourn of large-tricepted members of the Harvard crew's first boat, was said to have installed a mirror over Massachussetts Avenue inclined at such an angle that the elect might survey the commonality without themselves being seen. We of the D.U. had to settle for a squash court and a tiny garden where, in the fetid springtime, we paraded such women as we could muster before tables laden with glasses of champagne.

Like most of the final clubs, D.U. had once belonged to a national fraternity, but Harvard being what Harvard is, there came a time when the clubs cut loose from their brethren. In my day, D.U. members regaled each other with what is not, I hope, an apocryphal piece of history. A jerk from the Delta Upsilon chapter of some dismal college— perhaps Dartmouth—bounces up to the D.U. door and finds it locked. Hardly a fraternal situation. The jerk bangs on the door only to have it opened by a Chinese gentleman in white gloves. "I'm here to see my D.U. buddies," the jerk says, whereupon the Chinese gentleman asks him for his card. Because Dartmouth D.U.s don't know what a card is, the jerk finds Harvard's door closed politely in his face.

In my day there were no more Chinese gentlemen in white gloves. We did have a club steward, Bob Lloyd, who fed whiskey to Cambridge cops so that club members might park illegally on Dunster Street, outside the door. He also kept a camera, which he used to take photographs of D.U. members who, temporarily incapacitated by the liquid portion of their evening's sustenance, had paused for recuperative purposes on some club table or stairway. There is no recorded instance of Bob Lloyd attempting to use these photographs for his own financial advancement. Our assumption was that he kept them for private consolation, or to support his arguments with the stewards of other clubs as to who had the greatest burden to bear.

It is impossible to underestimate the importance of Harvard's clubs within the University community. There were, at that time, eleven of them, called "final" clubs because a student could be elected only to one, and then there was no other place to go. The clubs embraced about 10 percent of Harvard's undergraduates. Another 10 percent, it was said,

would rather have liked to belong. Perhaps 10 percent more
had heard of the clubs and couldn't care less about belong-
ing. That left a landslide majority in the University community who were unaware that these odd institutions existed at
all. Nevertheless, then as now, the clubs had their critics.
The prevailing leveling sentiment suggested that they were
as offensive and obsolete as Tyrannosaurus Rex and as
threatening to the tree shrews and protolemurs that constituted the serious part of the college. No matter that the
clubs were painstakingly discreet—their members were
hardly given to donning orange sashes and parading down
Mount Auburn Street—it was their bricked-in obscurity
that was intolerable to the laity. One apprentice journalist
writing for an occasional magazine announced that "clubbies" were unable to be frank with themselves, that the
clubs were "houses of silence" which had sapped the morale
not only of their members but of the student body as a
whole. Should, by some miscalculation, a good student be
accepted by a club, he would presently fail his examinations.

Who would have thought the lotos-eaters' island was so
close at hand? Where club men dream, with half-dropt
eyelid still, along the length of languorous afternoons.
Propped (if not on beds of amaranth and moly) in leather
chairs, the chill martini blossoms by their hands. I should
have been wild to join one had I not, in the fall of my
sophomore year, been quite so prudish. In my journal I
wrote: "Final clubs are in the air. My own attitude hangs in
the balance. I have heard more bad than good of them; I am
inclined to think they would be a colossal bore, yet there is a
flattering amount of social prestige connected with them.
This is their only asset, save cheap drinks." Furthermore,
the clubs were not rushing after me. Only the D.U. wanted
to take a look: "The pleasure of Mr. Prescott's company is
requested at a punch," the engraved invitation read. There
was a date, a time. "Someone will call for you. RSVP." "I have
not heard much good of the D.U.," I wrote. "A pretty rowdy
bunch."

I told my roommate of the year before, Henry Bercovic, that I was inclined to go. Henry had been punched by several clubs: Delphic, the Spee, D.U., Fox. "Ssshhh," Henry warned and looked around. We were finishing lunch in the Eliot House dining room. A nondescript fellow sat at the far end of our table; by straining his ears he might have heard what we were saying. "'What *is* this?" I asked. "You act as if I'm trying to touch the Ark of the Covenant." Henry gave me a disgusted look.

"You just don't talk about it."

"Why all the fear?"

"Don't you see that they don't like to be discussed?"

I looked at the guy at the end of the table. "You mean you're afraid of *him?*"

"Ssshhh. You can never tell who's listening."

For those who cared about this kind of thing, the punches inspired a certain amount of awe mixed with apprehension. "It is said that practically nobody leaves a club punch on his feet," I wrote, never having been to one. "People have been known to fall down the flight of stairs leading to the D.U. suite and lie retching at the bottom. They keep the drinks coming at you with an astounding regularity. The man you are with brings them to you from the bar and you are apparently expected to down them in good time, while he probably takes notes on your behavior. What a system. If they won't take me on three drinks, they can go to hell."

I approached my first punch fortified by aquavit, which had been served at a tea party given by the *Advocate* for its Radcliffe associates. The D.U. punch was held in a club member's room because we postulants were not considered fit to be admitted, even as guests, to the club we might be invited to join. I nursed three Scotches, each grimly thrust into my hand by the club's dullest and most aggressively ignorant member. Sweat broke out on my forehead, hands, and wrists—I was not then in training for heavy drinking— and at one point I felt it necessary to seize the back of a chair. Meanwhile, there was conversation to be coped with; it consisted mostly of long silences that I did not feel well enough to support.

"Insensibility holds no charms for me," I wrote in my journal a few days later. "And yet my contemporaries periodically go out with the intent of drinking themselves to this prostrated, nauseated state in which one wants only to die, to cease upon the midnight with no more pain than absolutely necessary." My roommate had just returned from a club punch. "At 6 p.m. he was joyous and bouncing with the prospect of hanging on a good drunk. At 10 p.m. he appeared at our door, suspended between two strangers, half undressed, wretched, pale as a sheet with a slightly green tinge, incapable of supporting himself, two great welts on his right temple incurred from walking into a door. He half fell into the bathroom and leaned miserably over the toilet, writhing fruitlessly in what is known in the vernacular as 'the dry heaves,' when all is thrown up, but the muscles of the stomach and throat still twist in agonized protest. And I look at him, wanting to help, feeling only sympathy and commiseration and a dull awe at that which is in man that makes him do this and rarely profit from the lesson.

"But what is really appalling is that people consider this great sport, not only to inflict upon themselves but to force on others. If you don't drink yourself into this state, others will pour this stuff down your throat to see that you don't welsh out on your share of the misery. It is the custom. One must be a man."

Full of doubts about the drinking life, I accepted an invitation to another D.U. punch—a Sunday afternoon outing for which we piled into cars and drove 35 miles out to a stretch of country on the North Shore by Cape Cod. The punch was held at a grand estate that stopped abruptly at a cliff which fell into the ocean. Waves broke against the cliff's foot; beneath us, yachts glimmered white against the blue of the sea. I stood on the cliff's edge in my tweed jacket with a Scotch in my hand (a before-breakfast bracer, as I had missed breakfast, and though it was now one-thirty, lunch was not to be served until three). With a great house looming behind me, the sea before me, and the wind in my face, I mustered some affection for the D.U. Club. It preserved, I thought, at least the framework of an aristocratic tradition now rapidly dying out. A sip of Scotch, a whiff of sea wind. Behind me, a uniformed steward tended a long bar set up on a terrace; a maid and a butler set out plates of crabs and oysters. Was not such an effort worthy of one's earnest support? If only to maintain a moribund tradition?

I turned to find that my cotraditionalists, people I hardly knew, had divided into two groups: one took off ties and jackets and threw a football back and forth; the other, glasses in hand, watched the former leap about.

That evening, in the course of a telephone call, the young woman I was courting and I fell into a quarrel. She complained of cruelty; I pleaded inadvertent ignorance; she hung up; I fumed. How to regain her attention? With half an hour to go before the Radcliffe switchboard closed down, I assembled within ten minutes half a sonnet:

> My anger and my love were once at strife;
> Each claimed dominion o'er the other's prize,
> And though their similar passions oft were rife,
> The latter dealt with truth, the former lies.
> But in the bitter flux to their surprise
> They found their goal was one. Who loves in life
> Is saved indeed, who lives in anger dies.

Pure puce, and given ten minutes more I might have finished the job, but I was persuaded that this woman was more important to my life than the tradition with which I had flirted all that afternoon, and so at a cost of $2.24—a reckless amount for me—I sent my aborted sonnet to her by way of Western Union. "Ha," I thought. "That'll get her. I'll just wait for the phone call." It got her. The phone rang. "Are you pleased with yourself?" she asked.

A week later, at the penultimate D.U. punch, Henry Bercovic was also brooding on more important matters than clubs. "I'm not ready for college," he said. "If military service

were only for twelve months, I'd take it. I need more matur-
ing. Every now and then I ask myself what I'm doing at
college, and the picture always seems to be Henry Bercovic
in a black tie and a drink in his fist. So I'm getting very suave
and sophisticated, but my education isn't worth a damn."

We were both in black tie, both with drinks in our fists, in
the Club of Odd Volumes in Boston's Louisburg Square. The
atmosphere was conducive to Henry's line of reflection:
handsome paneling, floorlength bay windows, engravings
from portraits by Joshua Reynolds, and books that were not
so odd, but seemingly permanently fixed in great shelves
along one wall. Sixty of us—club members, alumni, and
candidates—stood poised in little black-tie groups, making
conversation appropriate to the paneling.

"What would you like to drink?" an alumnus asked me,
reaching for my glass.

"No more for me."

"Ah, but if you *were* to have another, what would it be?"

Ah, and in a moment there was another drink in my fist.

"I hate to see anyone with an empty glass," the alumnus
said.

Within two hours, glasses empty and otherwise would be
shattered on the floor and bounced down the elegant stairway, but before that appointed time we sat down to roast
duck, wild rice, old Burgundy, and talk of Joe McCarthy's
censure in the Senate. As coffee replaced the ice cream,
meringue, and strawberries, Henry became expansive.
"There I was, with the best hand I ever held in my life. Ten of
hearts, jack, king, ace, and three of clubs. I put my hand
down on the table, threw out the three, and asked for one."
Long pause. Henry is waiting for someone to tell him what
he drew, but when no one does, he says, "The queen."

"Unbelievable," I said, meaning it.

Henry smiled. "One chance in five million. But the hand
was only worth forty dollars."

As cognac replaced the coffee, I told a story of a friend of
mine who seemed to have been bitten by a snake. He alter-

nated sucking his own blood and drinking slugs of whisky until, insensible, he was told that the snake wasn't poisonous. Henry then began an account of hunting elephant and tiger in India, and pretty soon, with the reappearance of the whisky and gin, the glass-throwing time was upon us. Henry and I decided to make a discreet tactical withdrawal. Pausing for a moment to rest his weight upon a Queen Anne serving table, Henry was shocked to find that unreliable female object shatter its legs beneath him. Increasing the speed of his withdrawal, Henry arrived at his room only to find that somehow a fifth of Johnnie Walker Black and half a box of cigars had become entangled in his coat. Rather than embarrass his hosts by bringing this anomaly to their attention, Henry prudently decided to say nothing.

In my journal I wrote: "At times I am terribly unsatisfied with my way of life, what I have accomplished thus far; I feel that what I am doing is not helping me at all, but only increasing my self-consciousness. Here I am, at 19, in the strength of my youth, posturing most ridiculously as Spengler's Faustian man, immersed in books and an artificial approach to life, trapped by artificialities and superficialities in myself which are being ground into my character. The imitation of life is not enough, and that, not life, is what is to be found in books."

And after the final black-tie dinner, during which the members of D.U. gave a final glance at the candidates they had assembled, I wrote: *"Les jeux sont faits.* Tonight they vote. I find myself interested and slightly satiated with the whole business. A little awed at the manifestation of young aristocracy enjoying the pleasure without the *noblesse oblige,* a little revolted by the organization that has no purpose, no thematic organization other than Society. Congenial fellows. I'm quite aware that I'm not really one of them, that I can enjoy them to an extent but no further. For me, this is form without substance, and those who can find substance in it are damned indeed."

I thought, that final night, that I would not be elected. I had not courted the club members. I could not talk easily to my fellow candidates who, at the final dinner, had discussed girls they planned to seduce over Christmas vacation, exchanging prospects and techniques with one another.

"Where do you go to ski at Christmas?" a member asked me.

"Well, I don't ski."

Courteous to a fault, the member regarded me with great interest. "I see, I see," he saw, passing my condition off as if it were normal. "Too bad. Great sport. Give it a try."

"You're ready for another drink," another member told me.

I sloshed the whisky in my half-full glass around. "How can you tell?"

"Your ice is melted. You're nursing it too long."

Then the singing began:

> Oh, every day is labor day
> At the Boston Lying-In.
> With shrieks, and groans,
> And spread-ing pelvic bones,
> Oh, every day is labor day
> At the Boston Lying-In.

Reader, I joined them. I had gone to bed that night at two-thirty, rating my chances at fifty-fifty. "Ridiculous to want it quite so much now," I wrote. "If you really had wanted it, you ought to have made your bid earlier." I thought I would be awakened at three or four by a bunch of D.U.s rejoicing in my election, but at seven-thirty no one had come. Had a note been pushed under the door? No. Into my mailbox? I put a coat over my pajamas and sneaked stealthily down the stair lest someone should catch me in this vain act. Nothing. Rejected, I went back to bed but was awakened a few minutes later with my acceptance which, according to law, could not be delivered before 8:00A.M. An answer was required before noon. As it happened, I had an eleven o'clock lecture on William Pitt, very vital, as I had done no reading and an exam was imminent, so I thrust my acceptance through the slot in the D.U. door. I hadn't walked twenty yards before the door opened and I was dragged into the guest room of the building to be fed milk punch for an hour—so much for William Pitt—while the members leaped after the little envelopes that came through the slot. Most of them were rejections. My friend Henry—he of the Queen Anne table—had been blackballed.

The initiation dinner took place shortly after New Year's. Old and new members assembled in Eliot House, where only Martinis and Manhattans were served. "Come now," said my host, "we are due at the club in ten minutes. You must have drunk two of these by then." There were more drinks at the club before we initiates were marched in alphabetical order upstairs to the living room where all but one light had been turned out. As the old members glowered at us, the club's president read a slightly pompous speech: Relax here . . . any time . . . be good fellows . . . offer sympathy . . . behave like gentlemen . . . broaden our personal contacts . . . share in a valuable experience. Names were called, affirmations made.

At dinner, served another floor up, each new member received a bottle of Piper-Heidsieck. We were required to aim our corks at the club's mascot, a stuffed duck hanging from the ceiling, and if one of us were to hit that duck, he would win a second bottle of champagne. Both bottles, of course, were to be drunk immediately. Incredibly, inevitably, I hit the damn duck. Because the young woman I was courting was presently to have a birthday, I tried to hide my prize bottle of champagne—a trophy I could not afford to buy her—but it was wrestled from me by a sharp-eyed D.U. alumnus who later admitted that he was an ex-marine who had taught his troops jujitsu. I had no reason, he assured me, to be ashamed of having to roll unsuccessfully on the floor with him—a floor already covered with Piper-Heidsieck and salt (thrown down to keep us from slipping in the wet), with olives, fragmented rolls, and mashed potatoes.

Priding itself as it does on providing an opportunity for students to meet and come to terms with a variety of people, Harvard will surely continue to rejoice in the final club experience, which alone allows an undergraduate in a tuxedo to wrestle with an ex-marine among olives and potatoes for a bottle of champagne.

Erich Segal '58

Erich Segal was born in Brooklyn in 1937. He attended Midwood High School before going to Harvard where he received his A.B. in 1958, and his Ph.D. in 1965. At commencement in June 1958, he was selected both class poet and Latin orator, the only person in Harvard history to receive both honors. His doctoral thesis became his first academic book: Roman Laughter: The Comedy of Plautus. *Though he went on to teach at Yale, then Princeton, then Yale again, in one sense Erich Segal never left Cambridge. His novels—*Love Story, Oliver's Story, Man, Woman and Child, *and* The Class*—all take place in and around Harvard.*

In September 1954 I and a thousand or so other freshmen gathered in Cambridge, sharing the confident assumption that, having been chosen for Harvard, we were, ipso facto, the best and the brightest. And that very first day we learned the most painful lesson of our young lives: most of our classmates were better and brighter. We spent the rest of our college years coming to terms with this and spent the rest of our lives trying to disguise it. This is the root cause of the infamous Harvard arrogance.

Many are the ways that eighteen-year-olds respond to their collision with fallibility. Some immediately drop out. In fact, by the second week of the term, one of my classmates had resigned and set himself up as a shoe-shine boy on the steps of the library. A few accept the truth about themselves with dignity and stop dreaming of the White House. The majority, however, go quietly mad, each in a special way, thus preserving for themselves a remnant of their uniqueness. Some attend classes and study. These, of course, are the maddest of all.

I had one friend, for example, who claimed his English course was too jejune. So to hell with going to classes. He retreated to the library to read "every nineteenth-century novel ever written." Unfortunately, he never officially enrolled in a course on this topic, and so he flunked out. I admired his intellectual independence; he would not bow to a tyrannical curriculum. He would not read what "they" wanted him to. He later went into publishing.

One of my roommates had been a superb high school sprinter. When the day came for track tryouts, he sat on our couch mumbling something about having left his spikes at home. Perhaps, he mused, he should go and get them. Home was, after all, about fifteen minutes away.

No, he decided. He'd just had lunch. He would rest a bit before going for his shoes and then begin rewriting the Harvard record book.

He stayed on the couch for two days.

Now he may have arisen for the occasional meal, but my recollection is that he spent the vast majority of the next forty-eight hours sitting on the couch of our living room, discussing the possibility of getting his track shoes.

To this day he is one of the fastest runners ever to have attended Harvard, though he never did go out for the team. I do think that, in addition to fear, there was an element of laziness in his philosophy, which, as a classicist, I recognized as Epicurean apraxia in its purest form. This conclusion I drew not merely from observation of his inert form on the couch (scientists never trust mere sense impressions), but from a dialogue between Fred (not, of course, his real name) and our Irish cleaning lady.

Yes, Virginia, there used to be cleaning ladies. Indeed, ours was the last class to have the benefit of their aid and counsel. Especially counsel.

This particular Sibyl (an allusion, of course, not her name) was the head of the maids' union and hence the very last to be forcibly retired. One day, as I was (I blush to say) returning from class, I overheard her speaking to Fred as she dusted around him on the couch.

"So what's yer major then?" she asked.

"Economics," he replied.

She looked at him with a wry smile.

"You sure picked it, didn't ya, honey?"

"Huh?" he said. Fred did not waste syllables if at all possible. It was tiring.

"If ya can't get out of here in Ec," she replied, "then ya can't get outa here in anything."

And she whisked out. I looked to see Fred's reaction. But he had fallen asleep.

Being a poor boy from Brooklyn and majoring in a subject the professors actually loved to teach, I worked like a fiend. My diligence did not endear me to any of my roommates, however. Perhaps it was because every evening I asked them to please not talk before 10 P.M. (because I was studying) or after 10:15 (because I would be sleeping). I was taking beginning Greek, and I was scared.

I was having nightmares about confronting texts in which not a single word was intelligible. I even took desperate measures, postponing my bedtime until eleven so I could spend another hour memorizing irregular verbs. I confided my panic to one of my roommates (not the sprinter). "Hey, I think I'm flunking Greek," I said.

He commiserated. "Then why kill yourself every night? Be smart—switch to social relations."

As our first set of final exams drew nearer, this alternative became increasingly attractive. It actually sounded jolly.

Normally, students would put stamped postcards into their bluebooks, so they could receive their final grades by mail, instead of waiting for weeks with bitten nails and spastic colons. I was too ashamed to insert a card. Instead I put in a thick envelope with a slip of paper.

One week after finals I was met at the door by my roommate the sociologist.

He greeted me by placing his hand around my throat and starting to squeeze.

"You lying sonovabitch!" he bellowed as I grew weaker and weaker.

"Gurgle?"

"You said you were flunking Greek!"

"Gurgle," I affirmed.

"You got a f——ng A!" he shrieked, rabid with betrayal.

How had he found this out? He let me go and allowed me to sink to the floor as he waved my (unopened) envelope at me.

"I held it to the light! You got a f——ng A!"

I got up slowly, desperately trying to concoct an appropriate apology.

"I'm . . . sorry. I really thought I was . . ."

But he had now stormed out to tell the rest of the dorm of my treachery.

Two things must quickly be said: from then on I roomed alone. I also got very few more A's. Perhaps it was a Pavlovian reaction to this violent—albeit not unique—college experience.

Traditional mythology places the epicenter of Harvard in the Yard. Here stands the majestic Widener Library, repository of the wisdom of all ages and all cultures. There is no denying this and no denying that I spent some of my college time wandering the stacks in quest of knowledge.

But with due respect, Widener is only the brain of Harvard. To me, its heart lies across the Charles River—in Dillon Field House and on the running tracks. To this day I am grateful to my distinguished professors of Latin and Greek. I owe a special debt to one unique teacher who, like Socrates, never published a thing.

His name is William W. McCurdy. His official title in the faculty handbook was track coach. But to those who knew him, he was psychiatrist, father confessor, spiritual guide, and moral example. And thanks to him, I learned a little about myself.

Camus wrote that his "*seules leçons de morale*" were learned on the playing field, and McCurdy was, in fact, a philosopher as well. He was hardly your stereotyped cigar-chewing, beer-bellied athletic mentor. Quite the contrary, he was in better shape than most of his runners and on occasion even raced them to prove it.

Also atypical was that, with a single exception, McCurdy

didn't give a damn if Harvard won or lost. All he cared about was that his "students" (sic) lived up to their potential.

The one exception was the Yale meet. But not because McCurdy was a wild Harvard chauvinist. Rather it was because his New Haven counterpart cared *only* about winning. "He's not a teacher," McCurdy would growl—though never to the press. Whenever possible he would endeavor to defeat Yale by huge, humiliating margins (often making his runners triple and quadruple events). At all other times, he would try to keep our winning score as modest as possible. This is how I got to run. If Harvard was too far ahead, he would throw me in, so the other team could go home with a few more points—and more self-respect.

Bill always claimed that he could see what was going on in a man's head by the way he was running. I never really believed this until I actually witnessed the incident I am about to relate.

We once had a freshman who was a genius at everything. Not only was he already a professional musician but he had legs as strong as his intellect. As a high school student he had already run a quarter-mile in 48 seconds. In those days, that would have put him a half-dozen yards from the Olympic team.

One winter afternoon, this young man sped effortlessly through a brilliant time trial on the tight indoor track. We all stood amazed. We had never seen so magnificent an athlete in a Harvard uniform.

McCurdy put his arm around the boy's shoulder, and they took a short walk on the infield. I assumed they were discussing the athlete's chances for a national title. I was wrong. Bill was throwing him off the team.

A few days later, I summoned the courage to ask him why.

"Because he's probably one of the smartest guys this school has ever had."

I know McCurdy was not aware that the likes of Henry James and Ralph Waldo Emerson had also attended Harvard—though, I suspect, slightly before his time.

"Then *why*, McCurdy? Why'd you bounce him?"

"Because he's flunking out."

"How do you know?" (This was well before exams).

"Segal, he's running nowhere near his potential. And if he's studying like he's running, he'll flunk. I thought I would shake him up by kicking him off. Maybe there's still time."

"McCurdy, you're crazy."

"I'm right, Segal."

And he was. The guy failed all his courses. He later achieved some renown in the performing arts, though he always vowed, whenever I chanced to come across him, that he was coming back to Harvard.

McCurdy should have been the dean.

He had principles. Idiosyncratic, but educationally sound. If you didn't try your damnedest, you could be an Olympic champion and he wouldn't give you the time of day.

To teach a "star" a lesson, he once ignored a national-class athlete (who was as lazy as he was gifted) and spent an entire month helping train the *manager* to break six minutes for the mile.

At the end of the month, the manager broke the tape in 5:58, and the star got the message. He thereafter became a very docile protégé.

I was not a mere bystander. In my senior year, I too incurred McCurdy's wrath for "not living up to my potential." He did not kick me off the team (although if he had, I might have done better on my general exams). Instead, he forbade me to speak a word to him until I had broken five minutes for the mile. (Please remember, sports fans, this was 1957). It was not that I hadn't been trying. But Mc-Curdy recognized that I had been having a clandestine flirtation with failure. His injunction to run that mile or else made me painfully aware of my neurosis.

Every day in November I ran a time trial at a mile—and every day I missed breaking five minutes by *less than a second*. In retrospect, it was a frightening, almost Dantesque experience. I did everything but fall down to keep avoiding success.

One afternoon, after I had clocked an even 5:00(!), Mc-Curdy very quietly ordered me to go off and return to the track in half an hour, for today was the day. Those were the first words he had addressed to me since the season began.

I returned in trepidation thirty minutes later.

To this day I can remember every step of that mile. There was total silence in Briggs Cage. French Anderson, our captain, led me through the first three-quarters in exactly 3:45—and then dropped out. I was on my own now, but if I could just keep up that pace, I would do it.

I heard a kind of universal pandemonium. Everyone was screaming, "Kick, kick!" McCurdy's voice was loudest of all. To my astonishment, I suddenly found myself running faster and faster. I covered the last quarter in 68 seconds flat. Mile time: 4:55. My face was soaked with sweat and tears. And I wasn't even tired.

I walked over to Bill McCurdy my teacher and said, "Well?"

Suppressing a smile, he answered, "You've started, Segal."

I had.

Thank you, Bill.

John D. Spooner '59

As the Class of 1959 at Harvard, we were part of the Silent Generation: too young for World War II and Korea, just too old for Vietnam. Daily maid service (the biddies) in the houses and the Yard had just ended prior to our freshman year. Eisenhower was President; we wore crew cuts, and you could not prevent *Playboy*'s first issues from disappearing mysteriously from your room. Freshman year I was thrown among brilliant strangers, General Motors Scholars, National Merit Scholars from Nebraska, Mississippi, Pennsylvania, California, New Jersey, and Texas. We were eight roommates, in adjoining suites for four. This was in Straus Hall overlooking the Square, opposite the old University Theater, the U.T., which one of my friends held up with a water pistol on a drunken dare. He was fired for a year, went into the Marine Corps Reserve and returned to graduate magna. Harvard will *almost* always readmit an offender. Harvard never likes to say she made a mistake with anyone. Every morning we were awakened by the bus dispatcher, below Straus Hall on Massachusetts Avenue, yelling, "Heights, Arlington *Heights*." One March afternoon a big California boy, benumbed by exams and studying German language flash cards, emptied a wastebasket full of water on to the dispatcher from a third-story window. He missed the dispatcher but managed to catch a crowd of townies assembled at the bus stop on their way to a hockey game. Enraged, they proceeded to break fifty-three windows in Straus Hall with snowballs. The big California boy was never caught or punished. It was enough that he suffered over his German flash cards. The boy was subject to fits of irrational behavior. He came from the lettuce country of northern California, *East of Eden* country, and never quite got used to the fact that there were bright, motivated students at Harvard considerably more sophisticated than he. He would brood about this in his room, with his flash cards, wearing a yellow terry-cloth bathrobe and not talking very much. The end of the 1950s was not quite the beginning of the sexual revolution. The Pill had not yet been invented. Many freshman classmates, at ages eighteen and nineteen, had not even dated, let alone had sexual experiences. One of our roommates came from Brookline, several miles from Cambridge. He had a car. He had a girl friend who owned twelve cashmere skirt-and-sweater combinations. The big kid from California, in his yellow bathrobe, blurted out in a late night bull session that he longed to leap into the room whenever the girl with the cashmere sweaters visited. He longed to leap into the room, whip open the yellow bathrobe and yell, "Stick 'em up." Some weeks later, when we had all forgotten his fantasy, the big kid from California heard a female voice through the unlocked fire door connecting the rooms. Without hesitating, he launched himself through the door, ripped open the yellow terry-cloth and yelled, "Stick 'em up," just in time to see the mother of one of our roommates lifting a teacup to her lips.

There was a selfish exuberance to our social life in those days, an exuberance generally unmarked by social consciousness. In retrospect, my friends and I were spoiled and romantic. This was true not only of the preppies from the eastern private schools but also of my freshman roommates, all public school boys. They were all brilliant, but they felt instinctively that they were special and had special things waiting for them in life. They felt that Harvard was the best, and no more than they deserved.

At the completion of fall hour exams, there was a tradition, the freshman smoker, a remnant of simpler times when the Harvard experience for many people was reminiscent of *Tom Brown's School Days*. The idea was to go en masse to Memorial Hall Auditorium and listen to a speaker who would amuse us enough to get us into a party mood. For several years the speaker was Al Capp, the creator of "Li'l Abner" and a Cambridge resident. Capp had been a long-time Harvard fan. But by the time of our smoker, he had become a venomous bully who delighted in insulting what he referred to as "spoiled adolescents, wet behind the ears, and a few other places too." Capp succeeded in whipping us into a frenzy, and, by the time he gave us the finger and stomped off the stage, we were whistling and stomping and throwing beer cans, ready for the main event, which was drinking warm beer in Memorial Hall until we passed out, got sick, made fools of ourselves . . . or all of the above. For many of us it was the first time we ever got drunk. Seven of us staggered home after midnight to be greeted by the one roommate who had refused to go to the smoker. He was a debater from New Jersey who made it clear the first day of school that he was not only smarter than all of us, but also holier. He always preached morality to us and swore that he would be a virgin at marriage. He was long and ungainly and appeared, when at ease, to be perching, rather than sitting, a sardonic bird of prey who cackled when he laughed and who read the Holmes/Laski letters for recreation. The one failing he would admit was the possession of a foul hairbrush that had never been cleaned. It sat on his bureau, full of dandruff and old tired brown balls of hair left over from grammar school, high school, and summers near the New Jersey Turnpike.

The night of the smoker he had hand-lettered a long sign, which he stretched across the door for our return. In large block letters it said, "Virtue is its own reward." We pushed through the sign into the room and were greeted by the debater, perched on top of his desk reading aloud from the Book of Psalms. In our subsequent cruelty, we held him down and poured beer on his head. Then we sacrificed his hairbrush, burning it in the fireplace and cheering as the remnants from his adolescent head sizzled and crackled. "Lips that touch liquor will never touch mine," he managed to cry before we stuffed him in the shower.

Does this sound childish? These were mostly public high school boys who had never been away from home. They had been highly motivated and competitive since kindergarten, told by parents and teachers and coaches that they had to be the best, that there were kids all over America breathing down their necks, waiting to take their place if they faltered. Many of my classmates, early in their Harvard careers, had never considered the possibilities of the word "relax." When that evening calmed down, we admitted to one another that we all wanted to write a novel. We agreed on a title, *Twelve Minutes to Park Street,* the words on the sign downstairs in the Harvard Square subway kiosk. We pricked our thumbs with a needle, dripped blood on a paper, signed our names to the agreement that stated that the title *Twelve Minutes to Park Street* belonged to whoever first sold a book to a publisher. F. Scott Fitzgerald had been published at twenty-two. This is the record for which we all were shooting. We scattered after freshman year. That random selection of roommates had been extraordinary. But there had been a level of competition difficult to sustain for four years. It was much easier to wrestle for possession of *Twelve Minutes to Park Street* without looking over one another's shoulders.

Harvard was a self-contained place in those years, socially very selfish and convinced that the real world, for us, would not be very different from our college experience. A boy committed suicide during Christmas vacation freshman year. He lived in the next entry and left behind a note that said, "The line between life and death is very thin." We all wrote that down, hoping to use it in our novels.

There was an innocence in the late 1950s that was not pretended. There were no social issues that galvanized us into protest. There was a draft for which we registered, expecting to serve in a peacetime military. But if we had been threatened with war we would have viewed it hero-ically, from a distance. As an opportunity it was a romantic necessity. Several friends of mine longed for the chance to fight. One of my sophomore roommates was a Haitian, handsome and moody with the soul of a revolutionary. His family went into exile after Papa Doc Duvalier rammed his way to power. My roommate, who was premed, said to me shortly after the school year began, "I shall either be dictator of Haiti by twenty-six. Or dead." He was an incredible dancer, the color of cappucino, and we could never keep control of our dates once they were introduced to him. I said to him one day, "I really like those slippers of yours, Jacques." Immediately he pulled the slippers off his feet and gave them to me.

"You like anything I have, it's yours," he said, adding that he would consider it an insult worthy of a duel if I tried to give the slippers back or refused to accept them. After col-lege he went to medical school in Paris, married a French girl and, in 1963, led a small guerrilla party into the moun-tains of Haiti, hoping for popular support against Duvalier. No one rose to help them, and they were hunted down in the mountains. Jacques was publicly executed in the main square of Port-au-Prince just before his twenty-sixth birth-day.

Another friend had grown up in Holland, took several years off from Harvard to join the Marine Corps, and came back to finish college. He was in my final club, the Owl, a club that had a reputation for attracting gentlemen jocks and whose living-room ceiling sported several cone-shaped electrical covers on the ends of which members had painted in red fingernail polish. They were called The Leeson Me-morial Tits. Pietr, the Dutchman, was short and baby-faced. Frans Hals would have painted him as a laughing choirboy.

Yet Pietr would lead members in black tie after club dinners into Boston's Combat Zone, the red-light district, to provoke fights in bars with the biggest, roughest-looking patrons. He also used to walk alone in Boston Common, purposely courting muggers whom he could then surprise with his fighting skill. Pietr was an expert in unarmed combat and the epitome of a sort of person quite common at Harvard, someone who appeared to be what he was not. At graduation, Pietr tried to interest me in going with him to Manchuria to fight against the Red Chinese. I declined and lost track of him for several years until a club mate called and told me that Pietr, looking for action, had become a correspondent for a French newspaper in Vietnam. He was tortured and executed by the Vietcong in 1965. There has always been a soldier of fortune element at Harvard, a strain of men with a romantic notion of themselves and a romantic notion of life.

The attitudes of eastern establishment prep schools remained important in the Harvard of the Silent Generation. Wholesale admission policy was still the norm for boys from St. Mark's, Milton, Noble and Greenough, Middlesex, Groton, and St. Paul's. There were virtually no Jews in the Hasty Pudding Institute of 1770 or in any of the better final clubs. There was no black visibility in the college at all, save for an occasional boy from Boston Latin who commuted between Roxbury and Harvard Square. If you were black at Harvard in the late 1950s, unless you were the president of Nigeria's son, you kept a low profile, did your work, and moved on quietly to the business of real life.

I remember being fascinated with the preppies, fascinated and delighted to be part of their games, which emphasized, as far as I could tell, two words: pleasure and irresponsibility. I found those two words impossible to resist. Violence and destruction were part of this world—violence and destruction for the sheer hell of it. Several incidents stick in my mind. I was at a house party in Concord with several dozen friends, all final club members from Harvard. The hostess was famous for her parties, for the quality of her

father's booze, and for her ability to round up former debutantes, future Junior Leaguers, who would not be ill-dis-
posed to getting into the back seats of 1958 Chevys. During
the course of the evening, windows were broken, tubs were
stopped up and overflowed on to the dining-room ceiling.
One member of the Porcellian, whose family owned most of
a major midwestern city, pulled the hostess's dress over her
head, tied her hands in that position, and left her in the
kitchen with two maids screeching at the top of their voices.
Several classmates left at 2:00 A.M. with a good portion of the
owner's wine cellar in their cars, including several cases of
hundred-year-old rum, which was used at club dinners all
through the spring. Two male guests spent the night in the
master bedroom's double bed with two Radcliffe sophomores who remembered nothing until the police arrived at
ten the next morning, summoned by the maids.

Another young man who staggered out of the party alone,
fell asleep at the wheel. Still in Concord, he awoke just in
time to avoid a telephone pole, parked his car, and broke into
the house nearest the pole. He lay down on the living-room
couch and went to sleep for the rest of the night. He had
written a note that he pinned to his chest. "Do not worry,"
the note said. "I am a drunken Harvard student, not a thief."
He too was awakened by the police, specifically a very
annoyed sergeant who held a Smith & Wesson .38 special
against the side of the student's sleepy nose. Is this story a
caution to parents against sending their boys to Harvard? Is
it an argument against the education of an economically
spoiled elite? It was social Harvard at the end of the
Eisenhower era, a time of the famous Fernanda Wetherill
coming-out party on Long Island where a mansion was
destroyed by college students. *Life* magazine printed pictures of that party, black-tied students swinging from chan-
deliers, champagne bottles crashing through windows. De-
structive behavior was the norm in those circles in those
days. There was status to be achieved by tossing what was
called "the biggest horror show." Social exhibitionism was

an area of competition. Who could be most outrageous? It was creative antisocial behavior in the context of the most congenial setting.

There were a lot of pants-droppers; one of my friends with this habit called himself "an *exposeur* of the first water." He was part of the Beat Generation at Harvard—aspiring poets, playwrights, and novelists who believed that Kerouac's *On the Road* was a masterpiece and that Ginsberg and Lawrence Ferlinghetti possessed the true secrets of modern poetry. My friend was tall and bearded, and his grunts passed as brilliant sentences among his set. Every night at about 1:30 A.M. he and his fellow beatniks would wander into an all-night cafeteria, one of several around Harvard Square. My friend would be wearing a raincoat and high-topped Converse All-Star basketball sneakers. And that's all. After he finished his English muffins, he would doff his raincoat, saunter to the counter, and ask for some "very merry huckleberry Jell-O." By the time the aged counterman could summon the police, the followers of Kerouac would be gone. One of my roommates, now a respected international lawyer in New York, would expose himself at cocktail parties, at dances, on blind dates, pretending total innocence, as if he had just returned from the men's room and had forgotten to zip up. I watched him one night in the bar of the Hasty Pudding, sitting with a group of clubbies and their dates. My roommate was drinking gin and tonic, holding forth on the male bonding themes of Hemingway, with his member resting on the round cocktail table in front of him, right alongside a bowl of peanuts. Everyone pretended not to notice. But the scene, in freeze frame, remains one of the most vivid recollections of my undergraduate career. Another of my classmates, nicknamed "the Beast" spent one entire year muttering only two phrases: "Every night is New Year's Eve," and "Tonight, *everything* goes." I saw the Beast remove an upholstered armchair one night from the senior common room in Lowell House, carry it over his head to Storrow Drive, and sit down on the chair. From this sitting position, he directed traffic with one hand while the other brought a bottle of Early Times frequently to his lips. Of course, the Beast was drunk, but he was also convinced that no ill could befall him. This feeling of invincibility as an undergraduate is not unique to Harvard; it is unique to youth. But we had a certainty that this was only the beginning of triumphs, that, like Prince Hal in *Henry the Fourth,* we would leave our roistering behind us and move on to accomplishments that were serious, far-reaching and special.

The annual Pudding show tour was, for me, the proof that life would indeed follow art. My senior year I sang Rodgers and Hart's *Love for Sale* in the auditions and was rewarded with one of the female leads, the Duchess of Wopping, modeled extremely loosely on Wallis Simpson. Erich Segal had written my junior year show, *The Big Fizz,* whose heroine, Bernadine Burpez, I always liked much more than Jenny, his heroine in *Love Story.* Joe Raposo wrote the music for that show. He later wrote the music for "Sesame Street" and several ballads for Frank Sinatra. If you starred in a Pudding show, you had no doubt success in the real world of show business would follow as a matter of course. How could Hollywood or Broadway be immune to the talents that had thrilled Cambridge, Massachusetts? The show ran in Cambridge for ten nights. It was staged, directed, and costumed by hired professionals and acted by exhibitionists of varying talent who appreciated good mugging if not good theater and who, above all else, appreciated parties and the thesis that life was a free ride. Indeed it *was* a free ride. After the first few nights, several members of the cast would invariably perform drunk. One male lead, a member of the A.D. club, who now paints in London and wears a gold earring in his left ear, chased a makeup lady from Radcliffe all around the dressing room before a performance, threatening to "bugger her good, what she deserves" and emitting high-pitched cawing noises like a crazed, randy crow. Often we had cast parties in the lounge upstairs after the show. One night I remember leading a kick line on top of the upright piano, assisted by three ladies from local junior colleges. I lost my balance on the chorus of "The Lady Is a Tramp" and pitched head first through a drum. The drummer fell on me for destroying his property and had to be pulled off by several pals. The slush fund paid for a new drum, and I was oblivious to the fall and the pummeling of the drummer.

When we didn't have cast parties we would all retire to the bar of the Casa Blanca, the Casa B, downstairs from the Brattle Theater. The word "gay" had not been invented in 1959. Neither had the term "black," applied as it is today. The only consciousness most of us had of homosexual presence was the graffiti on the backs of doors in the stalls of the men's rooms in Lamont Library. But all of us who played women in the Pudding show received notes on a nightly basis from a certain element in the audience. It was shocking at the time, and I mention it only because the seats along one end of the bar at the Casa B were considered the homosexual seats, even then. The Casa B was our Dôme, our Select Café. We had our cast recordings on the jukebox. We had our special bartenders. Each night we took over the bar and closed it, drinking stingers on the rocks, enough to ensure either sickness or the whirlybeds, and often both.

The show went on tour after the Cambridge run, to exotic places: New York City, Vassar College, Smith, Washington, D.C., New Canaan, Connecticut, Providence. We were put up in the best homes and apartments wherever we visited. Alumni opened their houses to us, their bars, gave us parties, introduced us to their daughters. I can recall going to a bash in Washington and being driven late at night in a government limousine out to the country. There are times in life when you awake somewhere not having any idea where you are or why you are there. I awoke at a farm in McLean, Virginia, and was served breakfast on a terrace with warm spring shining on my scrambled eggs with bacon and people on horses riding by, intent on the morning and the green fields. On that same tour, driving from Washington back to New York were four other cast members. We stopped at a phone booth on the New Jersey Turnpike. One of our friends called his father in the city about theater tickets for that night. We left the car near Broadway with minutes to spare before the curtain went up on *West Side Story,* which was doing standing-room-only business. We had fourth-row-center seats for the musical smash of the year, and the event remains one of the biggest thrills of my life. My friend's daddy naturally picked up the tab.

I pay for my pleasant surprises now, a reality that took me almost five years after Harvard to accept as a condition that would persist.

If there was a negative element to the Pudding tour, it was an event that produced a quotation I carry with me to this day.

While doing a show at Vassar, we were given a house to ourselves in Woodstock, New York, not yet a symbol of the sixties generation. The house belonged to my friend, Rupert, the ingenue in the cast. His parents gave us the key, a full liquor cabinet, a refrigerator bursting with goodies. There were three of us from the show and three Vassar girls, blind dates for whom we had high hopes. In those days, any women who would spend the night in an unchaperoned house were unusual. In the first five minutes alone in the house I asked my date what she wanted to drink.

"Scotch," she replied.

"Any Scotch?" I asked my friend Rupert.

He pushed bottles around the bar and said, "Nope, all we have is bourbon."

"All we have is bourbon," I told my Vassar date.

"Sorry," she said to me, picking up an old *Vogue* from a coffee table and flipping through it, "I *never* drink bourbon. But when I do, I *only* drink Jack Daniels." I think of that story whenever I enter a situation where everything on the surface seems perfect. And I also think of another Harvard moment whenever I need to put things into perspective.

The *Lampoon,* make no mistake, was a club. Precious and self-satisfied in its humor, the society of its members recalled the days of George Apley and the Gold Coast, with a suggestion also that perhaps comedy was queen. While a candidate for the *Lampoon,* you were allowed into the Flemish castle donated by William Randolph Hearst, for meetings, but only in that section of the building to the left of the Bow Street door. If you ventured into the forbidden parts you were automatically expelled from the competition. If you were elected to the magazine, you underwent an initiation night that preceded Fools' Week, five days of hazing and pranks, like chaining together the gates of the Yard or loosing pigeons in the main reading room of Widener. All of us were given fools' names, rhymed whimsy that we had to repeat whenever asked. My fool's name went this way:

> My name, sir, is, sir, Fool John.
> When I lean back my head and open my mouth,
> I can encompass an ass with my sterilized lips.
> Pull my ear harder and I flush sooner, Spooner.
> I am an utter, utter, fool, sir. And am in a
> state of the most abject terror, sir!

I think of my fool's name whenever events threaten to get too serious. The Silent Generation is still good at retreating into the fantasies fostered by Harvard.

Jonathan Z. Larsen '61

Jonathan Z. Larsen was born in 1940. He received his A.B. from Harvard College in 1961, and a Master of Arts in Teaching from the Harvard Graduate School of Education in 1963. For the next ten years he worked at Time *magazine, variously as a New York editor, a Hollywood correspondent, and a Saigon bureau chief. He left* Time *in 1973 and a year later became editor of* New Times, *a biweekly feature news magazine that had just started publishing. When* New Times *folded in early 1979, he returned to Harvard as a Nieman Fellow. Larsen and his wife now live in New York City, where he is news editor of* Life *magazine.*

In the first two weeks of January 1940, my father, then the president of *Time* Incorporated, made the news twice. First, in a Walter Winchell radio item about the birth of his third son and fourth child—myself—and second in a *New York Times* article announcing Roy E. Larsen as a candidate for the Harvard Board of Overseers. It is hard to guess which event gave my father greater joy, the birth or the nomination. Suffice it to say that from the moment I was born I was not just the son of another Harvard alumnus, but the son of a man who would remain passionately involved with his alma mater throughout his life. The day before he died unexpectedly in the fall of 1979, my wife and I stopped off at my parents' home in Fairfield, Connecticut, on our way to Cambridge, where I was to begin a Nieman Fellowship. From his sickbed, he shared a small joke with me—"Don't forget, Harvard is not as hard as it seems"—and then showed me a letter he had just received from Harvard's president, Derek Bok, inquiring after his health. The letter had clearly touched him, and he returned it to its honored place on his night table, along with his medicines.

As far back as I can remember, the word Harvard had been in the air. My parents made pilgrimages to Cambridge for Harvard–Yale games and reunions and often took us with them. I vividly remember, at age thirteen, watching my father step up to receive his honorary LL.D from James Bryant Conant. The magnetic field set up by this reverence was almost irresistible. Though my sister went to Sarah Lawrence and recalls that she never considered Radcliffe ("I wasn't the type"), my two older brothers and I followed in my father's footsteps as surely as circus elephants follow one another, trunk in tail, into the Big Top. Of the four of us, I was perhaps the child least likely to break ranks, as events would prove: I went on from Harvard College to the Harvard Graduate School of Education, a special interest of my father's that is today marked by a brick monolith in his name, and finally into Time Inc. itself.

Harvard, in short, seemed to be swirled into the pattern of my thumbprint. The only question was how well I would fare there. Ranked thirtieth out of seventy-six in my graduating class at Hotchkiss School, I was a diligent but mediocre student who had little faith in myself and not much more in others. And though I had enjoyed all the trappings of a quintessential preppy—governesses, summer homes, Topsider moccasins—I had never much enjoyed the company of children as privileged as myself. Barely five feet tall when I reached Hotchkiss at the age of thirteen and still not fully grown when I left, I had come to dislike competitive sports and almost everyone who was good at them. In the view of my teachers at Hotchkiss, I was simply retiring and unhappy. But in the view of my classmates, I was no doubt something of a prude, perhaps even a "wimp."

Over my four years at Hotchkiss, I had increasingly come to find its conformity and insularity suffocating. I could not dispel my vague sense that there was a more interesting, unbuttoned world beyond the dress shirt counters at Brooks Brothers and the tidy moorings of the Nantucket Yacht Club. And it was into this new world that I was eager to cast myself at Harvard. When it came time to fill out my application for freshman roommates, I wrote in a large, almost desperate scrawl: "Private or public school, anywhere in the U.S.A. Sincere, hard working."

If my intention was to rub elbows with the great un-washed, I succeeded in a way I had never intended. The first person to welcome me to Harvard, one of my two room-mates, turned out to be literally that—unwashed. A hunched-over adolescent of 6 feet 8 inches and 240 pounds, Bill (for so I shall call him) compounded his sheer mass with his clumsiness, thoughtlessness, and grossness. In the ten months that I knew him, I do not remember his taking more than a dozen showers or making more than half a dozen trips to the laundry. He broke almost every piece of furniture in the apartment, played on his dulcimers and guitars throughout the day, and incessantly smoked one or another of his collection of thirty pipes. I dreaded the morning when he would strop his straight razor to shave, because I knew it would send blood streaming down his well-pimpled cheeks, and I rejoiced when he left for his afternoon visit to the Leavitt & Pierce pipe store, because I knew he would spend at least an hour there, sniffing and smoking and mixing the various brands of tobacco.

I would like to be able to report that I suffered my new roommate gladly, but it would be a lie. His squalor and childishness, in fact, drove me to cruelties that often ex-ceeded his offenses. I would taunt him by asking him if he could smell something strange in the room, and then I would announce that the smell was getting weaker or stronger, depending on whether I was moving away from or toward his clothes closet (his habit was to keep all his laundry in one huge pile, which he would pick through each morning to find his "fresh" clothes for the day). Once or twice, I actually chased him about the room with a can of aerosol room freshener, spraying the very clothes on his back.

In the middle of this endless comedy was my other room-mate, Robert Fichter, a brilliant graduate of Lawrenceville who had spent a year at Oxford and seemed infinitely more worldly and wise than the rest of us. Fichter had as little use for my cruelties as he had for the squalidness of our very own Elephant Man, but he kept his tongue and even managed to maintain a modicum of order in the room. As the year progressed, he became a tutor and counselor to me, imparting at least a fraction of his own reverence for novels and classical music (hitherto, my musical scale had run from the Everly Brothers to Richard Rodgers).

Beyond the doors of Straus Hall, I found the universe of Harvard equally curious and exhilarating. Almost from the moment I passed through its huge wrought-iron gates, the qualities I most appreciated about Harvard were those that many of my classmates would come to lament: the college's enormity, its impersonality, its no-one-is-looking-after-you atmosphere. Here, at last, was a place I could get lost in. The world I had known at Hotchkiss was suddenly stood on its head: the eggheads and the oddballs had achieved parity with, if not superiority to, the jocks. For those of us who did not know, and did not care, who was supposed to take the relay from center field or how many years Ted Williams batted over .300, it was an enormous relief to discover that there were other terms on which one could be judged.

I now found myself not only stimulated but even intimidated by my new friends. Many of them were the sons of lawyers, doctors, educators, and diplomats and had grown up in highly charged intellectual environments. If they were not Merit Scholars, they were actors, musicians, or debaters of some accomplishment. And though my own parents had mixed with the great and famous in the world of arts and letters, little of this glitter had rubbed off on me. Few of their more celebrated friends made it back to our farm in Connecticut's fox-hunting country, and my father himself came home only on weekends. Before I was packed off to boarding school, I had spent most of my time in the kitchen with the Irish help. These gentle women had shared much with me—their humor, morality, and compassion—but they had not made it past grade school, so I in turn could hardly go to school on them. I learned only of County Cork and a few little ditties ("What's for dinner tonight, Nora? . . . Bees' knees and onions, turkeys' lips and chickens' hips"). Now, for the first time, I sat down to dinner fare that consisted of jazz, foreign affairs, socialism, health care, seasoned with words like "entropy" and "triage."

Gradually I realized that I was learning more from my classmates than from my classes. What I learned that year in Social Relations 10 ("childhood development," "behavior disorders") seemed nothing compared with what my friends told me about their own lives and families. Every day brought exposure to someone from a different culture, race, or religion, and every week began new friendships between people as different as God or Darwin could make them. There were, of course, limits to Harvard's melting pot and times when these new friendships would be sorely tested, as I was to discover early on.

Two of my closest friends freshman year were John Hancock and Joel Henning, all but inseparable drama students from the Midwest. Hancock, from La Porte, Indiana, would go on to direct plays on Broadway, and later movies in Hollywood, where he helped launch the careers of Michael Moriarty and Robert De Niro in a minor film classic called *Bang the Drum Slowly*. Henning, from Evanston, Illinois, would become president of the Harvard Dramatic Club, receive raves as Napoleon in Shaw's *Man of Destiny*, and go on to Harvard Law School. But at the moment they were just very bright, witty companions, as interested in their new preppy friend as I was in them. The three of us were given to roaming the streets of Boston that fall, ostensibly looking to pick up some stray ladies of the night, while in fact never wrapping our hands around anything warmer than a flat beer. On one such night, Henning and Hancock convinced me that I should invite them to my parents' Connecticut home for the Harvard–Yale game in nearby New Haven. They had heard about my parents and the rambling colonial mansion I lived in, and now they wanted to see for themselves how the captains of industry really lived.

Suddenly, there we were on my family's doorstep, a sight for sore eyes: Hancock, in preparation for a dramatic role, had not shaved for two weeks and looked as if he had just escaped from Alcatraz. Henning, as short and dark-complexioned as Hancock was tall and pale, no doubt looked equally suspicious as his sidekick. And I myself, pea green from premonitions of the impending disaster, looked for all the world like a kidnapped son being presented at gunpoint for ransom. Had I had any aplomb, I might have been able to put both my new friends and my family at ease, but it was not to be.

The house was full of my siblings' friends, all older and dressed in club ties, blazers, plaid skirts, and knee socks, swapping tales from the gridiron and the nursery. And in walk the three stooges in new campus proletariat garb, our tongues tied and our heads recently crammed full of Freud, Brecht, Marx, and God knows who else. My sister, trying to be friendly, kept offering Hancock a razor, refusing to believe his story about an upcoming role. My father gamely asked if Hancock was possibly related to the fellow who had signed the Declaration of Independence, and when he found out not, ran out of follow-up questions. My mother said almost nothing, neither then nor the next morning at breakfast, as we sat around our long dining-room table with both extensions in place. We chased down some hot coffee, climbed back into my Volkswagen, and crunched down the long gravel driveway, past my father's one-hole golf course, in silence.

If this startling glimpse into the future—the inevitable collision between my new, easily won ideals and the eternal verities of family, genes, and culture—produced occasional melancholy, it was nothing compared with the periodic depressions caused by another reality of those years: sex. It is arguable whether students of the late 1950s, repressed and sexually segregated, were more preoccupied with sex than today's students, supposedly liberated and undeniably sexually integrated. But sex was, in any case, a shadow that followed us everywhere—sex irrevocably confused with romance. Though the notion of women living in the freshman dorms and houses had not even been conceived, let alone suggested, there were plenty of attractive Radcliffe students in our classes to remind us of what was just beyond our reach.

Tantalus himself never had it so bad. The sound of two silk stockings crossing could obliterate the message of an entire lecture or drop one down a bottomless well of longing and self-pity. A brief glimpse of thighs silhouetted through a thin summer dress could provide the excuse if not the trigger for an all-night session with the bottle. Melancholia became not only a fashion but an art. The pain of our frustration was almost sublime, balanced as so many of us were on the razor's edge between boyhood and manhood, our desires and our bodies having long since surpassed our experience and opportunities and overwhelmed our reason. My only extended affair during those early years was strictly a platonic one and took place in the unlikeliest possible place: a pin bowling alley in the subterranean depths underneath the Wursthaus. There, almost every other day, Fichter and I would meet my Radcliffe inamorata and her friends to bowl away the afternoon, laughing, talking, flirting. It was an impossible match, my Radcliffe friend and myself, for she was far too bright and witty for me, and I was far too earnest and interested for her.

I exorcised my frustrations through athletics. By my sophomore year I had grown a few more inches and metamorphosed from a 140-pound weakling into a 160-pound health faddist. Now that I no longer felt in a competitive environment, I took up team sports, playing guard for the Lowell House football team, entering the occasional house swimming meet, or substituting in a game of house baseball. During the spring, I sailed for the Harvard team on the Charles River, and on winter weekends skied with my friends in Vermont and New Hampshire. In between, when I wasn't dabbling in squash, I would jog with Fichter down to the Mount Auburn Cemetery, take a lap around Mary Baker Eddy's tomb, and jog home. In those days, joggers were considered either a nuisance or a tourist attraction. I was once running along the Charles with another friend, Jonathan Sedgwick, when an old lady came into our path, stopped us, and asked if she could feel Sedgwick's rather large calf muscle (he said yes).

All this frenetic physical activity was paralleled by a new social life. My sophomore year I joined both the theatrical Hasty Pudding Club and a social club—I chose the Fly only after attending the final dinner at the Spee Club. Over the next two years, I spent a fair amount of time shooting pool and watching hairy-legged men dancing about as women at the Pudding, and eating lunch off tablecloths, playing all-night poker games, and attending garden parties at the Fly. At first, I was delighted to be taken into this international world of Latin American aristocrats, jaded Europeans, and what we liked to think of as the pick of the American students. I made some lasting friendships within the closed world of the Fly Club and passed some enjoyable nights puffing cigars, sniffing brandy, and laughing at the sort of jokes that get politicians kicked out of office. The problem was, I felt *too* comfortable. By my senior year, I realized that I had retreated from the heady egalitarianism of my freshman year and taken refuge among the monogrammed glassware and bound volumes of the final club system. I was a preppy recidivist.

What finally hurried me out the door had as much to do with taste as principle. It turned out that one of the Fly's Europeans, one of the richer and more infamous students at the College, had decided to play Pygmalion to a young, naive varsity swimmer from the Midwest. Almost every time I ventured into the club library, the scene would be the same: the European coaching the swimmer in some detail of history or gossip or simply gazing at him as he diligently read his course work. At best, the relationship seemed ambiguous, a page out of Henry James in which the more sophisticated European toys with and dominates an innocent American. At worst, it looked like a homosexual affair trying to come out of the closet that the culture was not yet ready to open. Whatever it was, it gave me that final push. During most of my senior year, I walked by the Fly Club on my way to Lowell House with barely a look.

There was another brick institution not far from Lowell House and the Fly that I managed to pass up altogether— *The Harvard Crimson*. Though it may sound strange for someone who became a journalist to admit, I never thought of working at the *Crimson* and seldom read it while at Harvard. University news did not interest me, and there were far better sources of information about the rest of the world. Instead, I joined the *Harvard Advocate* on its business side. I remember through the long tunnel of memory the difficulty of selling space in the *Advocate* to the local shops and restaurants of Cambridge—my first experience of what a precarious business magazine publishing can be. But the work was worth it, if only because it gave me a ringside seat for the illustrious authors and poets the *Advocate* would trot out in order to raise funds. Fichter was then on the editorial side of the *Advocate* and was soon to become its editor. Among his duties was the job of squiring our honored guests on to the stage of Sanders Theater. Or perhaps "pouring" is a more exact word, because, at least in the case of W. H. Auden, the job required an entire tumbler full of vodka, carefully disguised as drinking water (that is, Auden gulped it as one would gulp water).

Our surprise was not the amount of alcohol, but the notion that one could perform in spite of it. Social drinking had long since become a habit for us; drinking on the job was a new frontier. In those days, we all had fake IDs and seemed to be able to get as much liquor as we wanted, one way or another. Occasionally I would get so drunk that I would—for the amusement of whoever was around—eat glass. Not jelly-jar glass, mind you, but only the best crystal. I cannot honestly say whether I was after the attention of it or the danger of it, but in either case it became something of a habit. There were also less public displays that were equally self-destructive—hitting stop signs with my bare fists, for instance. I remember borrowing someone's motor scooter one night and running out of gas. In my drunken state, I opened the gas tank, struck a match, and then peered into the darkness with the light from it. Why I was not blown sky high I'll never know.

But these were just the moments of excess and depravity that were marbled through an otherwise somber and unexciting college career. Most free nights my sophomore and junior years found me over a cup of coffee and a baked apple at the Hayes Bickford or Waldorf cafeterias, talking with friends, or sitting in a front-row seat at a coffee house called 47 Mt. Auburn St. Club, listening to an undiscovered talent named Joan Baez. Baez was then singing traditional folk music, but with an emotional intensity that gave it a contemporary spin. She seemed to be feeling a pain she could not identify. Indeed, Baez and her music symbolized a growing but still unfocused sense of alienation many of us shared. Two years after we graduated she would startle a concert audience of fourteen thousand by sharing her stage with a new singer-songwriter, explaining, "Bobby Dylan says what a lot of people my age feel but cannot say."

What we were feeling, and trying to put into words ourselves during all-night bull sessions, was a case of existential malaise, a disillusionment with the whitewashed world of Norman Rockwell, in which one's social responsibility seemed to extend no further than the swath of one's power mower. This is not to suggest that "the sixties" had begun in 1960 or 1961. Certainly not. We were still politically and culturally naive. Black coffee was, for the most part, still the drug of choice, and our understanding of equality was that all Harvard men had to eat the same institutional food from the same central kitchen. Nevertheless, when the so-called counterrevolution broke later in the decade, it built largely on the establishment infrastructure that our generation represented. Men and women my age not only led the political awakening at the top but became its most outspoken apologists and interpreters in the media and at large. And many of us would remain loyal to those new ideals long after most of the college juniors and seniors who had taken over deans' offices across the country had renounced their own movement.

The Brattle Theater and the other art houses became the pulpits from which we took our sermons. The Sturm und Drang of Bergman and the biting social satire of Fellini—particularly in *La Dolce Vita*—matched our own dark vision. But as bad as we believed things were, we were still idealists and patriots through and through. When, halfway through our senior year, John F. Kennedy kicked off his administration with the words, "Ask not what your country can do for you, but what you can do for your country," some of us, at least, thought we had had a revelation. (It would be years before we discovered that JFK stole that line from his boarding school headmaster—"Ask not what Choate can do for you . . ."—or that the service we were being asked to perform was to save the Vietnamese people from their own nationalism.)

None of these issues, of course, seeped into the lecture halls or seminar rooms, at least not into mine. From the beginning of my freshman year I had decided that a curriculum of reading novels in my own language would constitute the shortest distance between the top of my head and a mortarboard with tassel. My goal, quite simply, was survival. Along the way, I sampled side orders of philosophy, sociology, fine arts. I did not realize it fully then, but courses I had chosen represented almost a mockery of a "general education." I had taken no history, ancient or modern, no economics, micro or macro. I had learned next to nothing about government or political philosophy. And even in my own field, English literature, I had left holes big enough to fall through. One of my tutors was to note for the file that, though I had some understanding of the novel, "Poetry and drama are still untrodden pastures for him. Nor does he seem to have any clear-cut critical method in approaching anything. He's a charming, sophisticated person, elegance his substitute for masterfulness." Another tutor, writing in the more concise style of Hemingway, put it thus: "Larsen is friendly and open and has a great deal of good sense and humor. I like him very much as a person. As a student of English he is quite dull."

I am afraid these harsh judgments were warranted. The only course that had truly inspired me during my first three years was B. J. Whiting's Chaucer. As for the rest, it passed through like so much Chinese food. It was not until my senior year that I moved to the edge of my seat and up from the back row. The reason was Richard Poirier, one of the "new critics" who believed in getting to know authors through a close reading of their words rather than through an autobiographical approach in which the books themselves were almost secondary. Poirier's course on Joyce, Lawrence, and Faulkner was the best experience I had at Harvard University.

As average as my grades were, I discovered halfway through my senior year that they were just good enough to allow me to graduate cum laude—if I wrote an acceptable thesis. With not much time left and with no topics at the top of my head, I turned once again to my guru, Robert Fichter. What should I write on? Without a moment's hesitation, he said, "Animal imagery in D. H. Lawrence."

"Done," said I. In two weeks I had read enough of Lawrence to begin writing. In another week and a half I had a finished thesis. Those who blessed it with an honors grade noted in the margin that I appeared to have been slightly overwhelmed by my extensive research.

The discovery of Poirier and the new criticism and the prospect of graduating cum laude were not the sum total of my blessings that year. I had also managed a Laurentian love affair. The morphology of older Harvard student–younger Radcliffe student had finally worked in my favor. Now instead of coping with the endless frustrations of sexless friendships, I experienced the far happier anxieties of a campus romance during those neo-Victorian years. Everything seemed arrayed against such an affair: parents, Harvard and Radcliffe parietal hours, steely eyed motel clerks. Once we drove hundreds of miles just to find any empty bed in my parents' empty house. But these obstacles simply heightened the intensity of the affair, as did our own tears, confessions, betrayals, and absolutions.

Indeed, everything seemed to be coming up magnolias and tulips during the spring of 1961, except, of course, plans for the future. Along with most of my friends, I took the Harvard Law School aptitude tests to see if that avenue was open. It wasn't, and perhaps that was for the best. Several of my classmates did so well on the tests that they immediately decided to enter law school, whether or not they belonged there. John Casey, a friend and classmate from Washington, D.C., sat through three years of law courses before he realized he'd rather write for a living. Years later, he delivered *An American Romance* and *Testimony and Demeanor* to high critical acclaim.

In any case, by the time I lined up to receive my diploma—ours was the first class to have diplomas written in English rather than Latin—I had nothing planned other than a sailing trip through Scandinavia on a twenty-five-foot Folk boat. After that, I assumed I would simply stand up to the great crap table of life and try my luck. Harvard had given me a measure of confidence, lasting friendships, and a thorough knowledge of what I had yet to learn. My four years had been unspectacular but very enjoyable, which was exactly what my freshman tutor had predicted for me. Recently, while thumbing through my college file for the purposes of this memoir, I came upon this prescient report, written back in May 1958: "Mr. Larsen should do average, perhaps better than average, work at Harvard. He is noncommittal, and does not reveal much of himself during counseling. He will in all probability have a smooth, enjoyable college career."

My view of my college years has only grown more sanguine as the years march by. I have some regrets about squandered opportunities at Harvard, similar to regrets I have about the years that followed, but they are minor. I have never second-guessed myself about Harvard itself or about the people I spent my time with. There has been only one occasion when I wished I had gone to, say, Williams. At the very beginning of 1979, *New Times,* a magazine I had been editing, folded, and I threw a hasty lifeline to the Nieman Foundation. And in the four months between application and acceptance, I grew very anxious. Several people I spoke to thought I would not get the fellowship, solely because I had gone to Harvard. The point of a Nieman, they told me, was to give a Harvard education to those unfortunates who had not had one. Oz Elliott, a Harvard and Fly Club alumnus, had once served on a committee to review the Nieman program. He told me that my chances were slim. Even my mother called with the bad news. Do not be too disappointed, she told me, but your father has heard that you will probably not get the Nieman. Finally, during a personal interview at the Faculty Club, this ugly prejudice surfaced. Why, my inquisitors wanted to know, did I want to return to Harvard, when there were other fellowships for journalists at universities like Stanford? Clutching my glass of orange juice—this was early in the morning and I had been drinking retsina wine not many hours before with my wife's family—I summoned up the proper amount of indignation and replied, "I want to come back here because I like it here. The Nieman is the best fellowship, and Harvard is the best university. And I hope the day has not arrived when a Harvard degree is considered a liability."

Andrew Holleran '65

Andrew Holleran is the pseudonym of a member of the class of 1965. He is a writer whose first novel, Dancer from the Dance, *appeared in 1978. He is a graduate of the Iowa Writers' Workshop, served in the army, and attended law school before turning to writing full time. He lives in Manhattan.*

Graduation from Harvard College in 1965 left me so depressed, that I went to bed and stayed there, speechless, for three days. Meals were brought. No one asked a question, a tact for which I was grateful then and admire now. I read the poem by Walt Whitman in which the bird has lost its mate ("O past! O happy life! O songs of joy!") and inscribed in the margin beside certain passages the date on which I felt I was finished with life. What could the world possibly offer after Harvard? It would never again be so civilized, so charming. Cambridge was what the father of a freshman roommate (just back from New Delhi on the business of a famous foundation) said with a sigh in the cab as we drove downtown the night he took us to dinner at Locke Ober: "What an *oasis* this place is!" I remember thinking that if *he* considered it one—a well-traveled New Yorker with an enviable career—then the world outside these shaded courtyards must be just as grim as I suspected.

Six months after my going to bed on graduation day, I stood in a rented room in Iowa City, reading with an open mouth a letter from a classmate who was now at Stanford and who wrote to say how superior the West Coast was to the East—and (blasphemy of blasphemies) how miserable he

had been at Harvard! What was more startling, I knew just
what he meant. "What a relief," he said, "to get out of that
neurotic atmosphere! Those dreary, ambitious, critical people and their monotonous irony! Those conversations in
which no one cared about the truth, but only wanted to score
a victory, the sarcasm, the coldness! I know having gone to
Harvard is supposedly a great privilege, but I was miserable
virtually my entire time there."

And five years after reading this letter, I decided while
walking home to my first apartment in New York that it
would have been far better for me to have never gone to
college, to have come straight to Manhattan and *lived*. This
opinion was just as fervent as the sadness of the senior who
loved Harvard (or feared the world) more than anything else
in life on graduation day.

It is hard to admit one was unhappy at Harvard—for it
was, to middle-class minds in 1962, the highest honor one
could earn before the age of twenty-one. "You are," the dean
of admissions assured us wittily at our first meeting in
Sanders Theater, "the greatest freshman class in the history
of civilization." We laughed, with the pride and released
tension of years of examinations, but wasn't it true? We
could die now, child martyrs, and it would be all right—we
would go straight to Heaven. We were Harvard undergraduates, members of a long and illustrious army. Harvard itself
was almost beside the point: getting in, having gone, were
the prodigious things. We took our fate so seriously that by
Christmas break, half the freshmen considered it tasteless
to reveal where they went to school; if asked, they said,
"Boston." Years later I encountered this bizarre form of good
taste as a joke in a Broadway play, where the students at a
girls' college, looking out the window at the autos parked
before their dormitory, recognize the Harvard men's cars
because they're the ones without any stickers.

So when I read my classmate's letter that night in Iowa
City, it seemed blasphemous—and at the same time liberat-
ing—for what he said was true: as much as the world hon-

ored Harvard College, I'd been miserable, too, a lot of the time there. If this conclusion seems a mean one, it was hardly the fault of the place; it was the fault of adolescence; and since my recollection of those years is a purely personal one—that is, I took part in no public, historical events—perhaps it has its own small weight.

I remember driving along the Charles River with my parents (their presence adding an emotional nervousness to the ordeal) the day of my arrival at Harvard with the euphoria of a knight approaching Camelot. By the time I entered my room in Matthews Hall, I was beside myself: I jumped up on the window seat, threw my arms out to the ivy-covered windowpanes, and said, "It's *just* what I imagined it would be! It's wonderful!" One roommate, a modest, sober graduate of Choate, rose from the desk at which he had been writing, aghast. As it turned out, he took the prospect of life at Harvard more calmly than the rest of us: he was a young man preoccupied with his parents' divorce, who applied himself—realizing he was no scholar—to off-campus jobs, and eventually became an office manager before going on to law school. Our third roommate was an extremely sarcastic Mexican (of Swiss and American parents) who intimidated me with the high moral dudgeon of socialism whenever he could and who, flapping his arms at lunch, decimated my faint arguments about world politics—with facts, I learned later, that were gleaned not from any monumental erudition, but from the latest issue of *The New Republic*.

I came to Harvard with the small margin of confidence bestowed by three years at a private boarding school in New England, but so did my roommates freshman year, and because they were nervier than I, they played Mrs. Danvers to my Joan Fontaine. I was in shock, anyway. One's first impression at Harvard is breathtaking: you are no longer the smartest kid in your class. *Everyone* is the smartest kid in his class. But even worse, I saw that life was more than taking copious notes at Professor Bailyn's lectures on colonial America; it was finding a friend to eat with at those long tables in the Freshman Union. I was very shy—sexually, emotionally, and intellectually ignorant of myself—and since I hadn't even decided on a personality, I became friends with people so contradictory they could not have been in the same room together.

At Christmas of my sophomore year at a lunch of the Harvard Club of Jacksonville, Florida, we students were asked to speak. I remarked that the variety of architecture at Harvard was matched only by the heterogeneity of the student body. This comment, to my surprise, drew laughter— and I think now it was because everyone who went to Harvard was impressed by the exotic aspect of his classmates. I had among my friends a graduate of Andover who summered in Maine, the son of a postmaster from the Bronx, an Oregon wheat farmer, a recluse from Vermont who spent his evenings listening to Bea Lillie records while smoking Gitanes, a scholarship student from Corsicana, Texas, a fellow from the upper East Side of Manhattan, the son of an English teacher, and the son of a famous cosmetics tycoon. I knew boys in yellow pants and tasseled loafers who belonged to clubs and mousy boys who lived in Lamont Library, working like drudges to get into law school, boys whose complexions were explicable only by fluorescent light. I liked people who considered effort tasteless and those who thought it their only hope.

I inevitably took from these classmates a style (whether a style of dress or wit or, more profoundly, character I am not sure) that was seldom what I'd dreamed it was: the boys I thought most stylish were cold and, gathered together at a cocktail party for aspirants to the *Lampoon,* so intimidated me that I slunk back to my attic room in Lowell House and waited for the inevitable rejection to be slipped beneath the door. The fellows at the *Crimson* were even worse. Everyone seemed self-assured, serious, and opinionated. The Master's teas, despite the best efforts of all, were as relaxed as a Noh play, and I went only out of a desire to learn composure, amused to hear, under the murmur of conversation, my roommate's cup rattling against the saucer in his trembling hand. (Everyone ignored it.) I remember telling my roommate sophomore year that Mozart had no melody. (And, because I was given advanced placement, I was allowed to skip those introductory courses in Greek thought that I realize now were what I'd have loved most. The advanced-placement decision once caused a teacher, on learning I planned to spend only three years at Harvard, to smile at me and say with a mischievous delicacy: "Ah. A young man in a hurry." For I left Harvard having read obscure novels of Charles Brockden Brown but not the *Iliad*.) My Mexican roommate told me American literature, my field of concentration, was inferior to European, and though I argued back, my response was merely patriotic. My tutor junior year accused me of being "feckless," and I had to go home and look the word up. He was right, of course: never was my ego so battered as it was at Harvard. I maintained in the face of another tutor's blinking frown that Henry Adams's wife committed hara-kiri. (My roommate had told me so at lunch.) My tutor did not even bother to correct me, embarrassed and appalled at my junky mind. (In fact Mrs. Adams drank chemicals from a photographic darkroom.) When we discovered our error, my roommate fell off his chair laughing over the gaffe I had committed that afternoon.

What does the ego do in circumstances such as these? It shrinks. It reassesses itself: can I survive this? So begins, soon after the exhilaration of acceptance to this august school, a slough of despond in which one's soul is virtually dismantled. The torment is private. College is such a flabby time anyway: misery expands to fill the time allotted to it. Not much is asked of one during these formless years except decent grades and occasional letters home. What worried my parents was not worrying me. Occasionally my mother would call: "You're not getting involved with those radicals, are you? You're not in any of those demonstrations?" I assured her I was not. I was lying in a stupor of depression after finishing Santayana's novel *The Last Puri-*

tan (which, though its hero leaves Harvard for Williams, evokes the melancholy strain of puritan idealism that seemed to me the Harvard ethos). I vaguely remember looking down on a crowd in Massachusetts Avenue from the cool, fluorescent vacuum of the top floor of Lamont Library, but I am not even sure why they were shouting. I remember more vividly the sight of a solitary rower on the Charles early one morning, or the first time I heard the horns enter midway through the first movement of Brahms's Second Piano Concerto. I was an aesthete who took copious notes out of guilt over such interests; they startle me by their completeness when I pull them out of a footlocker. On another occasion my mother said, "I hope you're not using drugs. Are you?" I was not. Inspired by a speech given by James Baldwin in Sanders Theater, I did enter the colored section of a liquor store in the southern town to which my parents retired after entering me at Harvard, and I got chased out. But that was all. I was not taking drugs, demonstrating against anyone, or becoming a radical. No, my apostasy was much worse than that.

I had a friend at school, an artist who had drawn portraits of several of our classmates; the two of us would walk down a street in Cambridge and turn to each other and say, "Now *there's* a face!" It was the deep, perplexing beauty of the faces in the street which galvanized my soul in a way no political question could. I became a student of eyes, mouths, complexions, smiles.

My roommate junior year hung a tie on his doorknob whenever he was making love with his girl friend; one would see them coming into the dining room just before the serving trays were returned to the kitchen, their faces flushed, smiling, starry-eyed, visibly altered by their hours that afternoon of sexual love. My own experience was more chaste. When I went to see a psychiatrist at the Student Health Services, the woman who interviewed me grew visibly distressed as she heard my reasons for suspecting I was homosexual; sympathy and sadness flushed her friendly face, and she made those cooing sounds, the tiny clucks and small regretful moans that women make when, watching the news on television, they hear of a family burned to death in their house, or learn of an airplane crash. Touched, almost relieved by her sympathy—it *was* a terrible problem; I *was* suffering over it tremendously—I went in the following week to meet the psychiatrist, a tanned and handsome man whose desk bore photographs of his sailboat, and who assured me these doubts were all illusory, that all I had to do was next time *kiss* my date at Wellesley. But alas, I did not, and I stopped seeing Debbie altogether, for it seemed a charade—a brittle exercise in politeness—to me. I can only surmise what she felt. And there I was: Student Health said I wasn't queer, so I went back to my library carrel.

How does one account for the behavior of that doctor? Did he sincerely believe my misgivings were illusions? Did he think that therefore to see me would be a waste of both his and my time? To this day, I haven't the vaguest idea, but that small act of courage (or despair), in turning myself in to Student Health, was my last for many years in this matter.

I could hardly bring myself to look up books under the subject "Homosexuality" in the card catalog at Widener, so frightened was I that someone would see over my shoulder that I was jotting down the call number of John Addington Symonds's *A Problem in Modern Ethics*. This slim volume and a few references in Plato were all I had to comfort myself as I sat in the Widener stacks staring out the window, marooned in a complicated adolescence. When I encountered the seven stages of the life cycle in Erik Erikson's course that spring, I could only conclude that four of them were not to be completed by the likes of me.

On the walls of the toilet stalls in Lamont Library (it seems a tale of libraries, after all: that was my Harvard) were written invitations to nude wrestlers. They were as real to me as the trilobites imbedded in the limestone sheets that separated the stalls. One evening a hand reached beneath the partition and stroked my leg. I rose in horror, pulled up my pants, and fled to my anthology of colonial American literature. I may have been in love with the beauty of men, but I was not about to be homosexual. It meant giving up the promise one had in life, a promise that Harvard itself symbolized; it meant to surrender the future.

To be a Harvard undergraduate was, I submit, in some way to be a snob—a fair number in every class think they may some day be secretary of state—and what Proust called inversion seemed to me the worst infirmity of all. One day after a lecture on American poetry by a favorite professor, a group of us asked if we could join him at his table for lunch, and he sighed: "If you promise not to ask if Whitman was homosexual."

Even Whitman—when John Addington Symonds asked him in a letter—denied this suggestion vehemently. Why should my professor discuss it? Homosexuality was dismissed, an embarrassing, tedious topic, by psychiatrist and English professor alike. Should I not dismiss it too? I was hardly going to tell mother the next time she called. When this professor—whose wit, affability and bachelorhood made him accessible—married in the spring of my junior year, I felt affronted, like a child deserted by his older brother. How could Professor X get married, at the age of thirty-five? "To widen the circumference of experience," he had written in a book, but this was not a sexual motive: it sounded like a trip to Greece. I felt lonelier, at any rate, for his marrying, and fell into that gloom common to homosexual youths before they have come to terms with themselves: the conviction that I was the only one in the world.

One morning after a sleepless night of studying for examinations, I looked through my window and saw proof that I was not: a classmate—the house playwright—walking into the foggy courtyard with his arm around another young man. There is a scene in Henry James's *The Ambassadors* in which the narrator sees Chad and Madame de Vionnet floating down a river in the country and realizes immediately they are lovers. The sight of these two classmates walking into the courtyard conveyed the same knowledge to me. Yet I did not rush out and say, "Hello! Help me!" No, I watched them pass the window in silence; they might have been angels for all they had to do with the rules of earthly ambition.

Yet this moment of affection was instinctively comprehensible to me even then: when else could two men walk this way except at that gray hour when everyone, Harvard itself, was asleep? Years later at dinner on Fire Island a friend recognized the figures in my story—had been the playwright's lover, too—and I was able, in that kitchen distant in time and space, to look back at college and understand things I did not at the time.

Now I understood my distress at the marriage in middle age of my admired English teacher and my friendship with the confident artist who drew those handsome faces—and his friendship with a bemused classmate who left school and was killed in Vietnam—and I wonder if his alienation and my own did not have something in common. No matter. It is too late. I've been back to Boston many times since then, and I've gone to its bars, beaches, and parks with a freedom I could not enjoy as an earnest, proper undergraduate going downtown on Saturday afternoon to hear the symphony, and I wonder now why someone did not lead me across the river to Sporter's, in whose large, noisy rooms I would have begun the aspect of my education that was wanting. But, like writers you can read at sixteen but not love till you read them again at twenty-eight, the timing of education discourages speculation. Perhaps the sexual void of those years was a useful dormancy. Could I have read Emerson with the same idealism had I been obsessed with the forearm of the bartender I had seen the previous night? Even now when faced with this dilemma in a youth whose sexuality is clear to others but not himself, one is not at all sure what is the better thing to do. One of the great scholars at Harvard a few decades before I arrived there, F. O. Matthiessen, wrote to his lover: "This is indeed the price we pay for the unforgiv-

able sin of being born different from the great run of mankind." Even this was published posthumously, however,
fifteen years after I left Harvard.

And having described this dilemma, it would be wrong to
dwell any further on it; it is hardly Harvard's fault that one
goes there a frightened adolescent ignorant of himself but
conscious that by the end of his residence in this vast,
international corporation, in the company of his sarcastic,
ambitious, and confident peers, he must make his way to
further achievements. Harvard students have dreams. "All I
want is a little house in the country," a friend said the night
we discussed our ambitions in life. And another in our group
who saw the Harvard psyche more clearly than the rest of
us, perhaps, replied: "All you really want is a little house in
the country surrounded by a crowd of people saying,
'When's he coming out, when's he coming out?' "

So the ambitious student, beset by sexual and social
doubts, falls back on what got him here in the first place—he
studies—and pretty much ignores a great deal of Harvard in
the process. Harvard became for me a search for yet another
room in which to read, a collection of libraries through
which I wandered, looking for the perfect chair, the perfect
lamp, as if that would make the book I was reading digest-
ible. From Lamont to Widener to the Lowell House library to
the lounge of the Catholic Club on Bow Street: I burrowed
farther and farther from the world. I began reading books of
literary criticism, which I could not remember a word of the
moment I finished the volume. Allegiance and passion were
missing. My heart wasn't in it. My heart was in meeting my
friends at eleven and going off to Elsie's for a piece of mocha
cake. On meeting the tutor junior year whose doctoral
thesis was a compilation of Melville's marginalia, I knew
almost immediately, as he crossed his riding boots before
the fire and sipped his sherry, that this man would not teach
me a thing all year. Harvard depends utterly, it seems to me
on reflection, on whom you meet: my sophomore tutor
showed me precision of thought and language; my tutor

junior year and I were two strangers in an elevator. The doctor I took my sexual fears to dismissed my case. What is fascinating is that Harvard, that vast corporation whose bursar sent me bills, whose glass flowers I never visited, whose possessions include a villa in Italy, a mansion in Washington, and God knows what else, consists primarily of those few moments you make contact with its representatives, and it is only as good, or as great, as those people.

And what happened ultimately is that it shrank to a few hundred living around a courtyard with two apple trees and an elm—as it was meant to, I suppose. Harvard finally came to me in Lowell House, where I needed only to walk to another wing to obtain a book, see a friend, eat dinner, or play a game of squash. This Harvard one could grasp. Worse, this Harvard one could love. Those doors around the courtyard which led me to a library, a friend, a squash game, a dinner—even as one reminded oneself, as all fortunate students do, that you were merely a lamb being fattened for slaughter, that the privileges afforded youth are to strengthen their bones for the marketplace which follows— were inviting. It was hard not to think that all one had to do in life was chirp like a bird at those long, polished seminar tables about moral choice in the novels of Henry James, contributing one last insight into *The Ambassadors* before scurrying off into the autumn night to dinner with friends or a game of squash. But just as you settled in, your time was up.

Yet nothing was resolved: I was still so unsure of what role I wished to audition for in life that when I saw, on entering the dining hall, two sets of friends at two separate tables— one history majors, the other crazies—I came to a dead halt of indecision. Was I going to be a lawyer or an artist? At Harvard we took our style from the boys from Andover in shells on the Charles, in khaki pants and clear-rimmed glasses. You felt for your precise placement in this motley society: I was a preppy, but not from an elite prep school; I was gentile, but Catholic; midwestern, but schooled in the

east; ambitious and shy. I was good at English, lousy at
math, and if I wanted to remain in the affluent, elite world of
Harvard I would have to go to law school, it seemed. So I
applied both to Harvard Law School and the Writers' Workshop in Iowa. I was certainly still ignorant as the end drew
near: at my senior orals, I said something about Harry
Truman just as defiantly wrong as my remark about the wife
of Henry Adams, and the same tutor was there blinking at
me as I said it. When I presented my thesis project to Robert
Fitzgerald one afternoon, he listened with an air of pained,
melancholy attention and then, on learning I had not read
Gerard Manley Hopkins, said, "Well, I suggest you *do*." That
offended shock—at an ignorance that would not bother the
larger world—was Harvard. It was also the tutor who
handed me my final essay before riding off around the
corner on his bicycle; beneath his compliments I read the
advice that "in life, passion *and* intelligence are everything."

Perhaps this was just a routine of his—perhaps it was just
the manner in which he gave me his credo scrawled on the
last page of my essay on Hemingway and rode off—but this
moment touched me then and remains with me still. How
tiny a sliver it was of the whole three years! How it
exemplifies the way we spoke to one another at Harvard
through a personal, and institutional, reserve—a reserve
whose coldness my friend complained of in his letter from
Stanford the autumn following graduation.

"In the case of artificial education," Schopenhauer says in
a book I found years after my own commencement, "the
head is, through lectures, teaching and reading, stuffed full
of concepts before there is any wide acquaintanceship with
the perceptual world at all . . . so it happens that education
produces wrong-headedness, and that is why in youth, after
much reading and learning, we go out into the world in part
naive, in part confused, and conduct ourselves in it now
with arrogance, now with timidity. . . . Correct understanding of quite simple things comes only when one is advanced
in years, and then it comes quite suddenly."

A walking, talking illustration of this text, I emerged from Harvard in a cloud of conceit and despair. Life after commencement was just as gritty as the senior in bed suspected: it was having to make one's living in a world that finds a use for you only because you can type. I soon found myself in an enormous, low-ceilinged room in a sea of ladies connected by earphones to Dictaphones, tapping out letters for a big insurance firm. I was like a prince disguised as a peasant in some operetta; the others did not know what I would never be so gauche as to confess: I was a product of Harvard College. Harvard College, in Boston. This was only the first of all those jobs writers take to pay the rent: I typed manuscripts for a professor of linguistics, taught remedial English, loaded trucks, waited on tables, tended bar, sold encyclopedias, and moved in those years further and further from the notion of Harvard as an avenue of success. For I did not accept the invitation that came to me in the spring of my senior year to enter the law school. It was just across the street from the Yard. But it was utterly foreign. It might have been my revulsion to exchanging the freedom of the undergraduate for the drudgery of the apprentice attorney—or just the suspicion that it was not the education I needed still—but there could be no doubt in my heart: I was suffocating in Cambridge and could not remain there one more fall, walking back in a trench coat with the Sunday *Times* to a cubicle in which yet more books had to be digested. Years later—long after that astonishing sadness that put me to bed for three days following commencement, mourning all I had loved about Harvard—I found words that expressed the motives for my decision to leave in Ecclesiastes: "There is no end to making books, and much study is a weariness of the flesh."

Were those years really as melancholy and intimidating as I have said they were in this little essay? Yes. Why then do I love to go back and walk through Harvard, and feel such a great pride in the place? A friend once said to me that the common error of writers is condescending to their youth—

treating it with too much pity, as if it could have been done so easily another and better way. (I doubt it could have; it took at least a decade to undo the knots in which my soul was tied as an undergraduate there.) I have confirmed his observation here: true, I was a middle-class, earnest, bookish fellow whose determination to make the dean's list and shyness confined me pretty much to a slender sliver of what Harvard offered. It was not till spring of senior year that I went down to the boathouse, for example, and did what I'd wanted to for three years: take a shell out. Yet I had much more. These memories are inevitably skewed, I guess, for I see in reading this piece that I have not even mentioned the friends I made there with whom I used to laugh so helplessly into the night I got sideaches. It was this laughter which made me very sad when I left.

Michael Barone '66

Michael Barone was born in 1944 in Highland Park, Michigan, and grew up in Detroit and its suburbs. After graduation from Harvard in 1966, he attended the Yale Law School and graduated in 1969. For two years after that he served as a law clerk to a federal judge. From that time on, his career has taken less conventional turns: he is principal coauthor of The Almanac of American Politics *(1971 and every two years thereafter) and has been associated with Peter Hart in the political polling business since 1974. He has also written for many periodicals. Mr. Barone lives in Washington with his wife Joan, who is producer of the CBS news program "Face the Nation," and their daughter Sarah.*

The word that best describes the Harvard I first knew is "confidence." In the summer of 1959, in Cambridge on a family vacation, we were escorted on a Crimson Key tour of Harvard Yard. The student guide was pleasant, fluent—and confident. His demeanor and carriage left no doubt that he knew Harvard was the best—and he assumed you knew it, too.

That feeling of confidence was one of the reasons I applied to Harvard. I grew up in the Detroit area, and I knew relatively little about colleges outside Michigan. But when I was accepted at Harvard, there was never any doubt in my mind about going. I entered in 1962.

Physically, Cambridge and Boston were almost a disappointment. The Detroit suburbs I had lived in were built almost entirely after World War II, and I had an unarticulated assumption that contemporary architecture and new buildings were good. Cambridge and Boston were almost entirely old then; there were almost none of the new buildings one sees today. In the early 1960s you could almost believe, as you looked around, that you were in the 1920s again. High Victorian buildings on Massachusetts Avenue faced Harvard Square, including the block between Holyoke and Dunster streets where the multicolored modern

Holyoke Center now stands, recessed from the street. The all-night cafeterias around the Square were still doing business—the Hayes Bickford with its alcoholic countermen and the wretched Albiani's, where I ate on my first night in Cambridge and never again. Brattle Street was still full of fussy old shops that catered to little old ladies, rather than the sleek stores that cater to the designer clothes–clad young women of today; the only hint of the future was the first small Design/Research store.

The MTA, with its dirty tiles spelling the station names and its antique dark cars and trolleys creaking on the rails, seemed to have changed little since it was built so many decades before. The skyline of Boston then had only one major post–World War II skyscraper, the old John Hancock Building, the one that looks like a squat Empire State Building, not the one whose windows fell out in the 1970s. The neighborhoods of Boston, too, seemed to have changed little since the 1930s. The West End had already been torn down and replaced with white tile high-rises, but other neighborhoods were still full of children with Irish and Italian faces, speaking in strange, sometimes almost incomprehensible accents. In Detroit, a city built in the automobile age, old neighborhoods are abandoned as soon as the generation that has been raised in them grows up; in Boston, obviously, though the city's population was already declining, people stayed in the same tight-packed three deckers generation after generation.

No one else at Harvard seemed to be concerned that Cambridge was not an up-to-date place, and I quickly cultivated a taste for it. I was particularly fascinated by local accents and contrived to pronounce vowels and r's as I heard them from Cambridge townies and Boston Brahmins and fellow students from Brooklyn or Philadelphia.

The Harvard I entered was certainly a confident place, at least as confident as I had expected; it was not, however, a particularly friendly one. It was not too hard to meet people in the freshman dormitories in the Yard or to talk with them in the Union, but it seemed difficult to get to know anyone half as well as I had known half a dozen people in high school. Getting to know women was particularly awkward, and at least after freshman year people didn't even say hello when they saw people who lived down the hall unless they had previously gotten to know them. There was an assumption in the air that you didn't have to meet new people, because you already knew lots of people, and of course this was true for the sixty freshmen who came from Exeter or the dozens who had known each other at Dalton or some other private school in New York; it was more difficult for many others. For many students, to make friends and have any kind of social and intellectual camaraderie meant participating intensively in some activity, whether it was the band, the intramural sports team, or the *Lampoon*.

For me it meant the *Crimson*. A couple of friends from my high school had gotten on the paper, and they urged me to enter the competition. I went out for the editorial board, which meant writing little pieces of political analysis and having them ridiculed by senior editors. Even before I was accepted ("elected," in *Crimson* language), I had grown fascinated with the place. If Harvard in general was confident, the *Crimson* was supremely confident; if Harvard was sure it was important, the *Crimson* was sure it was at the center of things.

And not only at the University. *Crimson* editors (everyone on the paper was called an editor) never seemed to forget that the paper went to the White House where, we supposed, it was read if not by John F. Kennedy, '40 (as *Crimson* form styled him; the only president was President Pusey), then at least by former Dean of the Faculty McGeorge Bundy. Editorials were written on the highest matters of foreign policy with some feeling that they might have impact on someone important, whether currently on the faculty or in Washington. I do not remember that President Kennedy was the focus of much adulation or even great interest from students generally; that the president was a

Harvard man was pretty much taken for granted. But it did contribute to the feeling of importance of students at the *Crimson*.

Confirming this feeling that we were somehow especially important were the large number of important people who took the trouble to come up to Cambridge to address *Crimson* editors in the upstairs conference room (an incredibly filthy and messy place misnamed the Sanctum) or at cocktail parties at which many editors and some guests got entirely drunk. James Reston discussing the President and Congress, John Kenneth Galbraith recounting his conversation with de Gaulle at the Kennedy funeral, Norman Thomas reminiscing about past battles—these were formidable conversation partners for college sophomores from places like the Detroit suburbs. Former *Crimson* editors, well positioned then as now at *The New York Times, The Washington Post, Time, Newsweek,* and *The New Yorker,* provided constant contact with the journalist gossip and trade talk of New York and Washington.

It seems almost absurd as I think back on it, but I remember arguing with fellow undergraduates at the *Crimson* and in dining halls about the future course of the Common Market and President de Gaulle's policies, and discussing which British periodical, the *Economist* or the *New Statesman* (there were partisans of both at the *Crimson*), provided the best view of what was happening in the world.

There was a lot of affectation in all this, obviously, but there was also a sense that was not wholly without foundation that we were—or were about to be—in control of the course of the major institutions of society, that the major decisions of the future were ours to make. We had confidence in our ability to rule as well as confidence in the people who then seemed to be ruling our nation and so much of the world. John Kennedy was not a personal hero, but his administration was all that most of us thought an administration should be, and in these years of the early 1960s a political consensus was forged at Harvard that had not previously existed. In the *Crimson* straw poll taken at the election of 1960, Harvard undergraduates had preferred Kennedy over Nixon by the less than landslide margin of 58 to 42 percent; the freshmen, apparently reflecting their parents' preference, had actually gone for Nixon. By 1964 Lyndon Johnson won more than 90 percent of Harvard's straw votes, and that kind of percentage stayed with Democratic presidential candidates through 1972. I remember that the Harvard-Radcliffe Young Democrats in 1964 had a membership of well over a thousand, including one-fourth of the undergraduate student body. Almost everyone seemed to share the basic goals—and the basic confidence of the national administration.

This was confirmed in what was then the college's number one academic course, Economics 1. Despite a variety of poor lecturers and a wide variance in the quality of section men, one-fourth of all students enrolled in it each year; in effect, everyone took this course, though it was not required. And although Ec 1 dutifully presented the views of several different schools, there was no question about the lessons the course taught. We learned that wise economists, many of them from Harvard, had discovered how to bring about national economic growth without significant inflation and that thanks to the Kennedy and Johnson administrations they had done exactly this. The facts, at least through 1966 when I graduated, seemed to confirm this emphatically. In economics, in civil rights, in every important area, government worked and it improved people's lives. And it was people like us who made it work.

But there were even in the early 1960s signs of trends that would diminish our confidence and change our point of view. I remember in 1962 hearing a speech at Harvard by Michael Harrington, the socialist, and I was struck by how much he expressed a nostalgia for the past and a sense that socialism may have been possible at one time but was not any longer. I knew then little of the history of leftist politics in this country, and I had little inkling—apparently, neither did Harrington—of the role he was about to play in our national politics. For at the time he must have been preparing, or beginning to think about, the *New Yorker* article on poverty in America which led directly to the antipoverty programs that captured the imaginations of so many of my classmates and contemporaries in the late 1960s.

It was not much later, in the spring of 1963, when Timothy Leary and Richard Alpert were fired from the Harvard faculty for using undergraduates in drug experiments after promising not to do so. I remember that I strongly supported the decision and took the point of view of one who must make a decision that affects a great institution, not the point of view of a young person eager to experience the effects of mind-expanding drugs. Yet it was not many months later that I got to know some classmates who smoked marijuana regularly and used other drugs as well. I remember seeing them at Hazen's, the luncheonette next door to Elsie's, late at night, after they had been smoking. Hazen's had recently been remodeled, with gleaming white Formica counters and walls, and my friends called it the White Place, and smiling would tell you about all the wonderful colors and patterns they could see.

One of the perennial topics at *Crimson* editorial board meetings, even in 1962 and 1963, was Vietnam. As I remember, the paper took at least three different stands on Vietnam when I was on it; I think I voted for them all. In the fall of 1963, as I recall, the *Crimson* was for pulling out American troops; it was big news among us when *Time* magazine recalled Charles Mohr from Saigon, and David Halberstam, then writing for the *Times* there, had been on the *Crimson* not many years before. In the first year or so of the Johnson administration's escalation policy, I think we supported the government's policy; I remember that I did, hoping that somehow we would get out of what seemed an increasingly bad mess. Later, we switched to opposition, though in my time the paper took nothing like the radical stands it did at the end of the 1960s.

Our perspective during all these debates, as in considering the problem of poverty or the issue of drug use, was that
of the policymaker. We did not think of ourselves as people
who could be affected directly by Vietnam, certainly not as
people who would be killed there. Yet there were signs that
our lives would be affected in some ways and that the institutions we had taken for granted would be transformed by
this war. I remember in my last year at Harvard, probably in
the early months of 1966, seeing buses in the open space
where Mount Auburn and Bow streets came together in
front of the *Lampoon*, waiting to take some students to an
antiwar demonstration. The protesters were milling around,
dressed in jeans and with hair that was then considered
long and unruly (but nothing like what would become com-
monplace among young lawyers in Wall Street firms a few
years later), when they were confronted by other, hostile
students, dressed in Weejuns and crew-neck sweaters.
There was violence in the air. I had seen the so-called spring
riots at Harvard—the occasions on the first nights warm
enough to allow students to go outside without shirts, when
hundreds of students would walk around and pretend to
defy the police—but those were essentially social exercises;
this was much scarier. Not much happened; the demonstrators got on their buses and went away. But I can remember
feeling that my world had gotten much chillier and less
comfortable all of a sudden and that it would not be getting
warmer again soon.

My year was the last year in which you could get through
college and graduate school without being drafted. In the
early 1960s the military needed so few draftees that undergraduates could take a year off and work or travel without
worrying about the draft. But by late 1965 that had changed,
and in early 1966 tests were given undergraduates, with
those who did less well supposedly to lose their deferments.
In fact this was one of several twists and turns of draft policy,
none of which was popular then or seems wise now. I
remember arguing several years later with my boss, who

said that the primary reason for the strength of the opposition to the Vietnam War among students was the draft; I thought that students were simply reacting logically to better and additional information. Now it seems quite clear to me that he was right. The Harvard of the spring of 1966, where no one was drafted, was skeptical about the Vietnam War, but only a minority—like the demonstrators and jeerers I saw—had really strong feelings about it. We thought we could keep getting deferments through graduate school and make it to age twenty-six without being drafted, which is just what I did; the war would not affect us. Two years later, undergraduates at Harvard assumed that they would be subject to the draft; that is when Secretary of Defense McNamara was surrounded by angry and apparently violent students. In my days, we had sipped sherry with these people; now they could no longer come on campus.

But government had not yet become the enemy in 1966. For the graduation issue of the *Crimson* that year, I wrote an article arguing that our generation of highly educated young people was characterized by an altruistic impulse that would affect their career paths and influence the course of society. I had certainly not gotten rid of the confidence that what we did at Harvard mattered. But the subject matter had shifted. In the early 1960s the issues that interested my friends usually concerned foreign policy. Certainly it was the tradition of Democratic administrations since Roosevelt and even of the Eisenhower administration that highly educated and well connected people were needed to conduct foreign policy; local politicians and labor-union pork choppers could be trusted with the drudgery of domestic affairs. The Boston that we saw around us in the early 1960s did not look like a very interesting place to work.

But as time went on, foreign policy became less attractive and domestic policy more so. Vietnam, certainly after the 1965 escalations, was one reason; students were not solidly against the war yet, but it did not seem like the kind of enterprise they wanted to be associated with. Impetus also came from the domestic initiatives of the national administration and from the civil rights movement. In the summers of 1963 and 1964 a number of Harvard students went south to work for civil rights. That experience and Michael Harrington's exposure of the "other America" convinced many that there was important, worthwhile work to be done at home to improve life in America and that young people could make a difference.

Brought up in affluence—and in about as secure a situation of affluence as any generation has ever experienced—these Harvard students set out to do good for the society that had done so much for them. "From those to whom much is given, much is asked," as President Kennedy said. Career choices were affected. Many more went into academic life, especially the social sciences, than in the past, for economics and sociology seemed to have the ability to provide answers for the problems that ailed us. There was an upsurge as well in the numbers going to law school; lawyers, after all, had played a key role in the civil rights movement, and they seemed determined to do great things for the poor as well. The goals of making money and raising a family seemed less important, as well they might to people whose personal histories seemed to justify taking these things for granted. The goal of helping society became more important.

Nevertheless, the mood I remember in my last months at Harvard in 1966 was less optimistic than the mood I had sensed a few years earlier. People hoped they could make a contribution, but they were by no means sure that they were running things or were about to do so, and over their futures loomed the specter of the war. The public policies that they had believed in so strongly seemed to be working just a little bit less well—and in a few years would seem to be working pretty badly indeed. This was a group of people less sure, less confident than they had been, less certain that the future would be everything they hoped it would be.

It is not supposed to rain at Harvard graduations, but it drizzled, lightly but perceptibly, on my commencement in 1966. The speaker was Averell Harriman, and there was a buzz of speculation in the *Crimson* that he would come forward with some startling new proposal for peace in Vietnam, just as another important administration official, George Marshall, had announced the Marshall Plan at Harvard commencement nineteen years before. Nothing like that happened; the ceremonies proceeded rather somberly. The rain was soft—not the hard rain that I understand lashed the class of 1968's commencement two years later—but it symbolizes to me the change in mood and perspective of my years at Harvard. Members of the class of 1966 have already had substantial achievements in the years since graduating, but for those who shared what seemed to be the consensus of that time, those years cannot have been entirely happy ones. We were not caught up, in our college years at least, by the turmoil and frenzy of the late 1960s, but unlike the undergraduates of those later classes we had also had some experience with the Harvard of an earlier time, a Harvard that seemed so confident—and seemed to have so much reason to be confident—that it had the answers and could solve the nation's problems.

James Fallows '70

*James Fallows was born in 1949 and raised in Red-
lands, California. He was a member of the class of 1970
at Harvard and lived in Adams House. He was on the
staff of the* Crimson *during all four years at Harvard
and in 1969 was its president. That year he also won
the Dana Reed Prize for outstanding undergraduate
writing. After graduation, he studied for two years at
Oxford as a Rhodes Scholar and has spent most of the
succeeding years as a journalist. During the first two
years of the Carter administration, he was President
Carter's chief speech writer; after that, he became
Washington editor for* The Atlantic Monthly. *His book*
National Defense *was published by Random House in
1981. He is married to Deborah (Zerad), '71; they live
in Washington with their two sons, Thomas and Tad.*

My Harvard problem is that, while I like many things about having been to Harvard, my memories of being there are almost all bleak. When looking on the bright side, I remind myself that I met my wife at Harvard, that many of my close friends are from those years (or are friends of Harvard friends), that the Old Boy network of the *Crimson* has been a help in times of trouble in my career. Given the imperfections of my character and the vanities of the world, I also know that if I had not gone to Harvard, I would have spent years sulking in California, certain that I was as good as those pantywaists on the East Coast but chagrined that I had not been admitted to the College of my Choice to have a chance to prove it. I count these things to the good. But when I think about actually *being* at Harvard, I cringe. For five years after my graduation, I found myself trembling whenever I set foot in Cambridge, which was as infrequently as I could manage. I considered it a victory when, in 1977, I was able to return and find all of it—the surroundings, the unchanging faces in Harvard Square, even the familiar building at 14 Plympton Street—an emotionally neutral setting.

The explanation for this reaction is that I have very few recollections of "college life" as such. I spent only half as much time at Oxford as at Harvard, but almost all my memories of normal college activities—kindly professors, student outings, sophomoric philosophizing about the meaning of life—come from those two years in England. At Oxford, I was a student; at Harvard, I was more an object of the upheaval of the times. As a result, the Harvard of my memory falls under two headings. I think of one, which covers my freshman year, as A Rube in Cambridge, and of the other as Wars and Blood Feuds of the 1960s. Neither is delightful in retrospect.

I arrived in Cambridge with a fuzzier sense of what to expect than some of my classmates possessed. I had grown up in Redlands, California, a small town with many rustic virtues but few contacts with the educational hierarchy of the East. In a nearby town there lived one central-casting Harvard Grad, a ruined society figure who wore plaid neckties and went on and on about the grand old days in "the Yahd." He was a Republican, like everyone else in town, but he had it both ways during John Kennedy's administration, railing against the policies but hinting that he could never be really mad at a fellow Winthrop man. True, my own father had gone to Harvard Medical School, and my mother used to rhapsodize about their days courting in Boston when she was a student at Tufts, but the job of exemplifying the real Harvard, that of the Pudding show and neckties over the doorknob, fell to the old grad and several of his friends. On the basis of what I saw and heard from them, I came to expect a student body consisting half of younger versions of the old grad, sandy-haired social-register offspring whose first names sounded like other people's last names, and half of wild-eyed over-achieving "liberals" from places like Great Neck. (To be honest about it, I had not heard of Great Neck—or Newton, or Scarsdale, or Shaker Heights—before I killed some of the miserable hours in Lamont Library looking through old freshman registers. Who were these people? How could so many of them be from Connecticut and New York?)

The liberals were the classmates who had me most worried, since liberals had been few and disreputable in my previous life. By common agreement, my high school class of 750 students was known to contain three liberals (and one Jew). I was for Barry Goldwater in 1964, which placed me in the mainstream in my town. The closest I'd come to political involvement before college had been to sit with fifty thousand other stalwarts in Dodger Stadium in the summer of Goldwater's glory and cheer as the candidate rode around the infield on the back of an open convertible. However widely I read, from *Atlas Shrugged* to *A Choice Not an Echo,* I learned that conspiring eastern liberals had denied America the conservative leadership it deserved. And now I was going to live in their midst!

The real problem with these liberals, I soon discovered, was not that they thought differently from anyone I'd known in the previous seventeen years, but that they knew a hell of a lot more about everything than I did. Like most of the other eager young things in the freshman dorms, I had done fine in high school, but I began to see that while Redlands Senior High School may have exposed me to a broader range of humanity than the specimens available at St. Paul's or the Bronx High School of Science, it had exposed me to many fewer books.

For my first expository-writing paper, I turned in an uplifting essay about the importance of optimism for today's youth. This subject had won me praise in local Optimist Club oratory contests; at Harvard, it earned me a C −. This was my first college grade, and I took it as an omen. The two courses that did most to convince me that I was in over my head were Humanities 6 and Soc Sci 2, the first taught by Reuben Brower and the second by Samuel Beer. Their content differed—poetry in Brower's case, historical analysis in Beer's—but their purpose was the same: to develop the students' abilities to weigh alternative explanations and use different analytical approaches to a given subject. To me, the idea of different analyses of the same facts was

completely novel. When I heard two versions of the meaning of the Magna Charta, I wanted to know which one was
right. By the time I'd expressed this desire a few times in
class, my section man concluded that I must have (in today's polite phrase) a learning disability. For me, trying to
understand Beer's lectures was like trying to see something
in the fourth dimension; my most frequent lecture note was
a big, scrawled "Huh?"

My response to confusion and failure was to become the
classic grind. When I go blind at forty, I will know it is
because of the hours I spent under the flickering fluorescent lamps in Lamont. By Thanksgiving time of my freshman year, I was living for the libraries to open, sneaking a
day's supply of lunch and snacks with me into the Widener
stacks. When I was evicted from the libraries at closing
time, I would hurry back to my room to keep plowing
through the books or to write homesick letters to my parents
about the cheerless new life I'd begun. One of my two
freshman roommates was Brian Carpenter, a young man
from Brownsville, Texas, who shared my sense of academic
disorientation but who responded with more self-possession
and dignity. Instead of descending to grade-grubbing, Brian
placed himself above such petty concerns and viewed the
whole situation with a Tennessee Williams–style archness
that I would treasure today but found insufficiently sincere
at the time. I was then in the fraudulent grip of the Evelyn
Wood speed-reading course, and I would come to the room
at midnight and ostentatiously flip pages, pretending to be
taking it all in. Brian would drily suggest that I buy a portable fan to help turn the pages, or he would dive across the
room with a kamikaze yell to seize my book.

These were only the academic joys of college life. I was
concluding at the same time that no one but the luckless
and insane would voluntarily live in a land to which such
winters came year after year. It was not until I was a senior
that I grasped the theory of fending off winter with a warm
coat, gloves, scarves, and so on; until then, I'd held on to my

western windbreaker, ideal for evenings in Laguna Beach,
and regarded anything more substantial as an affront to a
proper style of living, which meant being able to stroll outside at any time wearing the same clothes you'd had on
indoors. By the time I'd lived through one Boston winter, I
could not imagine that anyone willingly stayed for two.

I began to think that the symbol of eastern life was its style
of physical exercise. When bad weather brought the tennis
season to an end in October and lack of ability frustrated my
hopes of a place on the lightweight crew, I took up running
as my sport. This gave me "recreation" of the same sort a
caged rat enjoys when turning his little wheel. When the
rains and snows came, which is to say, during most of the
school year, the only place to run was on the upper deck of
Briggs Cage, overlooking an indoor baseball diamond.
Round and round I went, ten laps to the mile, always one
direction, grimy black dirt from the baseball diamond coating my mucous membranes, my spirits very similar to the
rat's. One evening in January, as I walked back across the
bridge toward dinner and a fun-filled evening in Lamont, I
found that my hair, still wet from the shower, had frozen into
a cunning ice pompadour. What was I doing here?

Relief came in two stages. One was a return to California
for the summer, where I spent a few weeks working as a
"copy aide" (i.e., flunky) at the *Los Angeles Times* and then
headed north with a high school friend who introduced me
to some of the countercultural practices that were then the
vogue. We loitered at the corner of Haight and Ashbury in
San Francisco (remember, this was 1967), we camped under the stars in Mendocino County, we said "Oh, wow!" at
sunsets over the surf. The other source of my salvation was
to escape the counterculture and drift instead into the
clutches of *The Harvard Crimson*.

I have since come to realize that most people who were
not on the *Crimson* find most things about the *Crimson*
repellant. My wife, who devoted her time at Radcliffe to
such wholesome activities as the Choral Society, tells me

that she and her friends used to get pains in their stomachs when they walked into the building to deposit a notice of choral practice, since they were always worried that some wise-guy *Crimson* editor would give them a hard time. My classmate Steven Kelman wrote about the self-important mystique of the *Crimson* in a book published in our senior year, a criticism I took with poor humor at the time. I replied with a nasty, so's-your-old-man review in the *Crimson*. Legend had it that the television program "College Bowl" never received more angry mail than after a special exhibition match between the *Crimson* and the *Yale Daily News,* on which the Crimeds not only went down to humiliating defeat but also gave drop-dead answers like "I want to be a club woman" when Allen Ludden interviewed them at halftime about their future plans.

I can understand the hostility. The culture of the *Crimson* was self-important and pathologically competitive. In a different setting, some of the people would have been the kind of drill instructors who beat recruits. Still I found the *Crimson* the source of far more happiness than anything else I did at Harvard.

I had drifted into the *Crimson* through the business board, working briefly as an advertising salesman and spending more and more time during my sophomore year laying out the ad dummy each night. The secret of the *Crimson* was that anyone seriously involved with the paper dabbled lightly in classes during the regular term and then crammed during reading period, when an undersized version of the paper came out only a few times a week. Late one night in January of my sophomore year, I was killing time in the basement of the *Crimson* talking with the pressmen and watching the presses run. (The *Crimson* was in those days printed on an antique press that handled only one sheet of paper at a time—essentially the same technology as the original Gutenberg press. From midnight until four or five in the morning, a jug-eared teenager from Cambridge would stand alongside the press and feed in some four thousand large sheets of paper one by one, and then remove each sheet and hand it to someone else for folding. Today, after two or three generations of new equipment, the whole press run takes about twelve minutes instead of five hours.) The "night editor," a harried figure who was tyrant-for-a-day in supervising each edition of the paper, came down the stairs to the pressroom, screaming that an undergraduate had been beaten up by a group of local toughs. Everyone was studying: who would cover the story? Wishing I could find a porkpie hat with "Press" tucked in the band, I volunteered. For the next forty-eight hours I divided my time between calling the hospital for updates and talking to sergeants on the Cambridge police. Later that week, I had my second big story—a fire in an aged building that housed part of the economics department, destroying the life's work of a man named Subramanian Swami. The police beat, fires, human tragedy—this could be fun.

As I spent more and more time on the *Crimson* and less and less on anything else, such good, clean, uncomplicated fun began to vanish. Nearly everything was complicated by the Vietnam War. I am sure there were people at Harvard for whom the years between 1966 and 1970 passed no differently than the years between 1956 and 1960 would have. There were still books to be read, chemistry experiments to be completed, concerts to attend. But such people were not drawn to the *Crimson*. To be part of the paper in those years, especially in 1968 and 1969, was to spend your time thinking not of chemistry but of Dow Chemical, not of Persians at Thermopylae but of the Vietcong at Da Nang. (Only we didn't use that name. We called them the National Liberation Front, or NLF, as in "Ho, Ho, Ho Chi Minh/NLF is gonna win!") Time was measured then not in semesters or classes, but in rallies and riots and public events. Even now I find it hard to reconstruct those years in any other way. For example, I met my future wife the week after Lyndon Johnson abdicated; my Harvard career ended ten days after the invasion of Cambodia, when rioting closed down the school.

This aspect of the 1960s is hardly unexplored territory, and I do not intend to belabor it here. What intrigues me most from ten or twelve years' distance is how difficult it is to keep those times in emotional and intellectual perspective.

As the events themselves fade from memory, the impressions that linger most clearly are of the extreme and painful behavior. I recall the *Crimson* editorial board meetings where debate raged on just how enthusiastically to endorse a NLF victory over the American forces in Vietnam, or how much support to give the Weathermen in their terrorist raids. I recall the Harvard faculty meetings where the ideological division was combined with the usual petty hatred of academic politics and thereby magnified tenfold. I recall the public appearances at which the great stone-faced Nathan Pusey tried to conceal his utter astonishment at the passions tearing up his university. (It was he who asked, "Can anyone believe that SDS's six demands are made seriously?") He clearly felt that in the snarling visages of the students he had seen the Hun at the gate. I was rarely on the winning, that is to say pro-NLF, side of the *Crimson* debates, but mere association with the paper was in those polarized days enough to earn contempt from a number of faculty politicians. A dozen years later, pockets of that bitterness remain, ready to spill out, like encapsulated pus, when sufficient pressure is applied. I recently encountered a professor of the social sciences who gave a splenetic lecture about the destruction the wild men of the 1960s had wrought upon academic liberties and standards. And look at all of you now! he said. You are lawyers, doctors, fat cats on the make. In 1969, when I was president of the *Crimson,* this man had been part of an attempt to wrest control of the paper from the students and give it to "responsible" alumni. He still wished the plan had worked.

Even if the bitterness comes first to mind, along with sensible regret for the extreme emotions on all sides, there are other elements that deserve inclusion in fleshing out the picture of those times. One was the note of farce or black comedy: I often wonder how any of us kept from bursting out laughing during one of the *Crimson*'s exclusive interviews with President Pusey. This one took place after the University Hall occupation but before Pusey announced that he was going to resign. I took with me to the news conference Nicholas Gagarin, a free-spirit member of the *Crimson* of whom I will have more to say. Nick had come under the influence of the Esalen Institute; his prescription for Harvard education was heavy on Esalen-style fun and games. We would have an open university in the Harvard Yard—street dancers, jugglers, a festival of learning including spontaneous courses on Freud and Gertrude Stein. He wanted Pusey's endorsement, and he thought that a few moments of sincere face-to-face explanation might do the trick. As Nick described his plans, Pusey looked at him as if he had come from Mars. When it was over, he adjusted his mouth and said something like, "Well. I see." Thank God there was no presidential tape-recording system in those days or no Garry Trudeau at Harvard to turn the whole thing into a cartoon parody.

I presented a similarly dignified spectacle in my last appearance as a scholar, when I faced my oral examinations in American History and Lit. This was in mid-May 1970, a few days after the Cambodian invasion, when the school year was about to be canceled and chants of "Pass/Fail!" filled the air. In the previous few weeks, I had pounded out a thesis about the U.S. Department of Agriculture and its offenses against southern blacks in the 1930s and 1940s. It was earnest and well intentioned, but scholarship it was not. The interviewing committee, which included Bernard Bailyn, was looking for a polite way to make just this point when I walked into the examination room in Holyoke Center with a red "Strike!" armband on my pea jacket. Bailyn looked as if he wished the 1960s would be over soon. (Technically they were, of course, but they lasted in spirit for several more years.) He asked gently, "Could you please tell us, Mr. Fallows, just what you think the armband will accomplish? Just what are you protesting here in this room?" When it came down to it, I wasn't protesting anything in the room, and I had the fleeting wish that the last year or two of school had involved something closer to real academics. I didn't know what to do with the band, so I left it on my arm, where it remained during the orals like some enormous stuffed fish I'd inexplicably brought along but that everyone else was too polite to gawk at.

Along with the black comedy, there was also an element of uncertainty and disorientation that is easy to overlook, now that we all know how things turned out. Perhaps everyone else at Harvard had a much clearer sense than I did of what it all meant—the student protests, the events in Washington and Chicago and Vietnam. My own sense was of being on a gyre of history whose final resting point no one could safely predict. Another civil war between blacks and whites? The recriminations of history visited upon America's "good Germans" for going along with an immoral national policy? Who could tell? If others could, I certainly could not, and I suspect there were many like me. As a result, people were unmoored from any secure knowledge of which degrees of resistance would look wise in the perspective of history and which would seem excessive and shrill. Others of our generation came under far more immediate and tangible sorts of "pressure"—the life-and-death pressure of combat, the economic pressure few students at Harvard faced. I do not mean to equate these experiences, but I do believe that this sort of pressure, exerted on privileged students with overwrought notions of morality, took its toll on people's ability to act "moderately" at all times.

There was one other element that, ten years later, accounts for much of what seemed brutal in those times, but which I have also come to consider one of the luckiest things about being part of that generation. It was the extraordinary, blind confidence that Harvard students then possessed, as individuals and as members of a group. Their— (our)—feeling was different from that of the generation that

came home from World War II to take over the management
of America's institutions, since it was tinged with cynicism
about the basic precepts of American life. But there was
among students in the late 1960s the same sense that young
veterans possessed in the late 1940s—that of preparing to
take over and of being comparatively untroubled by fears of
failing to find a place in the economic order. I am talking not
about mere self-satisfaction in the I-have-made-it sense,
which has always been an unfortunate part of the Harvard
culture and probably always will be, but rather about the
psychic and (most of all) economic confidence of the generation that had been reared in the summer of America's time.
The only limit to our nation's power seemed to be the wisdom with which it was used. The most pressing problems in
our careers seemed to be choosing among the possibilities
laid before us.

As is obvious even in the retelling, such confidence spilled
over all too easily into the smugness, arrogance, and astonishing wastefulness of students of that era, who sometimes
looked upon the richness of a Harvard education as if it were
all a plot to trouble and vex them. But it also equipped them
with the healthy form of arrogance that emboldens its pos-
sessors to take risks rather than avoid them. This kind of
confidence enabled students to leave college without admission slips in hand from law and business schools (although
many took that route, of course), because most shared the
quiet assumption that the opportunities would come again.
Perhaps all young people should feel this freedom to experiment, but they don't; perhaps this was a privilege that went
with a Harvard pedigree rather than a broader trait of that
era. Still, I think those times were different, and on balance I
prefer the arrogance of my contemporaries to the hesita-
tions and uncertainties of those who followed us by six or
eight years. People felt they could gamble—in challenging
the government or the University, in laying plans for their
careers—and could survive even if they lost. As I write, I am
one week away from my tenth college reunion. I am not sure

how much of this confidence remains. I will be surprised if there is not still quite a bit there.

I was reminded of this element a few weeks ago, when someone I had known faintly in college wrote me to discuss a movie about Harvard in the late 1960s, called *A Small Circle of Friends*. I thought that the movie did a good job of depicting some of the confusion and ordinariness of daily life at the College in those extraordinary times, and I had said so in a review. My acquaintance wrote to say that the movie might have been true to parts of reality, but there was a whole side of life it left out. To illustrate what he meant, he sent along copies of a few pages from *Windsong*, a pastiche of fiction and reportage that my friend Nicholas Gagarin had published one month before our graduation in 1970.

I suppose that to those of worldly sophistication (or broad reading in the works of Evelyn Waugh or Anthony Powell), Nick Gagarin might have seemed almost a stock figure. He was the aristocratic scion with fey, elegant charm who beguiled and mystified his friends. This is not the place to tell Nick's full story at Harvard (nor do I pretend to know it all), which began with his friends' thinking him the most fortunate of creatures and ended with their crying over him as martyr, after he shot himself to death in 1971. His book seemed to be one of the turning points in this progression; Nick was exalted by the prospect of its publication and then cast down when the book was panned nearly everywhere it was reviewed. I remembered that harsh reception and had not opened the book in ten years, since I feared that it would not have aged well. Yet when I looked through those Xeroxed pages, there was . . . something to it, a quality that Nick's writing revealed. For example, a few days after the occupation of University Hall, the crowd at a mass rally in Soldiers Field roared its approval of a resolution saying, "This body repudiates the right of the Harvard Corporation to close our university." Nick wrote:

> In one sense, this vote set the tone for the days of the strike to come. For what the resolution says, beyond its outright repu-

diation of the Corporation, is that Harvard is 'our university.' And for many students this realization has been sudden, staggering, and of monumental importance for the future of their education here. We are on strike. We have shut down the university. But we have also opened a new university, our university, a free university. . . .

[The first Harvard] is a bunch of buildings. Many of them—particularly the libraries—are great buildings. But by themselves they run the danger of being nothing more; and most of the time the first Harvard is nothing more: it has no soul.

The second Harvard—'our university'—is very different. It is us, the students and faculty. We are its guts and its soul and the strike is the fact of our liberation. The students who liberated University Hall had to pay for it with a bloody police beating. That is because University Hall is the first Harvard's turf. Harvard Yard, however, is our turf—and now it is the headquarters of the second Harvard. . . .

The carnival nature of some aspects of the strike springs from the fact that in the first time in recent years we find ourselves with some breathing room. Suddenly we have won a victory. Suddenly we find that the cycle may not be closed, that we may not be doomed by the system to lives of corporate boredom. Suddenly we are free and we find that education is not what we have always been told it is. Suddenly everything is open, there are bold new directions in which we can walk, and we feel ourselves a little more fully because we dare to explore them.

Injudicious? Yes. Self-dramatizing, immoderate, insensitive to the demands of academic freedom and the traditions of an independent University? Yes, it was all those things, and so were many of us. But the confidence of it is astounding. It is there in every line. We can do it; things will improve; we can take the risk even of looking like fools. Maybe we should regret the immaturity of it, but in reading these pages I felt satisfaction, even pride. Something *was* going on in those days. I hope that the sharp memory of the excesses and extremes does not extinguish an appreciation for the live, daring spirit behind them. Ten years ago, parents, teachers, and leaders of the University seemed to mistrust and fear the demons loosed among the students. Should they not finally be prouder of implanting such confidence in their children than of almost any other influence they could have had?

Steven Kelman '70

Steven Kelman graduated summa cum laude from Harvard in 1970. His book on student radicalism, Push Comes to Shove, *appeared that year. He received a Ph.D. in government from Harvard in 1978 and now teaches at the Kennedy School of Government there. His most recent books are* Improving Doctor Performance *(1980) and* Regulating America, Regulating Sweden *(1980).*

For me, it is most appropriate to begin memories of Harvard with memories of high school. This is so because, among the people with whom I spent the most time in high school, "getting into Harvard" was about the most important goal a person could have.

I was class of 1966 at Great Neck South Senior High School, in Great Neck, Long Island, outside New York City. The high school was mostly Jewish, and over 80 percent of graduating seniors went to college. Harvard took one (or sometimes two) out of our graduating class each year, something we considered terribly unfair, since we were certain that ten of our graduating seniors could easily be among the top students at Harvard. We felt victimized by "geographic quotas" that, we assured one another, were anti-Semitic (without, I think, any great conviction or emotional resentment, since probably none of us had ever personally experienced anti-Semitism in our lives). We half-growled, half-joked about the groups the Harvard admissions process favored—kids from small towns in Montana and rich prep school types from the right families. (This was before the era of affirmative action for minorities, so that question never came up.)

But the difficulty of obtaining the prize of admission to

Harvard made the prize so much the more valuable. There were certainly students at Great Neck South for whom getting into a good college, much less getting into Harvard, was not a preoccupation, but there was a surprisingly large number for whom it was.

My recollections of Harvard are infinitely more favorable than my recollections of high school. A combination of frequent exams (we had five academic courses, and between them we usually had about an exam a week) and the importance of grades for getting into a good college sufficed to give one a more or less standing bout of nervous stomach. Many of my most vivid memories of high school surround tests and grades. I remember students taking up twenty minutes of class time after a test was handed back to argue over one or two points on the test. (Once a student who was a particularly tenacious disputant announced in chemistry class that he had a headache and wanted to go to the nurse's office, at which point the teacher said, "You stay right here. You've given me a headache all year.") A teacher we had for two straight years in "special" (advanced placement) math made it a practice never to give partial credit for answers in math exams where the student showed by his work that he understood the principle of the problem but made a calculation error somewhere. "Partial credit?" she would ask the class sarcastically, with a salty Nova Scotian accent that was a favorite for student parody, "Would they give an engineer partial credit if he did a calculation wrong and the bridge collapsed?" We laughed, albeit nervously, and we gnashed our teeth. To this day, I have a recurring dream (that, I understand, is relatively common among workaholic types) in which I show up for an exam and realize that I have forgotten to attend the classes all semester or in which I am about to appear in a play and realize that I forgot to learn my lines. The venue of such dreams, to this day, is high school.

By contrast, the academic atmosphere at Harvard during the years I was there (1966–70) was remarkably low-keyed. People never talked about grades. (Generally, one didn't know even one's own roommates' grades.) Exams were infrequent—a midterm and a final in each course. Courses were interesting. On that dimension, I experienced Harvard just as it was in the storybooks: as a chance to have a rewarding intellectual experience while still getting that perpetual knot out of my stomach.

Another way in which it was clear, from freshman year on, that Harvard contrasted favorably with high school was in the lack of social barriers among students. Looking back, it absolutely amazes me how much high school society was a divided society with high walls of insecurity keeping people apart. Our high school newspaper ran a piece once about students at Great Neck South being divided into "beats" (who sang folk music at parties and competed for good grades), "poppies" (who were fashionable and who dated a lot), and "hoods" (who were juvenile delinquents not headed for college). I didn't know a single "hood," and, while I knew some "poppies," I regarded them as socially so superior to me that it was senseless to try to get to know them (especially the girls).

Life in a Harvard freshman dorm (I lived in Matthews South, at the corner of the Yard closest to Harvard Square) was designed to smash such barriers. Suddenly one was placed in close physical and intellectual proximity with kids the likes of whom one had never met before. The strangest thing was meeting for the first time the children of hereditary wealth or hereditary fame, the aristocratic types against whom one had vague prejudices but about whom one knew little.

They *were* different. One guy told me that he had only recently learned that not everybody had a coming-out party; he had thought that even in the ghetto modest such parties were held. Others told of summer homes and winter homes and estates their parents lived on when not at either. I wrote an article during my freshman year for *The New York Times Sunday Magazine* on my freshman class; one of the most exhilarating parts of researching the article was talking with "famous children," or, rather, children of famous parents, in the class. It seemed as if, for the first time, I was on the inside looking around rather than on the outside looking in. (As an incidental note, the attention that article received when it came out—and the fact that, to this day, people I meet of my approximate age frequently remember that article—served, and serves, to remind me of the special place Harvard occupies in American life.)

All this was different, but the confrontation with a different world did not, as it had in high school, produce anxiety or insecurity. There were those final clubs, off somewhere, that I knew about and knew I would not be invited to join. But, frankly, it didn't bother me in the slightest. (I endorsed the saw that the people who were upset about not getting into the Porcellian Club were not people like me, who stood completely outside the club system, but those who had "only" made it into the Fly.) The differences were exciting, not depressing.

In a sense, things were made easier because I attended Harvard at a unique moment when, for a brief instant, the cultural role model for significant portions of the Harvard student body—including a not-insignificant number of the aristocrats whose cultural style at an earlier point had dominated—was the New York Jewish kid, intellectual and radical, perhaps even coming out of a family of 1930s radicals as well.

That in turn, of course, was related to the student politics of the late 1960s. The class of 1970, of which I was a part, caught the wave of student radicalism as it was forming and rode with it until it crested with the Cambodia and Kent State protests of May 1970. The fall of 1966, when I was a freshman, marked the beginning of the dramatic growth of SDS (Students for a Democratic Society). The fall of 1967, with the sit-in at Harvard against job recruiters from Dow Chemical, marked the beginning of the radicalization of SDS. The fall of 1968 marked the beginning of the SDS campaign against ROTC, which culminated in the sit-in and "bust" at University Hall in April 1969. And the spring of 1970 saw trashings in Harvard Square and a shutdown of Harvard following the Cambodian incursion and the Kent State killings. Starting with the fall of 1970—when our class was gone—campuses across the nation began to cool down. If you look at lists of contributions to the Harvard College Fund by class, you will see that there is a marked dip—compared not only with classes before but with classes after as well—in the proportion of members of the class of 1970 who give to Harvard. Our class was prototypical of the student radicalism of the 1960s.

One might have predicted that all this would please me just fine. First, I was addicted to politics. My parents had me out distributing literature for Adlai Stevenson and for local school-board candidates by the time I was four. During the 1956 presidential campaign they dressed me for Halloween in a big diaper, bedecked with Democratic party buttons and a sash reading "Time for a Change." That same year I gave a speech for Stevenson to my third grade class and was depressed that my arguments were not convincing enough to get a majority of my classmates to vote for Stevenson. Given a lifelong addiction to politics, I should have rejoiced in the hyperpolitical environment that Harvard became during the years I was there. Never before (or since) had I been lucky enough to have so many others share my own passion.

The second reason that it might have been predicted that the politics of the late 1960s at Harvard would have pleased me just fine was that I was, by my own definition, a radical. In my junior year in high school, I joined the Young People's Socialist League (YPSL), the youth group of the Socialist party of Norman Thomas and Michael Harrington. I went to Harvard determined to start a YPSL chapter there.

In fact, by the time I graduated I had succeeded in becoming the single undergraduate most hated by SDS. A book I wrote on the Harvard strike, *Push Comes to Shove*, appeared during Cambodia/Kent State, and SDS flooded the campus with leaflets denouncing it. Several months before the book came out, I had entered the competition for undergraduate English language commencement speaker, a competition open to any senior, with the winner selected by some professors in the Classics Department. I won, and when my selection became public a month or so before commencement, SDS began a campaign to have my selection (which they ludicrously saw as an administration conspiracy) annulled. There were threats to storm the commencement stage, and on commencement day a phalanx of faculty members supposedly was there to block entrance to the stage. The effectiveness of the phalanx was vividly demonstrated when a group of eight demonstrators from a Cambridge community group took over the stage, shortly before it was my turn, to protest Harvard's policies in the city of Cambridge. The takeover did, however, take some of the heat off my appearance. When I finally did give my commencement speech, it was interrupted by virtually constant heckling, and a small number of students walked out. But there was nothing more serious. (My parents commented afterwards that the success of the community demonstrators in storming the commencement stage, outdoors in the vastness of Harvard Yard, hardly inspired their confidence in the security arrangements designed for me.)

Despite my self-proclaimed radicalism and my addiction to politics, the late sixties at Harvard were, politically, a depressing time for me. Depressing, I should add, in an intellectual sense and disappointing in an emotional sense—although still exciting and exhilarating, with the excitement coming from the rush of ideological polemic and the proud feeling that one was standing up for what was decent and right despite hostility and contempt.

The origins of my idiosyncratic response to the politics of Harvard in the late 1960s were, again, in the special nature of my experiences in high school. Great Neck, New York, was an atypical American community. It was an upper-middle-class, predominantly Jewish community where there was a good deal of political activity, much of it on the Left.

Many old Communist party members or sympathizers, now older and more settled but still not so different ideologically from what they had been during the 1930s, lived in Great Neck, and their children were my classmates in high school. Several years before the flowering of the anti-Vietnam protest movements and of the New Left, the dominant political point of view among the significant number of political activists at Great Neck South was already the kind of radicalism that was to attain similar prominence in many college campuses around the country only by 1970. I remember well the after-school discussions in the Forum Club, a political discussion club that was one of the school's extracurricular activities. In 1963, at the time of the anti-Diem demonstrations in Saigon and two years or so before the antiwar movement began to stir, basically *everyone* was against American involvement in Vietnam. We had a fair number of students who were already then enamored of Mao's China; a pro-Mao book by someone named Felix Greene, *Awakened China*, was eagerly read, and Felix Greene appeared as a speaker sponsored by a local adult group where many of the old Communist party types tended to congregate.

Within that environment I was, already in high school, a dissenter. I defined my politics for myself in the middle of tenth grade and planted my tree right there. I was a democratic socialist or a social democrat in the tradition of the socialist parties of Western Europe. That meant that I was for democracy, against communism, not anti-American. It meant that I supported the labor movement and the Democratic party. Like other ideologies on the Left, mine gave me an answer (a sort of informal party line) on most political questions. I proclaimed my political self-definition in an article I wrote during the summer between my sophomore and junior years in high school on the political life of Great Neck South, criticizing procommunism among intelligent high school students. I sent it unsolicited to *The New Leader*, which was a political statement in itself, for *The New*

Leader was an old socialist, strongly anticommunist magazine that made the older generation of communist sympathizers see red (no pun intended). *The New Leader* wrote
back that it wanted to publish the article, making that day
probably the happiest in my sixteen-year-old life. After the
article came out, William Buckley wrote a column about it,
the local newspaper ran a lead story about it, and I was
promptly notorious.

The late 1960s "radicalized" many students, at Harvard
and elsewhere. But I wasn't the only one who came to
Harvard with ready-made politics. I remember my first
weekend in Matthews South, just after my parents returned
home after depositing me and some belongings in Harvard
Yard. I ate dinner at the Hayes Bickford cafeteria just outside the Yard across Massachusetts Avenue with Mark
Dyen, a boy from the dorm. ("The Bick" was later replaced
by a Chinese restaurant.) Dyen was from New Haven, and
his father taught at Yale. He had spent some time in Indone-
sia with his parents, and we spent a good part of the evening
arguing about President Sukarno: Mark thought he was
great, and I thought he was a tinhorn dictator. Dyen also told
me about his involvement in efforts to run an independent
Left candidate against Congressman Robert N. Giaimo of
New Haven, whom I had never heard of before but whom
Dyen described to me as an "establishment liberal." I didn't
think people should run candidates against "establishment
liberals," at least not in a general election where it might
help elect a Republican. Dyen later became an SDS leader
and after that for a short time an underground Weatherman
terrorist; now he works for Massachusetts Fair Share, a
quasi-populist community organization where many old
Harvard SDSers ended up. We became (and remain, I
think) fast enemies.

Much of the core of SDS leadership—especially the group
that, when SDS factionalized, became known as the New
Left caucus—came from hereditary radical, or at least hereditary political, backgrounds not dissimilar to my own. I

suspect that all of us who were like that shared a certain feeling of separateness, at some deep emotional level, from the hoards of previously apolitical or nonradical students who became radicalized by Vietnam, or by going away from home and being exposed to new ideas, or by a sense of personal alienation from parents and/or from society, or simply by being at Harvard during a time when our best and brightest were, the common account told us, demonstrating and even occupying buildings. We who brought our politics to Harvard were quicker to engage in obscure polemic, more conversant with Marx, more likely to know where the dividing lines were on such faraway questions as the Kronstadt Rebellion, the role of the Social Democrats in Weimar Germany, or the actions of Ho Chi Minh in 1946. We were, in a sense, more European and less American: we lived and breathed in a world where half the people we knew called themselves socialists or radicals, not one where the figure was closer to half of one percent. Something that I think I never fully appreciated as I worked to organize a chapter of the Young People's Socialist League on campus was that anyone willing to take the major step of identifying himself, in the United States, as a socialist (even SDS never used the word "socialist" in its name) was unlikely to be sympathetic to the quite restrained and moderate and very outspokenly anticommunist politics the YPSL was offering. In Europe it would have been no problem: there were lots of socialists there, and many of them were quite restrained and moderate and anticommunist. But we were in the United States, not in Europe. And we were not living in a time when people were interested in social change because of an ongoing commitment that did not get born yesterday; we were living in a time when such commitment was born of burning threats and searing alienation.

During the four years I was at Harvard, SDS became both much bigger and much more radical. By junior year SDS regular meetings could go a good way toward filling Burr A, which had a capacity of about two hundred. (I knew the capacity of various lecture halls superbly well because we had to go through the difficult task of trying to estimate meeting and, above all, lecture crowds when scheduling YPSL meetings with the office of the dean of students— more particularly, with Miss Jean Douglas, a short Scottish woman utterly devoted to Dean Watson, who got along with me far better than she got along with other campus radicals, particularly the undergraduate Trotskyist leader, for whom she had a special dislike.) In contrast to SDS meetings, YPSL membership meetings were typically held in various classrooms in Sever that had a capacity of fifty or so. We had speakers fairly frequently, however (more often than SDS did), who drew large crowds. Michael Harrington could fill Lowell Lecture Hall, which had a capacity of eight hundred or so. We got almost two hundred to hear Al Lowenstein speak in Harvard Hall to tell us about his plans, not yet fully formed then, to try to "dump Johnson" in 1968. And —my proudest achievement—we got, with the help of extensive and creative publicity, over a hundred people to pay a dollar each to hear Max Schachtman, of whom nobody had ever heard before, speak on the fiftieth anniversary of the Russian Revolution (his topic: "Workers' Paradise Lost"). Things like that were important to us then.

SDS became bigger. It also became much more radical. A sort of diminishing-astonishment principle was at work within SDS. Some small vanguard scouting party would tentatively stake out some position further and further to the Left. Once the position had been staked out, it no longer seemed quite as daring or unthinkable. Through repetition, gradually it became part of everyday SDS vocabulary. Thus, pro-Castro and pro-Mao positions were advanced very tentatively by some of the more "far out" elements within SDS when I was a freshman, and by senior year they had become the standard line within the organization. Sophomore year, in connection with the sit-in against a Dow Chemical recruiter, tentative talk about the unimportance of "bourgeois civil liberties" began. By senior year, this too became standard. Finally, like a supernova exploding and destroying itself, the now sectarian and factional national SDS organization at its Chicago convention in 1969 divided into several organizations, one of which went underground to bomb buildings and another of which announced that anybody who did not "support" North Vietnam, Albania, China, and Cuba (I think that was the whole list) was "no longer a member of SDS."

Meanwhile, I became—and the friends with whom I associated became—increasingly obsessed with SDS. Although the YPSL leaflets we put out about SDS—filled with accusations of "pro-totalitarianism," "elitism," and "contempt for the American people"—were regarded as hard hitting and even extreme by many students on campus, the leaflets actually reflected mild and sanitized versions of our feelings. Just as we psychoanalyzed the SDS members (in our private discussions) as "crazy" (some were self-hating; others were playing out bad relationships with their parents), so they psychoanalyzed us as being resentful of them because the YPSL was never able effectively to challenge them as a student organization. I can't render definitive judgment on the quality of our psychoanalysis of them, but I think I can say that their psychoanalysis of us was wrong. We thought that their political views were evil and that, if adopted in America, they would make our country a terrible society. Their growth on campus made us obsessive because it made us despair for the future of America. But, given the trends in the country at large at the time, we were quite proud of ourselves that we amassed about sixty dues-paying members and twenty genuinely active members for the organization. We had more active members than the Young Democrats (which dissolved after Humphrey was nominated in 1968) or the Young Republicans.

Looking back on the feelings we had then, several things stand out. We certainly overestimated the threat SDS posed to the future of Western civilization. I remain convinced that its leaders were as bad as we thought they were, but I think we didn't need to be as worried about them as we were. Our obsession with them honored them by overrating their importance. Second, I think we tended too much to take the idealistic mood—of which the growth of SDS was a twisted but nonetheless unmistakable product—too much for granted. We assumed that students would be idealistic and concerned and that it was all right to devote most of our attention to the twisted forms such idealism was taking. The current vogue of reactionary chic—the opposite of the 1960s' radical chic—testifies all too vividly that such concern and idealism cannot be taken for granted. Third, I am amazed and amused, looking back on those years, at just how sectarian all of us were. We in the YPSL as well as those in the various SDS factions genuinely did have a "line" on most political questions, a "correct" answer that it was important to adopt, even in its details. We could argue at length about—and be very worried about—slight changes in wordings in a resolution. The YPSL nationally, and the top leadership of the Harvard chapter locally, had a complex position on Vietnam that was very careful to avoid a call for unilateral or unconditional American withdrawal. We held a YPSL majority at Harvard to this position through three years of escalating radicalism and opposition to American policy. Finally, in the fall of my senior year—the fall after the 1969 strike—a membership meeting of the Harvard YPSL chapter voted, by a relatively narrow vote, to adopt a policy favoring unconditional American withdrawal. Even though the resolution was peppered with the (for us) compulsory words of opposition to North Vietnam and the Vietcong, I nevertheless regarded the passage of the resolution as an immense personal defeat, a failure of our meticulous efforts at indoctrination in our "line" on important political topics.

Finally, I think that both we in the YPSL and those SDS leaders who were hereditary radicals failed really to appreciate the personal and emotional animus that impelled much student radicalism in the 1960s, or the uninterest of many vaguely radical students in the detailed ideological disputes that were so important both to SDS people and to us. A significant number of students were angry and unhappy about their lives, and , though we saw the anger around us, we had a hard time emotionally identifying with it. (Looking back ten years later, that anger seems even harder to empathize with, since it now seems to be gone.) Moreover, much of the arcane ideology with which SDS tried to reach the student body went in one ear and out the other. Students had a vague sense that SDS kids were "idealistic" and that they were "putting their bodies on the line" by doing the things they did, but most students had no idea what SDS really was advocating. This probably made most students believe that YPSL warnings about SDS were shrill and incredible, and this infuriated us. But it probably also infuriated SDS people, because they were not making ideological revolutionaries out of many students.

On a personal level, one of the distinguishing features of living a student life so centered on politics in a highly politicized time is that one's friends were in effect chosen for one. Most of my closest friends were people active in the YPSL. That in turn consisted of people who, for whatever reason, were attracted to our ideas and wanted to become politically active. Especially around Adams House, where I lived, I also became friendly—mainly in terms of dining room companions, with whom one did spend, admittedly, very large quantities of time, especially at dinner—with a fair number of people to my right politically, with whom I shared mostly hostility toward SDS. There was an economics tutor who was opposed to the war in Vietnam because he felt that the United States should not donate the services of its army to foreign countries (if they wished to purchase such services, that was all right). There was a history and literature tutor who drove all the way down to New York to cast a ballot against Mayor John V. Lindsay (voting absentee didn't give him the same thrill) and who bordered on being a racist. Arthur Waldron, my roommate for a year, was an anglophile who persisted in wearing a suit with a pocket watch to dinner most nights and dreamed of becoming the first American to master both Russian and Chinese, thus ensuring a successful career in the CIA. (I found out when I visited Hong Kong in 1971 that any number of foreign service officers knew both Russian and Chinese well. Arthur went on to get a Ph.D. in Chinese history at Harvard.) We spent a perhaps disproportionate amount of our time around the dinner table telling SDS horror stories.

The high point of student radicalism at Harvard was, of course, the student strike in April 1969. SDS had been preparing for it during the entire academic year with a campaign to get ROTC off campus; several weeks before the strike, the Progressive Labor faction of SDS began a campaign against Harvard's activities in Cambridge, which they saw as part of a plan to make Cambridge into an "Imperial City" (which I promptly dubbed "Emerald City"). In the week or so before the building occupation, my friends and I began feeling increasingly desperate because there seemed to be no way to stop SDS from taking over a building. We discussed among ourselves having a group of students link arms in front of the entrances to University Hall, so that SDS would have to commit violence against us in order to get in. I cannot now recall why the idea was rejected, but it was. The night of the University Hall takeover the YPSL executive committee met all night in my room in Adams House B entryway to draft a statement. We sent representatives to some meeting of "moderate" students going on in the Yard at the same time, using the student ID of a freshman member, Rob Patullo, because the Harvard police had closed off the Yard to all but the freshmen who lived there.

For me, the strike was a time of exhaustion and depression over what had happened at Harvard, mixed with a certain weird exhilaration. YPSL put out reams of leaflets—literally tens of thousands—distributed in connection with the various mass meetings at Harvard Stadium and distributed in the Yard. Officially, we supported the initial three-day strike endorsed the morning after the University Hall "bust" at the student meeting in Memorial Church. Actually, most of our inner circle did not really even support that brief a strike; I can't remember whether we actually pronounced the phrase at the time, but I know that my attitude took off on the statement of the American commander who talked about destroying a village in Vietnam in order to save it. We supported the strike in order to try to destroy it. We officially opposed continuing the strike beyond the original three days.

That summer and fall, I wrote *Push Comes to Shove,* an account of student radicalism at Harvard that culminated in the strike. It came out in May 1970, just a month before I graduated, and it got a fair amount of attention. While Harvard was on strike over Cambodia, I was traveling around the country promoting the book. The book was severely critical of the pro-SDS stance *The Harvard Crimson* took. Instead of assigning one of the more blatantly pro-SDS editors to review the book, they gave it to Jim Fallows, outgoing president of the *Crimson.* Although Fallows had been involved in something the *Crimson* tried to organize called the Conspiracy against Harvard Education, he had generally been a relatively retiring and fair-minded type. Fallows succeeded in penning an absolutely vicious review. At one point (this was before the gay liberation movement rendered such comments unacceptable) he suggested that my hostility to SDS might be due to an unrequited homosexual love for Mike Kazin, an SDS leader in the class of 1970

I was out of the country for two years after graduating, and in September 1972 I returned to Harvard to attend graduate school in political science. One of the magazines to which I took out a subscription on my return was *The Washington Monthly,* of which Fallows was a contributing editor. I found that, in spite of myself, I liked much of what he wrote. Sometime in early 1973 I got a letter from Fallows. He had been looking through the mailing labels at the magazine to see who in Cambridge subscribed. He came

upon my name and address, and he wrote to apologize for
his review of *Push Comes to Shove*. The review was one of
the most embarrassing things he had ever done, he concluded. I wrote back that I appreciated his letter very much
and accepted his apology. In 1977 in Berlin, I attended a
conference at which Fallows, then President Carter's chief
speech writer, was also present. We hadn't seen each other
since graduation. He told me he was very hesitant about
ever going back to Cambridge, because there were so many
unpleasant memories associated with it in his mind. I told
him that was funny, because I didn't feel that way. We talked
more about Harvard in those days, and I felt a bond growing
as between two people who have been through a difficult
experience together. But I also realized how the 1960s were
finally becoming part of the past, something one talked
about in terms of "how things were then." It was, in a sense,
on that day in Berlin that the 1960s at Harvard ended for me.

William Martin '72

William Martin was born in Cambridge in 1950. He grew up in Boston and graduated from Harvard in 1972. After Harvard, he worked for two years in the Boston construction business, then moved with his wife to Los Angeles. He received his Master of Fine Arts in motion picture production from the University of Southern California in 1976, won the Hal Wallis Screenwriting Fellowship in that same year, and has since written several screenplays. His first novel, Back Bay, *was published in 1980. He now lives with his wife and son in a Boston suburb*

We lived, that freshman year, in Thayer Hall, the dormitory that looks like a textile mill looming beside University Hall. One night in April, after we had finished studying, a group of us were sitting around sipping coffee and talking about basketball. Boston and Los Angeles were about to meet in the NBA playoffs, and my money, quite a lot of it, said that the Celtics were going to win. A friend from the West Coast, who made coffee each night around eleven o'clock, was betting ten dollars against me. He said that the money he was going to win would pay for all the coffee I had drunk during the year.

It was not an unusual conversation in Thayer. Like any dorm, Thayer had its cliques, and every clique had its favorite topics of conversation. The bridge addicts talked about bridge, the premeds about Chemistry 10, the New Yorkers about how much better everything was in New York. But certain topics gave us common ground: the Celtics and Red Sox, the Beatles—whose White Album could be heard someplace in the dorm at any time of the day or night—overbearing section leaders, and girls.

Most of us in freshman year seemed to do more talking about girls than with girls, and many of us couldn't quite understand why, after almost a year at Harvard, we had not been able to meet the right girls—that is, girls who would be impressed that we went to Harvard. As freshmen, we still had several preconceptions about the power of the Harvard name, and about girls, that experience would later erase.

I considered the Red Sox a special talisman because, until spring training, I had had few conversations with any of the prep school graduates from old New England families. I had made friends easily among the students from the Northeast, mostly middle-class Jews and Irish Catholics, like me, and among students from the rest of the country who enjoyed forcing me, as a Bostonian, to defend Boston's weather, its streets, its drivers, its politicians, and its accent. But shaving into the same mirror with a Hallowell each morning became much more interesting when we discovered that we were both concerned about Carl Yastrzemski's batting average and Jim Lonborg's knee. Out of the frustrations of following the Red Sox had grown a New England tradition that crossed all boundaries, even at Harvard.

From time to time in that freshman year, we also discussed politics. We could not avoid it. At Harvard in 1969, politics seemed to mix naturally with the oxygen, automobile exhaust, and cannabis smoke that formed our atmosphere. Nationally, we'd had Nixon to kick around for three months. Locally, the SDS was rumbling about ROTC and University expansion, while an outsider from the radical fringe named King Collins had been making *Crimson* headlines by disrupting a social relations class and charging that social study, when not accompanied by radical social action, was a fraud. And if that was not enough politics, we had only to think back a few months to 1968.

The war in Vietnam, Gene McCarthy's Peace Crusade, Lyndon Johnson's decision not to run for President, the assassinations, the racial unrest, the Columbia takeover, and the Chicago convention had combined with seven months at Harvard to instill various degrees of political consciousness in the members of our freshman class.

Some in the class were "politicized," a term that, in the

late sixties, was used interchangeably with "radicalized." It described those who suddenly decided that they were among the first to recognize the immorality, hypocrisy, and stupidity of the establishments in power, then turned to the Left and signed up to distribute radical pamphlets in Harvard Square. Those who decided that Richard Nixon had all the answers and went off to join the Young Republicans were not considered politicized.

Others in the class had attained a higher level of consciousness. They were "politically aware," which meant, basically, that they were on your side and spoke eloquently in support of your opinions. To a Young Republican, other Young Republicans were politically aware. But more commonly the term referred to a member of a radical group who was committed to the goals of his organization, always tried to look serious, seldom displayed a sense of humor, and *wrote* the pamphlets that were distributed in the Square. The politically aware spent their time trying to politicize the rest of us and make us see the light.

But the rest of us were too busy trying to confront the more demanding, if more mundane, aspects of our existence—Nat. Sci. 10, Expos., freshman mixers, life in a dorm, and meals at the Union. We read the pamphlets, formed our opinions, then went back to our apolitical lives.

I tried to avoid labeling myself, but, when I thought about it, I considered myself a liberal. I was willing to listen to anyone argue any side of an issue for at least five minutes. I took most of my political attitudes from Robert F. Kennedy's book, *To Seek a Newer World*. I had spent the previous summer working as a tutor in Harvard's Upward Bound Program, where black teenagers taught me more than I taught them. I opposed the war in Vietnam, but I didn't think that, if I were drafted in three years, I could do anything but obey the law. I tried not to think that far in advance.

Few of my friends, in April 1969, were either politicized or politically aware, but we were aware that the noises from the

SDS were growing more ominous, and some sensed that the disruptions by King Collins, trivial though they were, foreshadowed something more dramatic. Nonetheless, most of us agreed that there would be no building takeover and that, if there was, the police would not be called. We believed in Harvard's ability to solve its problems, in the ability of rational people to settle their disputes through rational argument.

With that in mind, we had not taken the increasing tensions too seriously. We had responded to all the political debate we'd been hearing by creating a mock organization called the TVG or Thayer Vigilante Group, a cabal of rightists for whom we formulated satirical reactionary responses to every SDS position. Although the TVG did not exist outside the imaginations of a few of us in Thayer Hall, we felt that our slogan, "Tradition unhampered by progress," was as good as anyone's.

"You've got to have a good slogan," Mike Leahy, one of the founders of the TVG, had explained. "Everyone around here has a slogan. A good slogan is more important than knowing what you're talking about." Leahy—tall, slender, with long hair and a sharp eye for pretension—believed that taking *anything* too seriously was bad for the health. That attitude, and the Red Sox batting helmet he had been wearing since the beginning of spring training, would give him a pair of distinct advantages when the rhetoric started flying and the clubs started swinging.

Around eleven o'clock on that night in April, our conversation about basketball was interrupted when we heard the sound of people chanting someplace outside. I looked out the window toward Widener Library. Hazard lights mounted on sawhorses were flashing yellow, warning of a half-filled pipe trench that snaked across the near corner of the Yard. Portico lights, like votive candles lit at the temple of learning, illuminated the pillars and steps of Widener Library. The rest of the Yard was in darkness, and the chanting was growing louder. Then, more lights appeared near Widener Library as a group of students marched out of the shadows carrying lanterns and signs and shouting "Rotcy must go! Rotcy must go!"

I turned to my friends, who were already hurrying outside for a closer look. One of them, a military school graduate, was strapping on his garrison belt as he went. A garrison belt is a thick piece of leather with a lethal-looking buckle; it has been known to be a favorite weapon among street gangs.

I said to him, jokingly, that the TVG wouldn't be needed tonight. He said that he still had to hold up his pants, and he rushed out. Considering his military background, I thought that his action seemed more like reflex than bravado. He was responding to a threat. Although we seldom admitted it, many of us felt threatened by the radical students. We had arrived only seven months before, and we were still awed by the University, by its history, its prestige, its "tradition of the life of the mind," as one professor had put it. In assailing the administration, the radicals were challenging our preconceptions about Harvard, and my friend, at least for a moment, was ready to meet the challenge with his garrison belt.

Outside, about a hundred demonstrators had gathered in front of the statue of John Harvard and were climbing the front steps of University Hall. Nervous University policemen protected the doors of the hall. Freshmen poured from their dorms to see what the commotion was about. Others, who were trying to study or sleep, screamed out their windows for quiet. But the demonstrators continued to chant, "Rotcy must go!"

The night was cold for April, and I was shivering as I walked among the demonstrators, studied their faces, and wondered if they had the courage to take over University Hall. Then, from the edge of the mob, I heard familiar voices begin a counterchant. I looked toward the noise. My friends from Thayer were laughing as they shouted, "Rotcy must stay! Rotcy must stay!"

What we saw that night was just a rehearsal, a little dumb

show before the play. The SDS dispersed, the garrison belt was unstrapped, and we went back to the dorm and talked until two. We joked about the counterrevolutionary tactics the TVG would employ if a building were taken. We discussed the administration's tactics. And we decided that the SDS wouldn't do it. We were wrong.

By noon the next day, the SDS was in University Hall. The sun was shining brightly. A mob of students filled the yard. An SDS leader with a bullhorn exhorted them. Many jeered. Others impulsively joined the SDS. Leaflets littered the ground. The Beatles' song, "Revolution," was blaring from a stereo in Weld Hall. Moderates and conservatives were arriving with more leaflets. Mimeograph machines were spinning crazily all over Cambridge. Students were chanting, "Rotcy must go!" Others were chanting "SDS get out!" And both sides were struggling to find the ultimate chanting weapon—a slogan that rhymed.

Mike Leahy, just back from lunch, his pockets filled with fruit, sidled up to me and suggested that we go into University Hall. I hesitated. He said that the SDS had "liberated" the hall for all of us. I could never argue with Leahy's sarcasm, and together we went in.

We walked first into the foyer of the freshman dean's office, where a WHRB reporter was preparing to interview one of the SDS leaders. Leahy, in the best tradition of Harpo Marx, offered the radical a banana. He was politely refused. I left Leahy to distribute his fruit and went upstairs to the faculty meeting room, where the SDS had convened.

The scene there reminded me of something from *A Tale of Two Cities*. The portraits and busts of Harvard's presidents, the gentlemen who had presided over three hundred and thirty-three years of orderly education, gazed down on a motley mob of students who, now that they were in possession of the hall, didn't seem quite sure of what to do next. I resented these students because they felt that their political beliefs gave them the right to disrupt the functioning of the University and interfere with the academic freedom of the rest of us. Although I later grew to admire their courage and realized that I agreed with many of their positions, my resentment colored my responses for the next week.

Around four o'clock the next morning, after a few hours of fitful sleep, I was awakened by the electric scream of the fire alarm. The students in University Hall had sensed that the bust was coming, and they had pulled every alarm in the Yard to rouse reinforcements. The freshmen again poured from their dorms, and hundreds of students, many shrouded in blankets after sleeping a few hours in hallways, swirled and darted around the floodlit University Hall. The wind was whipping debris around on the ground, it was a chill forty degrees, and the SDS bullhorn was working again, its shrill tones reverberating across the Yard.

As the crowd grew, SDS students and sympathizers ran from dorm to dorm asking for sheets and wastebaskets filled with water; they were preparing for a teargas attack. My military school friend and I were standing on the steps of Thayer when we were approached by a radical student who explained that they were going to cover their faces and hang wet sheets in the windows of University Hall.

"Wet sheets aren't going to stop teargas," said my friend. "I've been gassed, and I know what it's like. Your eyes'll burn and you'll start to vomit. It'll kill you. And if you put sheets on the windows, you'll just be making a gas chamber for yourselves. If you think there's going to be a bust and they're going to use gas, get out now."

Today, a conversation like that would sound rather bizarre in Harvard Yard. That morning, it was simply one more touch of surrealism.

Around five, as the sky turned leaden gray, the police arrived in a convoy of yellow school buses, which rumbled down the driveway between Thayer and Memorial Church and pulled up in front of Sever. The state police, with their helmets and clubs and baby blue uniforms, climbed out of the buses and formed their phalanxes across the yard.

For a few moments, the huge crowd of students outside the hall was stunned, silent. My friends on the steps of Thayer had made no jokes about the TVG since the takeover. We had all hoped that somehow, the issue could be resolved without an army of police. Then, the crowd began to roar its anger. One of my friends, a rather quiet, conservative student, began to scream, "I can't believe this is Harvard! They've brought in the pigs!"

The police marched forward, and Harvard was politicized.

By seven o'clock that morning, students had gathered on the steps of Widener for the first of many mass meetings. The first student to speak suggested seriously that we all go over and stone President Pusey's house. I left the meeting and went to breakfast.

In the next few days, we would hear many stupid suggestions and a litany of chants and slogans. By eight o'clock on the morning of the bust, we were told that we should "Strike Now" and "Shut it Down." The list of demands grew. The University had once more proved Mao correct: political power came from the barrel of a gun. If you weren't part of the solution, you were part of the problem. The strike vote was taken in sunshine at the stadium. The Red Fist. The Black Fist. Mass meetings. Ad hoc committees. Guerrilla theater. Leaflets, counterleaflets, position papers. Embattled deans in bow ties, with close-cropped hair and close-clipped accents, defending University policy in forums filled with hostile students. The world turned upside down and right on the edge of craziness.

The craziness was exemplified for me in an incident that occurred a few days after the bust. I was having lunch with my friend from military school in the Freshman Union. As we talked, a member of a radical guerrilla theater troupe appeared on the balcony above the dining area. He fired a loud cap pistol several times into the air, then began to play a scene. Another actor, dressed in a stylized police uniform, ran down the center aisle of the dining hall firing his cap pistol. For a moment, no one in the Union was sure that the scene was not real.

As the phony policeman rushed toward us, I looked at my friend.

His face seemed blank, without emotion, as though he were functioning on automatic. He grunted, "Enough of this," then picked up his dinner knife, methodically wiped it off with his napkin, as though he were cleaning off a bayonet, gripped the knife like a weapon, held it at his hip, and began to stand.

Fortunately, the actor on the balcony "shot" the phony policeman, who fell before he came too close to the knife. Realizing what he had almost done, my friend sat down, shook his head, and cursed all the radicals who had kept the University on edge for days.

That week in April became one of the watersheds of our Harvard lives. Afterward, invincible Harvard seemed vulnerable after all. We realized the tenuous nature of peace on the campus and the potential impact of politics on our everyday lives. Some students were politicized enough to join the revolution. Others, who had participated in the strike and realized their capacity to effect change, returned to their work until motivated again. And few of us any longer felt awed by the University or threatened by the radicals.

As I thought about it in the following months, I began to see the incident in dramatic terms, as a series of stories about the people around me and as one major conflict between the administration and the SDS. As a dramatist tries to understand the complexities of experience, he recognizes certain truths: protagonists are not often without flaw, antagonists are seldom evil, and both have their motives. Most characters take action because they believe their position is right, but much human activity occurs in a gray area where right and wrong are relative concepts. The SDS acted from conviction and a sense of moral necessity. The administration responded from a position of legal right and responsibility to academic freedom. Each believed in the rightness of its own position. Each discovered that there are few simple solutions, few simple motives. And Harvard itself, the protagonist, was changed.

The TVG dissolved at the end of that freshman year. My

military school friend moved to Mather House, mellowed considerably, eventually became a tutor in one of the houses, and earned a Ph.D. in biology. He has remained nameless here because he is sometimes embarrassed when we recall the garrison belts and dinner knives. Mike Leahy moved to Eliot House. He wore his batting helmet most of the time, for protection, he explained, if the sky started falling; he tried to convert us all to Pabst Blue Ribbon, and he held forth most nights on the comic absurdity of everything going on around us. After Harvard, he joined the Peace Corps and eventually became a physician. I moved to Kirkland House, where I spent three rewarding years.

Life at Harvard was not, as it may have seemed to an outsider, an endless stream of political demonstrations and upheavals. Once I had accepted campus politics as potentially disruptive, I was able to develop a healthy cynicism about the objectives and activities of the campus radicals, about the stubborn attitudes of the administration, and, with each year, immerse myself more deeply in my work.

I had always been fascinated by motion pictures. At the beginning of my sophomore year, I decided that, if I could muster the courage *not* to go to law school after I received my A.B., I would try to become a filmmaker. Although Harvard had no film major, I had chosen Harvard because, like most people, I felt that four years there would prepare me for anything I wanted to do. Moreover, I wasn't completely certain, until my senior year, that I wouldn't outgrow my fascination and actually *want* to go to law school. So I majored (or "concentrated," as we said at Harvard) in English, and without any difficulty created my own unofficial "minor" in film studies.

The serious examination of motion picture history and criticism, especially when it focused on that so-called poor relation of art, the American popular film, should have seemed rather unconventional within the framework of a Harvard degree program. But I was seldom discouraged by professors or departments when I wanted to link my interests with theirs. I was always respected as someone interested in a new discipline.

As a freshman, I felt that Harvard could use a few courses in film history. I organized a group of students, and we petitioned the University in support of several junior faculty. To my satisfaction, we were rewarded with Humanities 197, Film Analysis. In my junior year, David Reisman encouraged me to study America's social character through its films. And in my senior year, the English department allowed me to write an honors thesis that related the films of American director John Ford to the works of James Fenimore Cooper and philosopher Josiah Royce. As long as I met its requirements, the department was willing to accommodate me—except that not one of the senior faculty was familiar with the work of John Ford, and every thesis must be read by at least one senior faculty member. The junior reader had studied Ford's films and gave the thesis a summa. The senior faculty member, who had spent his life with literature and thought little of films in general, admitted in his critique that he had seen only one of Ford's films, and that on television. He didn't like the film, dismissed Ford, and focused rather harshly on my discussions of Cooper and Royce. The thesis did not receive a summa, but I was allowed to do the work that was important to me. That was all I could ask.

The Harvard I remember most warmly, and the Harvard where I learned the most, was not in the classroom or on the political barricades, but in the Kirkland House Junior Common Room, where I directed four plays. If I'd had an option, I would have been making movies, but film was expensive, there were no regular screenings of student films, and, given the equipment and time available, it was impossible to make anything longer than a fifteen-minute silent film in a semester. In house theater, we had budgets (and, after my first production, a willing patron in Master Arthur Smithies), live audiences to respond to our work, and the opportunity to mount full-length productions.

As a sophomore, I directed Samuel Beckett's *Happy Days,* a play that William Alfred introduced me to in Humanities 7. As a junior, I directed another comedy revue. And in my last year, I directed a production of *The Taming of the Shrew* that appeared at Kirkland House and the Loeb Experimental Theater. For three years, I had a forum in which to learn about actors, staging, scene structure, and the rhythms of dramatic storytelling. And I learned lessons that I still draw on, even though most of my storytelling now takes place between hardcovers.

They were, by Loeb mainstage standards, fairly small productions, but each play had its anecdotes, its conflicts, its good and bad notices, and every time out, I learned something new. I remember the intensity of the work, the consuming energy that each show demanded, the excitement of mixing logic and intuition to solve a problem of staging or character, the depression that arrived at that point in rehearsal when I feared disaster, the resolve that made me continue, the nervousness, the bad temper that sometimes cost me friendships, the fulfillment, and finally, the exhaustion. I learned that once I had committed myself to a show, I couldn't hold anything in reserve.

I suppose that, even if I had not pursued a career related to the theater, I'd still be glad for the experience. Because, more than my studies and more than the strikes, those four plays taught me about myself and helped me to grow up.

In April of 1970 we were working on *Happy Days* (which, because of the upheavals of that spring would run for just two performances). I was rehearsing with the actress in the Kirkland House Senior Common Room when I glanced out at Boylston Street and saw, once more, phalanxes of state police in riot helmets. The rehearsal stopped in mid-line.

A mob of radicals had marched from an antiwar meeting on Boston Common and were trashing Harvard Square.

It was a frightening night of teargas, shattering glass, fires in Harvard Square, mobs running down Dunster Street ahead of police riot troops, the Kirkland House gates locked to all but house members and their friends.

At one point, I ran up to my room to try to wash the teargas out of my eyes and found a young man and his wife standing in my living room. They were definitely not students. In an era when jeans and workshirts were the height of fashion, he looked like something from the windows of J. Press, and she looked as though she had just stepped from the pages of *Town and Country*.

I asked him, not very hospitably, "Who the hell are you?"

"My name is Arthur Kopit."

The young Broadway playwright, author of *Indians* and *Oh Dad, Poor Dad*, had been dining in Lowell House with a group of students, including my roommate. After dinner, he and his wife had innocently stepped into the middle of a police charge. They had been clubbed and, along with my roommate, pursued to the gates of Kirkland House.

While the state police were firing teargas canisters all around Kirkland House, I told Arthur Kopit how much I had enjoyed *Indians*. We agreed that we would have to talk about theater sometime in more relaxing circumstances. I offered the playwright and his wife the use of my room for as long as they cared to stay; then I went back downstairs to watch the riot. Only at Harvard.

On the street, it was a night of craziness and fear. These rioters were hard-core revolutionaries and street toughs. They were not bringing serious demands to the University; they were bringing anarchy. After that riot, the radical movement at Harvard never again carried the force it had wielded in 1969.

A few weeks later, however, Harvard was once more politicized by Nixon's invasion of Cambodia and the Kent State killings. Harvard students joined with students across the nation in a massive protest to let Nixon know that there would be no more business as usual. I didn't think that Nixon was listening.

Perhaps the strike did have some effect on Nixon's policies. Perhaps the unrest at home did cause him to hasten his withdrawal from Vietnam. But after 1970 there were no more strikes. Nixon's decisons to mine Haiphong Harbor and bomb Hanoi drew protests, and I seem to recall another building occupation that was largely ignored during my senior year, but by my graduation in 1972, the seventies, for better or worse, had begun.

When I graduated, I was glad to move on to the next phase of my life. I had hoped for years to tackle the movie business, and the West Coast was now before me. But my memories of Harvard, both good and bad, did not bleach away in the California sun. As I grow older, specific incidents and emotions seem to become even more vivid.

I can remember the compassion of William Alfred for the characters in Arthur Miller's *A View from the Bridge* as he lectured on their inability to express themselves. I remember the incredible excitement of the final forty-two seconds of the 1968 Yale game. I can recall my first hangover, after a party at the Kirkland House Master's residence; I recall that three double bourbons on an empty stomach were the cause. I remember the awe with which I listened to Walter Jackson Bate's lectures on Samuel Johnson. I was never sure if I was more overwhelmed by Johnson or the brilliance of Bate's scholarship and presentation. I prefer not to think about my embarrassment when, during my senior oral exam in English, I could not describe for Professor Bate the transition from the Classic period of English literature to the Romantic. I enjoy remembering the times we had after I met my future wife, and I laugh about the dates who shot me down.

I have my regrets over things I did not do, resources I did not use, but they are balanced by fulfillments. I sometimes wish that I had been forced to explore academic areas that are now alien to me, like math and science, but I was able to study whatever mattered to me at the time. Had I arrived in a more tranquil era, I might have been able to read more literature and study more history, but I would have learned far less about the complex nature of political action and would not have been on the periphery of a political struggle as it unfolded. It was not an easy time to go to college, but it wasn't boring, either.

I think I should close with a few words about Kirkland House. In an era of political unrest, it was good to have a small island of normalcy. For me, it was a comfortable, loosely knit community that demanded only what you were willing to give, a place where you could be as isolated or as gregarious as you wished, and by turns, I wished to be both. I had the requisite share of personality conflicts, mostly with roommates, but I made good friends, enjoyed good parties, and spent many a quiet night studying in the house library. Whenever I went to a meal, I knew that stimulating conversation with my friends would distract me from the food and teach me something as well. I met some fascinating people and some people I couldn't stand, and in some way, I enjoyed all of them.

When my wife and I were married a year after graduation, we decided that no place had better memories for us than Kirkland House. We held our reception in the courtyard.

Mark P. O'Donnell '76

Mark P. O'Donnell was born in 1954 and graduated from Harvard in 1976. He wrote his class ode and delivered the Ivy Oration on Class Day. As an under-graduate he studied with William Alfred, an experience he calls "too exalting to risk describing." After traveling in Europe on a fellowship, he worked briefly at Esquire, *leaving to write and participate in a late-night cabaret at the 1978 Spoleto Festival in Charleston, South Caro-lina. His humor, cartoons, and poetry have appeared in* The New York Times, Esquire, *the* Saturday Review, New Times, *the* Soho Weekly News, Ploughshares, Canto, *and many others. He contributed to the book* Junk Food *and, with classmates Kurt Andersen and Roger Parloff, wrote* Tools of Power. *His play* Fables for Friends *was produced at Playwrights Horizons in 1980. He is the recipient of the Lecomte du Nouy prize.*

I grew up in Ohio, which to the East Coast mind is somewhere between Oklahoma and Missouri. No one I ever knew, or met, or even smelled had had anything to do with Harvard. On my street in Cleveland, you might as well have referred to Shangri-la or Sherwood Forest—ideology is definitely not the basis of comparison here—because real people who breathed were in no danger of going there. "Harvard" was used by the smart alecks at Clack's Candy as a comic superlative: "Hey, we could send that mutt of yours to Harvard, Tony." The notion of it adorned our lives as trivially and immaterially as the notion of igloos or Grauman's Chinese Theatre. Ambition, even to travel, has always shamed the Irish of heart, and although my schoolmates wrote "Save this autograph till I'm famous" in one another's yearbooks, it was in playful surrender to the unlikelihood that their auras would ever illuminate more than one zip code.

My twin brother and I had been recruited, circus fashion, for Exeter, but as our permanent-record cards affirm, we went to public high school to stay with our three thousand friends. It's difficult to remember what an Ohio adolescence was like, since I romanticized it so scrupulously to others once I got to college that I can no longer distinguish truth from its attractive anecdotal derivatives. The myth of bizarre wholesomeness, of lockers, shaky marching bands, and wholeheartedly inept instruction—all true enough but not innocent in the way cosmopolites suppose—I have since exploited among gullible sophisticates eager to believe there are living Andy Hardys and hence, salvation. You never know what you are until you have to explain yourself to those who are different from you. (Why we paid the Harvard comptroller seven thousand dollars a year for the privilege of gawking at one another is somewhat more obscure.)

But I'm getting ahead of myself, a favorite Harvard calisthenic. Back at John Marshall High School (home of the infrequently victorious Lawyers), twin Stephen and I parlayed our genetically identical blarney into a bouncy species of local stardom. Perhaps it was a factor of our singular doubleness, but the powers from the right side of the tracks who had considered us for Exeter this time proposed the Big H. We had never excelled with this in mind; we were merely enthusiastic about entertaining ourselves. My co-zygote was hesitant; since Kalamazoo was such a funny word, he had wanted to wear its sweatshirt. He'd also liked the girl on its brochure. My school newspaper's adviser warned me, "It'll be the end of your sense of humor"—I guess he had met a Harvard grad—but we finally opted for the Unknown, hoping it might be less work than the Known. Besides, this was a brand name after a life of house brands, the academic Mallomar in a sea of mere gooey cookies.

One ends up at Harvard, I assume, only if one's toilet training was very easy or very difficult. (I won't be specific about which extreme was mine, but I do arrange all my colored pencils according to length.) The anal in-betweens lead affable, unacceptably rational lives, while those from the end zones proceed to selfishness, psychosis, and public office. There are exceptions: if a distant ancestor had so mortifying an introduction to personal regulation that he compensated his way into the presidency, his well-adjusted descendant can coast into Harvard and move off campus as quickly as possible. People who grew up comfortably steeped in Harvard lore seem the least buffeted by it, though Nature in her occasional fairness tends to provide those so advantaged with underweight and insincere friends.

I had imagined (with sad little squeaks, when I was alone) that my future classmates would be egregiously rich, skilled at levitation and the transmutation of base metals into gold, and handsome to the point of causing boulders to weep and donate to the class fund. At worst, they would be crew-cut geniuses who had traded their puberty to the devil in exchange for a marketable death-ray formula. Curiously, though neither type exists in the pure sense (maybe the swimming requirement keeps them out), in my idiot savoir I had intuitively pre-experienced the quality most Harvard grads wish to project: *I'm intimidating, but forget it, I'm just plain accomplished and meticulous, but intimidating, don't forget.* This is a complicated life's work, and few master this one-and-a-half whammy contortion until the obsessive calculations of corporate behavior succeed those of schooling and family life.

I didn't live in the Yard, which featured women for the first time with my class, but off in one of the all-male Union dorms, ill-featured and flung to the side like the bad kids hiding out from choir practice. The segregation, bare light bulbs, and washroom-green walls of Greenough fixed in my mind the belief that the administration perceived those it placed there as potentially violent. Judging from the human noises that enlivened my radiator pipes all winter, this may have been true of those who inhabited the suites upstairs.

The first few days were humid with pretension. The air surged with mass job-interview hysteria and the clacking sound of soft young antlers in nervous ritual combat. I put on a Rachmaninoff record as I unpacked, hoping to win points thereby, only to hear a snide passing voice in the hallway remark, "Not Rachmaninoff. *Come on!*" I soon realized I was hopeless: I'd assumed that liking Renoir was a credential, I voiced the *g* in Modigliani, I rhymed Brueghel with bugle, I mentioned Roy G. Biv in a discussion of ultraviolet rays, I had a Mormonesque flop of hair that is spotted at more ol' swimmin' holes than in espresso houses, and I'd inexplicably taken to understand that tank-top T-shirts were smart fashion if worn over long-sleeve shirts. My jeans were too short and too new, and so was my family tree. I considered crying myself to sleep after realizing all this: it seemed wonderfully autobiographical, and I'd learned to do it for a little theater production of *Our Town*. As I recall, I had an extra piece of pie at dinner instead.

Fortunately, the Psyche-out of the Innocents lasted only a week, after which tensions were released with daringly banal water fights, decorative outdoor toilet-paperings, and the season's first performance of "Holworthy sucks!" My initial sense that I didn't deserve to be at Harvard was democratically expanded to include most of those around me, especially the ones who folk-danced and ate sprouts. Classes commenced, and the signing of study cards brought a marital tedium to the surroundings. An arid, grubby phase followed, in the depth of which many of my classmates realized they wanted to write for the *Crimson*.

Within two weeks I had calmed down about the unlimited food, though I still marveled that you could have all the chocolate chip ice cream you were willing to stand in line for. Meals punctuated and directed my days like a "Pogo" character's. Otherwise, my first freshman semester was spent writing coy, manic letters to hometown friends I wasn't destined to keep, tending a wry but I-hoped-poignant diary of all that wasn't happening to me, and playing word games until wee hours with people whose parents even played word games. I proudly accustomed myself to mental furniture like Freud, Marx, Darwin, and dichotomies. The Greenough gang argued about whether an ostrich egg is the largest single cell, and we even phoned a professor at three in the morning to get his highly equivocated answer. Imagine such youth as to stay up all night out of interest and not anxiety.

In 1973 the new mood on campus was still new, though it wasn't interesting to hear about it then, either. Going bare-foot was still a political statement, and the final clubs were still bashful about their elitism, but the fear of abandonment that would lead to *Self* magazine was already eating up the baby boom's will to Worry About Others. The *Lampoon* was rumored to have wild parties, and its members were said to be "sick," which meant, I suppose, that they were willing to make light of illness and death in a way only those who are young and experienced with neither have the luxury to do. I had no compassion for such lack of compassion. As a profes-sional high school student, however, I longed for An Activ-ity, and as a tourist, I wanted That Which You Can't Get At Ohio State. What drives men to extracurricular involvement may well be sexual deprivation—I mean, look at senators' wives—but like the Widow Douglas to the snake-oil man, I turned to the *Lampoon*.

The Castle has been for over seventy years a Delft-tiled spiritual tree house for the disillusioned, or at least for those who thought it would be attractive to try to be. She adds to her slouching ranks with a long competition, culminating in a week-long simulation of birth trauma that a fraternity would call hazing, but since it has reputedly mystical under-pinnings, the rite is called Phools' Week, and no one has to apologize. Many a Pinocchio has climbed on to its mule wagon and lost all hope of ever becoming a Real Little Boy, and me, oh God, I'm one.

With only a sleepwalker's sincerity, I would walk to the *Lampoon* of an evening and deposit a few hastily drawn Bic-pen cartoons on the Sanctum floor. Then I would try to forget that I had, so later rejection would be meaningless.

Months passed. I shaved. I shaved a second time. Then, one Thursday, I was invited to a *Lampoon* cocktail party. It was my first taste of liquor, a lovely disorientation height-ened by the circular library that is the Castle's public room. I had never shared an event with people in black tie before, and under bourbon's first soft instruction, my head became

a diving bell, weighty but suspended, and lively, oblique
people darted past me, shimmering with privilege. A corner
of myself disapproved; my background had taught me to be
dubious and dismissive of highfalutin malarkey like social
events, precise speech, doctors, lawyers, their children, government, and any desire exceeding three square meals a
day. As with so much else I encountered, I didn't like the
Lampoon, but I wanted it to like me. After they abducted me
for Phools' Week, though, I experienced that intense onrush
of devotion that binds kidnapped heiresses to their captors.

First of all, officer, they forced me to skip classes, and I
was never to recover my governing passion for perfect attendance. (One of the few gentlemanly things about the
Lampoon is its tradition of absolute scholastic negligence.)
Then I was invited, along with a dozen other callow initiates,
to watch the long-standing members make jokes about us. I
knelt, catsup-spattered and sleepless, for a week of point-
edly unfounded insults from the reigning upperclassmen,
primarily Jim Downey and Sandy Frazier. They so dazzled
me with their gleeful, mock-heartless improvisations, as
hellishly blithe and banal as the recreation directors on the
Flying Dutchman, that I resolved to win their friendship.
Standing bare-chested with my head up the fireplace flue
singing selections from *Oklahoma!* for their diversion, I
plunged into the epiphany that occasionally enlightens
mortification—the *Lampoon* was suddenly my puppy religion, my first cosmic crush, and by the time I entered the
candlelit Great Hall as a member I couldn't remember not
caring whether I got on.

Life at the Castle taught me many things, chief among
them that on a color television even the black and white has
orangey-green edges and that roaches, like young men
away from home, only like to eat what's bad for them. It
opened a world of adult irresponsibility to me that my sterling childhood would have swooned at rather than imagine.

Morning, compliments, and outside friends were for
brownnoses. Those who impeded your self-indulgence were

assholes, unless they were Poonies, in which case you struggled not to disclaim them, usually in vain. No one was
responsible for this tenor; the place just possessed its tenants like any other eerie old house might. Still, real sentiment was awkward to express there, because boredom was
the apparent hallmark of awareness. There was a magazine
sporadically, yes, but the central event at the office was the
stylish open-ended loiter, carried on in shifts as if to break a
Guinness record for gross sexual patter conducted by vir-
gins. Some people were afternoon idlers, some midnight.
Yours truly Hungry Jack just had to witness both, since it,
like the dining hall food, was unlimited and free. For three
years I grew in my knowledge of the *Lampoon's* trivia, like
an eager immigrant or second husband, and only when I
was exhausted into simplifying my life did I reappraise its
music. But, for a while, I knew the playful, industrious
abandon shared elsewhere only by orphans who take over
the orphanage and don't tell anyone.

My other varsity nonsport was the Hasty Pudding show.
Perhaps the student council prez in me wanted more club
photos for my coffin wall; maybe the tourist in me wanted
more postcards. Whichever the case, like the fabled nervous
defendant who stabbed someone in the back, I did it acci-
dentally, three times.

To the world at large, which for Harvard's purposes is
New York and Connecticut, the Hasty Pudding show has a
sad potency as the symbol of how preppies used to be so
enviable and ridiculous in their simple love of an offensive
good time. Like tennis and the Lacoste shirt, it has democratically taken in the huddled masses in recent years, but it
still makes a Binky-it's-me-Kendall impression when you
flip through the program and compare the cheerful bank
ads with the career ambitions listed at the end of the flip
little autobiographies. The Pudding most characterized me,
certainly; it was practically Dracula to my Lugosi, even if I
always felt like the Chinaman at the barn raisin'. In my
journalist's way, I wanted to disdain the let's-sing-show-

tunes-till-real-late crowd as ineffectual, but I secretly loved their decent energy, and my fantasy has always been to get close enough to that set to hear it admit its fear of death. The Pudding had a few of those energetic decent musical buffs and a few back-of-the-class deans of the Funny Voice, but mostly it regarded its charm as antitheatrical, and an audience that understood that was never disappointed. Its abundance was as simultaneously chintzy and unrestrained as the Rose Bowl parade. If I wrote, "Enter the villainess disguised as a wedding cake," by gar, they whipped up a wedding-cake costume. It was intoxicating, though like most intoxicants, it thrilled and depressed at once, somehow, as one stood in those dim, musty corners among the discarded sequined remnants. There was a precious strangeness in hearing my own words (more or less, often less) like distant barking, drifting from a glitzy, misted-over stage, night after phantasmic night, uncoiling for a possibly uncomprehending audience of optometrists.

The shows I have seen since graduating, paradoxically, frighten me without managing to interest me, rather like witnessing a Masons' initiation or the *Satyricon* as performed by some Young Republicans. Why do they still wear women's clothes? Let's face it: the folks in Kenosha will want to know. Maybe, like wacky greeting cards, it's a way to purchase temporary and safe insanity, the joke told on the subway on the way to the Manufacturers Hanover of life. Maybe it's perpetuated by the tension of ambitious men's fear of emasculation, or their fear of women, or, most likely of all, like those outdated laws against grazing cows in Harvard Yard, it's just never occurred to anyone to strike it from existence. Whatever its reasons, the Pudding has spurted regularly and spectacularly for some time now, and if long routine history augments your idea of a fun thing to watch, this is the next best attraction to Old Faithful.

Still, it was good clean fun. Thanks to the Pudding, I can now be unimpressed by klieg lights, free champagne, strangers in formal dress, vanity records, and Bermuda. It let me

run with the Loebies and eat in Adams House without
having to attempt suicide. And at the cast parties there were
unlimited peanuts and maraschino cherries, plus roommates' Wellesley girl friends who flattered me by declaring
me out of my mind. During all this I told myself I was
gathering material for a series of articles, that I was myself
in youth, that this was only the courtesy-car provisional me.
Like most, I expected maturity to find me without any
cooperation on my part.

Academics, the discerning will notice, don't seem related
to my Harvard. The people who spent their time in libraries
didn't seem to be from Harvard; they were more like intellectual townies. I never took any "guts," I will hasten to
remind my grandchildren, but I admit I did take some
mighty nebulous creative writing seminars, most of which
featured wine and cheese and no required reading. A few of
them veered into ill-advised Esalen-style confrontations
("What is Art?" "Why don't you take that poison you carry
around in your purse and find out?"), but mostly people sat
Indian-style in instructors' bohemian-boutique apartments
and made like poets. Since Smattering wasn't offered, I had
to major in English. Is it because actors used to have to sleep
in the barn that Harvard could never bring itself to grant a
major in theater arts? Maybe it seemed too simian—all that
running around perspiring and pulling faces. The consort-
ing with foreigners, the gunpowder, the codpieces—it just
isn't history of science. But, since there is no gym requirement, let's not be ungrateful too quickly. At least all the
theater at Harvard is guaranteed to be for the love of it. No
one need toady or tally unless that's what he loves doing
best. Better a joy ride than a driven cast, throbbing and
posturing with the drama-school stiffness of Those With
Their Futures On Their Shoulders. Harvard theater may be
pudgy, but it is as unpressured and available as a public
cemetery. Anyway, a Harvard degree already testifies to a
talent for self-presentation.

But let's rejoin my classmates in linear time, whose

winged chariot turned on the meter and hurtled us, for lack of a more problematic word, forward. I acquired Latin and Shakespeare texts and thrilled at their unviolated repose on my bookshelf. I drank cappucino in the studied starkness of almost-remodeled basements along Bow Street. I nodded knowingly. The house dining halls gave me my final preparation for modern adulthood: self service, kindly voiced gossip, cavalier manners that contained unspeakable ambition, and of course, the unlimited food again. I never learned how to make the most of the hair God gave me, but otherwise I think I eventually got the Harvard experience. I even saw the glass flowers. I guess I can say that's my Harvard, at least pending my final loan repayment.

So, how can I, still wet from my encounter with it, distill my years at Harvard so that generations after me won't have to go there? How can I separate the inevitable traumatics of adolescence from the specific trauma of Cambridge? Since I pretended to come to conclusions all through my time in college, I am amply prepared to pretend to come to some conclusions now: Harvard is probably not all that important. This will come as a relief to those graduates who still haven't bought a mug. No, especially if you think about it right before bedtime, Harvard seems a tad inconsequential, though when you consider the imploding universe, what doesn't? Still, to paraphrase Pascal, Harvard may be no more than a reed, feebly trembling in the wind, the weakest thing in all Nature, but it still beats the hell out of Tufts.

John H. Adler '81

John H. Adler was born in 1959 and educated at Haddonfield Memorial High School in Haddonfield, New Jersey. He graduated from Harvard with an A.B. in government and a passion for Shakespeare. At Harvard he served as president of the Signet Society and as a senior editor of The Harvard Independent. *He entered Harvard Law School in the fall of 1981.*

I guess I just wanted to see what was so great about the place. Full of conceit, I had long before decided that I deserved to attend the best college in the country, and Harvard's claim to that position had been clear to me for years.

Thurston Howell III had convinced me of Harvard's greatness. Howell, the snobbish millionaire on television's *Gilligan's Island*, had attended Harvard. Whenever a savage appeared on the island, Howell would note the man's barbarism as a sign that he "must be a Yale man." Without either then or now ascribing any cultural or social value to *Gilligan's Island*, I somehow accepted the underlying philosophy of Harvard's pre-eminence.

I arrived in Cambridge very determined to discover the secret of Harvard's greatness. Up to that point, I had only the words of a sit-com, but I took the seven-thousand-dollar-a-year gamble (later eight, nine, then ten thousand).

From the first moments my enthusiasm waned rapidly. Rain graces Cambridge autumns the way sunshine accompanies Florida winters, and during my freshman year God granted Cambridge extra grace. Harvard fell into a somber, drizzling silence such as the one that so endeared itself to Faulkner's Quentin Compson. For two months we, the already homesick freshmen, endured incessant rainfall. Harvard hadn't mentioned this in the brochure.

Months later, the weather offered a grandiose apology in the form of two successive two-foot snowfalls. For the first time ever, snow closed Harvard, providing a recess that revealed the hidden immaturity of thousands of normally (perhaps abnormally) serious collegians. With all car traffic forbidden in the state, pedestrians and skiers claimed Mass. Ave. in a prolonged display of communal warmth and giddiness. Brother Blue, the somewhat bizarre master of myth, stood atop a huge pile of snow to recite *Macbeth* while showing Lear's crazed disregard for the elements. Undergraduates sculpted amazing ice figures, including an enormous, extremely detailed phallus complete with sticks for pubic hair.

The University had mentioned its diversity, so before arriving I expected to room with a southern black or an urban Jew, someone to contrast with my suburban background. Instead I drew Guy, an acerbic socialist, and Gene, a reclusive communist. Although from a Republican town, I considered myself in the mainstream of Democratic liberalism. My grasp of truly leftist politics, however, extended only as far as a vague feeling that communism was pure evil. Suddenly I found myself confronting disciples of the Devil, cruel freshmen skilled at turning bad arguments to their advantage. For my unwillingness to join the revolution, I was forced to defend ITT, the Pentagon, Exxon, and the Catholic church, institutions I had previously been ever ready to criticize.

This ideological conflict did nothing to ease my transition into college life, so I withdrew into the dwindling solace of a deteriorating hometown romance by correspondence. Faced with an unsatisfying fidelity, I turned to light drinking, which led to socializing, parties, and nonintellectual detente with Guy. Gene never managed to join the fun, usually hiding in his bedroom whenever we had guests.

Regrettably, my strongest memory of closeness with

these roommates occurred during the first in a series of demonstrations designed to end apartheid in South Africa. Activists held other guilt-exorcising protests over the seeming demise of Afro-Am and consciousness-raising fasts for Cambodia, but the main issue of my undergraduate years was apartheid. Leftists demanded complete divestiture of holdings in companies operating in South Africa. Conservatives, myself included, supported a University role in shareholder resolutions relating to South African conditions. All of us seemed to agree on Harvard's moral and economic influence . . . and on our (the undergraduates') ability to convince or coerce Harvard.

We started with an afternoon rally outside a discussion by the corporation of shareholder responsibility. The weather suggested a platonic ideal of spring. I could easily have protested forever in such a climate, or, as exams were still some time away, at least for the rest of the week. The demonstrators, a thousand strong (along with about a dozen weaklings), felt outraged when the corporation decided not to divest immediately. We vowed to continue the fight.

Later that week, in actions that coupled the euphoria of our snow holiday and the rancor of Vietnam protests, we undertook a midnight candlelight march and subsequent siege of University Hall. The march drew thousands of sincere undergraduates offering a peaceable expression of disgust over the injustice of apartheid. Accepting the herd mentality, no one noted the absurdity of thousands of upper-middle-class elitists singing about the solidarity of the "people."

What followed destroyed much of our naiveté in short order. After the march, the real activists spent the night in front of University Hall while the sunshine patriots, myself among them, trundled off to bed. By nine the next morning the crowd had returned, diminished in number but fortified in intent. Some blocked the staircases; others slowly circled the building in a patient chain. Pressured by my roommates, I dutifully took my place in line, chanting the anticorporate

slogans ("GM, 3M, ITT; all South Africans must be free!")
and the obscene invectives ("Bok Fox Epps!"). Deans stayed
away from the demonstration, and we had won a great
victory over apartheid by successfully closing Harvard's
central administration for a day.

The corporation's seeming indifference to this moral triumph sparked a more violent response from the activists,
who in turn alienated the rest of us. As President Bok
crossed the Yard one day to enter his Mass Hall office,
students, led by Guy, blocked the door, forcing him to rush
through Johnston Gate into the Square and the safety of a
Harvard police car. The activists, not to be denied their
chance to harass the president with impunity, surrounded
the car, rocking it up and down before it screeched away;
Gene was among those sitting on the hood. Having lived
with the half-joking promise that my roommates would be
willing to kill me for the revolution, I sympathized with the
victim rather than with the aggressors' forgotten original
motives. I wondered how an assault on Bok would ease the
plight of many South Africans. From that day, my Harvard
remained its own godless, amoral self of old.

Still, I was sorry when, in the housing lottery, both Guy
and Gene chose the Quad, the traditional home of leftists of
all denominations, while I picked Winthrop, a river house
with apparent warmth and suburban homogeneity. None of
this explains how I landed in Lowell, suffering every Sunday at one when crazed sadists rang the tower's Russian
bells with an arhythmic vengeance that frightened even the
local roaches.

Often I thought the bells were a divine punishment for
my failure to attend services at Mem Church. From my
Thayer window I had overseen and overlooked a year's
worth of devotion, and God wanted to get even in Lowell
House by driving me insane or deaf. I should have wor-
shiped regularly, if only to hear Peter Gomes, a black
preacher with Brahmin manners and British accent.
Gomes's extraordinary charm and aristocratic suavity

should have made religion painless enough. He even offered to lunch with me at the Signet Society for each Sunday I prayed with him in God's house. He fought hard for my soul, occasionally letting me wait table and wash dishes at his dinner parties. In these ways did I grow close to the man once mentioned as a write-in candidate for pope.

I had already gained valuable experience in the table-waiting game during my freshman year. I waited on all the big shots at the Signet Society, gaining literary insight with each meal. David Updike never talked, thus saving his strength for short stories in *The New Yorker*. Caroline Kennedy never cleared her plate and chain-smoked like Pittsburgh. Maura Moynihan, by contrast, was effusively friendly, living on the edge of the punk music world in a totally black wardrobe, an optimistic answer to *The Sea Gull*'s Masha, in rhapsody for her life.

As surly waiters do, I injected my thoughts into each day's literary debate. In the kitchen I was daunted by the imperious intelligence of Kate Tait, the Signet's steward and the daughter of Bertrand Russell, but among the members I displayed the cool facade of an intellectual fakir, and though I had written only two presentable articles for the *Independent* and had never read past the death of Prince Andrey, I became a Signet member early in my sophomore year.

Because membership to the Signet is based ostensibly on literary merit, I felt compelled to justify myself to my electors. My reputation seemed to rest with my performance at the initiation, a ceremony consisting of readings, by candlelight, of selections of prose or poetry. I worked up a ludicrous piece of specious reasoning that showed how I, as waiter of the leading group in the leading university of the leading country, ruled the world. Somehow this two-minute, one-gag jest produced sustained laughter, especially the contagious cackle of John Marquand, senior tutor of Dudley House and a likable, ridiculous figure of Falstaffian girth, appetite, and good humor. Thanks to the reassurance of applause I managed to finish and earned my rose, which, according to Signet tradition, I must return with a copy of my first published work.

About this time, I began performing my long-running tragicomedy, "How to Fail with Women Despite Really Trying." After an unspectacular tryout in the Yard, the show opened to feminine indifference in Lowell, with weekday matinees at the Signet. Not that there weren't pretty women at Harvard—I counted nineteen all together—but every one I met had a boyfriend or a headache. Perhaps because I was once nominally (if unwillingly) loyal to a girl at home, I got a reputation as a "fun date." Some fun.

Responding as can only a young man enduring involuntary abstinence, I tried new approaches to meet women of intelligence, compassion, beauty, and moral weakness. I took the names of ugly girls in hope of meeting their pretty roommates. I often almost talked to women from neighboring schools. In acts of drunken desire I once stalked Pine Mattress, climbing fences to avoid campus police. At Lesley I scaled a fire escape to bang on second-floor windows.

Finally giving up, I chose a less satisfying alternative and began staring. Along with four similarly depraved and deprived friends, I institutionalized this ocular entertainment in a weekly Rotary Club dinner in which, dressed in coat and tie, we occupied the dais overlooking Lowell's dining hall and viciously ogled the Cliffies. On a beauty scale of one to ten, our scoring, like the College's grading, inflated the girls' ratings, and seldom did even the homeliest creature receive less than a two.

Only when I acted unexpectedly did I have resounding success. Once during a power blackout I decided to brave the snowy, cold darkness, beer and flashlight in hand, to visit a woman in Eliot. I found her at an invite-only cocktail party, stole her away, and was still in bed when the lights returned with absolutely no respect for our privacy. I waited for months for another blackout before dismissing power outages as a causal device in my love life. In the meantime I fell in love with a different Harvard woman every week and was dismayed when each failed to ask me out.

I would be happy to say that I cleverly channeled my frustrated energies into my academics, but I am sure I could have managed both women and work. Fortunately studies did fill much of the time, but I escaped the prevailing attitude of joyless grade-grubbing that produced a great many extremely tedious people who will undoubtedly make millions of dollars and someday return for reunions to recall the good old days they never had. One roommate, who will remain nameless (even among his closest friends), celebrated the completion of a paper or an exam by reapplying himself to the minutiae of his other courses. And so it went with many others.

This pervasive wonkishness made me admire the people who really seemed to like being at Harvard. Ed Redlich, disgusted by the general pomposity, sometimes ate with his hands and often toured 33 Dunster Street, the restaurant, begging food from total strangers. Anything worked to relieve the tension created by overly ambitious classmates. The few of us who disdained this pressure, and I for one never let academics disrupt more important matters, gathered together, seeking humor in everything and laughing hysterically at a huge puddle of spilled milk or a particularly scatological line from Aristophanes.

I never quite managed to avoid intellectualism altogether, but I did limit it to the Signet and to formal dinners in particular. One night, James Thomson, the curator of the Nieman Foundation and the evening's toastmaster, sat beside me, the holder of the hardly contested Signet secretaryship. When the cigars came around, I turned for guidance to this man who had clearly been born with one of Havana's finest between his teeth. Leaning back in his chair, Thomson began an empassioned discourse on the art of cigar smoking. Following his example, I pricked a hole in the round end, lit up, and inhaled deeply. Coughing violently, I turned to him like a spurned cur. "Oh, by the way," he added, "beginners shouldn't inhale."

At a later dinner I studied both artistic and academic bad manners. Now the incoming president (the New York vote

had carried me over the top), I drew as a dinner companion
John Ashberry, the featured poet, who introduced himself
with "I'm John Ashberry, but then you knew that." At one
point, he needed a guide to show him the nearest bathroom.
While there, I recounted for him Norman Mailer's hilarious
bathroom scene in *Armies of the Night.* Ashberry listened
with disdain, and I was relieved later when groupies from
the *Advocate* moved their chairs opposite him at the head
table and hung on his every pronouncement. When he
finally rose to present his reading, he was incomprehensible, and even the most mannerly professors perked up when
he announced his last poem.

When Ashberry finished, Alan Heimert rose as toastmaster to introduce Gail Parker, once his teaching assistant.
Heimert, whose proud contempt for undergraduates made
him an almost comic figure as Master of Eliot, began his
remarks by saying, "Calling Gail Parker an educator is like
calling Hester Prynne a seamstress." He later so badly gar-
bled an award presentation to Amyas Ames that the citation
had to be taken from his hands and read by someone else.
From just this literary laboratory I learned the dangers
inherent in the rough-and-tumble world of after dinner
speech-making.

I already miss those Signet dinners. I miss reading period;
in real life one can't postpone everything until the end of the
semester. For four years, I obeyed the parable: "If God had
been a Harvard man, during Creation he would have slept
for six days and then pulled an all-nighter." When fall exams
move to December, as they inevitably will, generations of
future undergraduates will lose that wonderful safety net,
without which I could never have gone to Fathers' (a bar)
every Wednesday night.

One thing I shall not miss, however, is the curious respect
people show me when they learn I'm from Harvard.

That, after all, will go on forever.

About the Editor

Jeffrey L. Lant received his B.A. summa cum laude from the University of California, Santa Barbara and his M.A. and Ph.D. degrees in history from Harvard, where he was Woodrow Wilson Fellow, Harvard Prize Fellow, and winner of Harvard College's Master's Award. He has established Jeffrey Lant Associates, Inc., a management and consulting firm in Cambridge, Massachusetts. Before forming JLA, Mr. Lant taught and administered at Harvard, Boston College, and Northeastern University. He has written more than 300 articles, and his recent books include Insubstantial Pageant: Ceremony and Confusion at Queen Victoria's Court, Development Today: A Guide for Nonprofit Organizations, *and* The Consultant's Kit: Establishing and Operating Your Successful Consulting Business.